THE AMERICAN PEOPLE
AND CHINA

Published volumes in the series,

"THE UNITED STATES AND CHINA IN WORLD AFFAIRS"

ALEXANDER ECKSTEIN

Communist China's Economic Growth and Foreign Trade:
Implications for U.S. Policy

A. M. HALPERN (EDITOR)

Policies toward China: Views from Six Continents

A. T. STEELE

The American People and China

THE AMERICAN PEOPLE AND CHINA

A. T. Steele

A VOLUME IN THE SERIES,

"THE UNITED STATES AND CHINA IN WORLD AFFAIRS"

PUBLISHED FOR THE COUNCIL ON FOREIGN RELATIONS BY

McGRAW-HILL BOOK COMPANY

New York · Toronto · London

The Council on Foreign Relations is a nonprofit institution devoted to the study of political, economic, and strategic problems as related to American foreign policy. It takes no stand, expressed or implied, on American policy.

The authors of books published under the auspices of the Council are responsible for their statements of fact and expressions of opinion. The Council is responsible only for determining that they should be presented to the public.

Foreword

This book is one in a series on The United States and China in World Affairs being published by the Council on Foreign Relations as part of a three-year program, begun in 1962 under a generous grant from the Ford Foundation. This program comprises discussions, studies and publications arranged by the Council to encourage more active and better informed public consideration of one of the most important areas of U.S. foreign policy.

The Council's program, which has been guided by a Steering Committee under the chairmanship of Allen W. Dulles, does not aspire to produce a single and simple set of conclusions. The phenomenon of China's role in the world, including the question of Taiwan, is far too complex for that. Each study in this series therefore constitutes a separate and self-contained inquiry written on the responsibility of its author, who has reached his own judgments and conclusions regarding the subject of his investigation and its implications for U.S. policy. The list of authors includes persons with a variety of backgrounds in Chinese affairs and foreign policy. Some have had long personal experience in China. Others have studied China and Far Eastern problems during recent years or dealt with them as officials and administrators. They represent a variety of viewpoints and have, in each case, been able to consult with a group of qualified persons invited by the Council on Foreign Relations to meet periodically with the author.

No recent aspect of American foreign policy has aroused greater passions in the United States than our relations with China.

Ever since the failure of U.S. policy during the Chinese civil war and the Communist victory in 1949, the role of public opinion in influencing the China policy of the United States has been the subject of much controversy. The charge has been made that emotionalism has weighed heavily on our China policy and that there has been inadequate public debate of the issues. On the other hand, it is claimed that public opinion, aroused by the behavior and hostility of the Chinese Communists, is firmly and rightly in support of present policy. The problem is further complicated by the difficulty of being adequately informed about developments in China. The absence of normal contacts and exchanges between the two countries and the severe control of information by the Chinese Communists make it doubly difficult to get a full and fair picture of developments on the mainland. The strong emotions with which the available information is often interpreted add to the complications.

For all these reasons, it has seemed important, as part of a general examination of the relations between the United States and China, to give special consideration to the way in which public attitudes toward China and China policy have been shaped, what they are today, and what influence they have on policy decisions. This is the purpose of the present volume by A. T. Steele, a distinguished American foreign correspondent for many years. He has based this study on his own research and interviews conducted across the country. To complement his work, the Council on Foreign Relations, in the spring of 1964, commissioned the Survey Research Center, University of Michigan, to conduct a comprehensive nationwide survey.

Mr. Steele spent the years 1931–49 in China, where he represented at different times the Associated Press, *The New York Times* and the *Chicago Daily News*. Later he traveled widely throughout Asia and elsewhere for the *New York Herald Tribune*.

Robert Blum *
The United States and China in World Affairs

* The work on this volume was substantially completed and the Foreword written before Dr. Blum's untimely death. Professor Lucian Pye, Massachusetts Institute of Technology, succeeded Dr. Blum.

Preface

The author acknowledges with gratitude the invaluable assistance received from a large number of individuals and organizations during the course of this study. He owes a special debt of appreciation to the late Dr. Robert Blum, whose friendship and wise counsel were from the beginning a major sustaining influence.

Meetings with a study group on American Attitudes toward China, established under the auspices of the Council on Foreign Relations, were also most helpful. There were three such meetings, each producing a lively and useful exchange of ideas on the content and handling of the study program. Members of the group were Everett N. Case, chairman; Hamilton Fish Armstrong, A. Doak Barnett, James R. Basche, John Cooley, W. Phillips Davison, Tillman Durdin, Lloyd A. Free, Samuel B. Griffith, A. M. Halpern, Philip Horton, Porter McKeever, Joseph Slater, Howard P. Whidden, C. Martin Wilbur, Richard S. Winslow, and Frederick C. T. Yu.

Many other persons gave generously of their time and knowledge to help bring the project to satisfactory completion. We wish particularly to express our thanks to those specialists who took time out from busy schedules to read and comment on parts of this report while it was still in draft form. Their corrections, criticisms and suggestions enabled the author to avoid many pitfalls and wrong turnings. The scope for differences of opinion on this subject is, of course, very wide. In some matters of judgment the author has yielded to the superior wisdom of his friendly critics, in some he has chosen to stand his ground. This point is mentioned only to make it clear that the writer takes full responsibility for the views expressed in this book, except where otherwise attributed.

We are grateful, too, to the scores of persons who submitted to interviews, often on very short notice, and to the others who responded to questionnaires, letters and telephone calls and thereby cheerfully inconvenienced themselves in order to help provide missing bits of information needed for this report. The author wishes it were possible to mention by name all those who have lent a hand in the study. The list, however, is extremely long, and it would be unfair to mention only some of those to whom thanks is due.

Completion of the study undoubtedly would have been more prolonged and difficult but for the unfailing cooperation of the Council on Foreign Relations and its staff. The Council's library facilities proved indispensable. We are indebted, also, to a number of other institutions and organizations, notably the Roper Public Opinion Research Center, at Williams College, Williamstown, Massachusetts, for assistance given.

Finally, a word of respectful appreciation for the indefatigable members of the Project's office staff, who labored uncomplainingly, for long hours, in the deciphering, typing, re-typing and editing of the author's manuscript. And let it be said, in grateful postscript, that any award for stamina and forbearance in this undertaking has been earned, unquestionably, by the author's wife, Esther.

Contents

x   *Contents*

Introduction

Any attempt at accurate assessment of American public opinion on a subject as controversial as China is assured of difficulties. For one thing, this is a relatively uncharted field. Also, experience shows that Americans have tended to react intensely and emotionally to developments in China, with sudden fluctuations of feeling ranging from admiration to disillusionment, from sympathy to antagonism. This highly emotional element complicates the analyst's task.

While this study is concerned primarily with American public opinion about China and about United States policy toward that country, it ventures also to explore the triangular relationship between public opinion, the Congress, and the administration in policy formulation. It seems apparent from our findings that the American public is becoming increasingly favorable to a re-examination of our China policy but that the legislative and executive branches of the government are lagging somewhat in their response to the public mood. How this situation came about and what can be done about it are matters of importance which receive considerable attention in this report.

The ups and downs of public opinion on China become understandable only against the historical background and the heritage of assumptions, expectations, emotions, traditions and even illusions and legends which have contributed to our present attitudes. Thus, we have devoted no little attention in this study to the past

1

record. The main body of the book, however, is devoted to the present and the future. We have relied less on the printed than on the spoken word, as captured in interviews and public opinion polls. Very early in our survey it became evident that any meaningful study of public opinion on China would have to take into account not only the attitudes of the general public but also those of opinion leaders. Our data have been derived from two principal sources:

A nationwide sampling of public opinion carried out by the Survey Research Center at the University of Michigan. (The Survey Research Center's report of its findings appears as Appendix A of this study.)

A series of more than 200 interviews by the author with Americans occupying responsible and leadership positions throughout the country.

The two approaches complemented each other with the opinion survey posing a uniform list of questions to a sampling of the entire population and the interviews following no set pattern and concentrating entirely on persons of standing and leadership in their respective fields. Thus, the interviews provide information of a highly individual nature from an influential and relatively well-informed sector of the population, while the survey gives statistical backbone to the book and provides a basis for comparing present-day opinion with opinion at other times over the past thirty years as shown in the results of previous polls.

The national survey was conducted by the Survey Research Center during May and June 1964. The sample of persons interviewed consisted of 1,501 individuals chosen by advanced methods of probability selection to be generally representative of the adult American population.

During his interviewing of opinion leaders, the author visited fourteen cities: New York, Washington, D.C., Chicago, St. Louis, Memphis, Tulsa, Dallas, Topeka, Los Angeles, San Francisco, Portland, Oregon, Seattle and Boise. In each community the first step taken was to seek out one or more citizens of recognized responsibility and to obtain from them suggestions as to the names of persons representative of various professions and viewpoints with whom productive interviews might be arranged. From the names offered, the writer then made a choice of persons likely to provide a reasonably good cross section of informed opinion. They included business executives, professors, members of Congress, government officials, politicians, labor leaders, editors, doctors, lawyers, clergymen and others. Some had a special interest in and knowledge of China. Most did not. Interviews varied in duration from half an hour to as long as three hours. In a few instances they were devoted largely to a single aspect of the China question, while in others they ranged through a very wide spectrum. The record of these interviews is contained in about 100,000 words of notes taken during travels between late spring 1963 and early summer 1965.

Because of the sensitivity of the China issue, many persons are reluctant to express their innermost thoughts on it publicly. Therefore, we gave assurance in most interviews that the names of the persons questioned would not be used. Without this assurance, some of these individuals undoubtedly would have been less outspoken—or would not have permitted quotation at all.

Apart from the souces mentioned, scores of other persons were sought out, written to, and queried on specific points of information. The author also made extensive use of the collection of public-opinion polls at the Roper Public Opinion Research Center, Williams College. At one stage of our inquiry, questionnaires were sent out to a representative list of 150 newspaper editors across the country, of whom sixty responded. A similar, but not identical, set of questions was mailed to fifty-eight television and radio executives, of whom twenty-six replied. A survey was also made of the amount of space given to China news in a varied selection of twelve newspapers over a one-month period in March 1964. Additional perspective was provided by a more impressionistic survey of opinion which Samuel Lubell conducted in late 1963 and then supplemented with a few further soundings in 1965.

Throughout this study, we have been conscious of feeling our way through an area that has not been extensively explored. Even China specialists, when interviewed, often hesitated to venture an assessment of public thinking on China, except with respect to their immediate circle of friends and contacts. There are, in fact, significant regional differences on the China question: viewpoints, that is, tend to vary somewhat from area to area. Moreover, China is a subject on which people are not only inclined to be volatile but are also quite capable of reaching contradictory conclusions from the same set of facts. This is understandable. They are, after all, groping for comprehension of a behemoth they cannot clearly see. In the circumstances, we have approached the subject with caution. Readers of this book will not find hard and fast answers to the dilemmas raised, but they will find numerous signs pointing toward new directions in American thinking about China.

A few words about the organization of the book. The initial chapters are mainly historical and trace the undulations of American opinion regarding China from the years of our earliest contacts with that country to the recent past. The second part is devoted to an examination of present-day attitudes, while the third part deals with the related problem of improving the flow of information about China into the United States and, more specifically, of getting more of this information to the public at large. Part IV is concerned with the impact—or lack of impact—of public opinion on our government with respect to the shaping of China policy. The study concludes with a summary of findings and the author's conclusions and recommendations.

PART ONE

The Past Is Prologue

CHAPTER ONE

Traditional Attitudes toward China

It was mainly during the nineteenth century that the foundations were laid for the huge and conglomerate edifice of truths, half-truths, assumptions, legends, prejudices and contradictory opinions that make up our present-day outlook on China.

But even earlier, in colonial times, there was some awareness among Americans of the remote celestial empire as a source of tea and silk, of exotic art and interesting ideas. The admiration for Chinese ideas and things which had been characteristic of the so-called Age of Enlightenment in Europe was not unfamiliar to those Americans who kept up with the works of Leibniz, Quesnay and Voltaire.

China, of course, was already an ancient, a great and a highly civilized nation long before the United States was born. It is perhaps well to remind ourselves that the times of George Washington were the times of the Emperor Ch'ien Lung, probably the most cultured ruler of his day. Ch'ien Lung was a poet and patron of the arts. He surrounded himself with men of talent and scholarly distinction. An achievement of his reign was the compilation of an anthology of the finest in Chinese literature—a prodigious project which involved copying by hand 36,000 volumes of books and manuscripts. Yet Ch'ien Lung had despotic ways in which Americans will find haunting similarities with the regime now in power in Peking. Not the least of these were his ruthless repression of political criticism, his arrogance toward foreigners, his lofty belief in the innate superiority of Chinese civilization over all others.

The American Revolution, which occurred toward the end of Ch'ien Lung's reign, must have seemed to him but a petty squabble between white barbarians at the remote outer fringes of his empire, if, indeed, he thought about it at all. And certainly the founding fathers of the United States of America were too busy with the affairs of revolution and nationhood to be concerned with the cultural activities of an Oriental potentate at the other side of the globe. By the time of the celebrated tea party at Boston, the Age of Enlightenment had gone into decline. In Europe and America a healthy skepticism was replacing the former adulation for things Chinese. But Americans had not forgotten that China was the place where tea and silk came from. Seafaring Yankees wasted no time in cutting in on the lucrative China trade, previously a European monopoly. The good ship *Empress of China* made the first American commercial contact with China in 1784. Returning seamen brought home exciting tales of the Orient and its riches. Interest grew, and trade expanded. In 1789, the year that Washington took his oath of office, there were fourteen American ships in Canton.

So began our relationship, as free Americans, with China. It was not a very broad contact—only one port was open to American and European traders. But it was the beginning of a tradition of involvement in China and her problems which was to become an increasing preoccupation of Americans during the ensuing century and a half. After the merchants came the missionaries. The first American missionaries to reach China arrived in the early 1830s, to be followed by a growing procession until, a century later, there were more American missionaries in China than in any other country in the world.

American contacts with China developed haphazardly under the spur of three main motivations—to turn a profit, to further our national interests and, as some saw it, to rescue the Godless millions of China from misery and damnation. Almost from the beginning the American involvement in China was charged with emotion and sentiment. The early American traders were down-to-earth men who resented the restrictions imposed upon them by the Manchu authorities. The missionaries, who followed, were more articulate, more emotional and, in the end, more numerous. It was the humanitarian urge, represented by the missionary effort, that left the deepest marks on popular thinking.

The impact of American missionary activity on China—how much of it was constructive, how much of it disruptive—is a matter of controversy. We can be much surer about the impact of the missionaries on American attitudes toward China. It was considerable. The stories the missionaries brought home about life among the heathen, their impassioned appeals in churches, in Sunday schools and in public meetings, deeply conditioned American thinking about China in the nineteenth century and left a residue of ideas and notions which still colors our views. To this day there are few Americans who have not been touched, in one way or another, by the missionary influence.

The impression the missionary made on his fellow Americans was, of course, quite different from the impression he made on the Chinese. Americans saw the missionary as a dedicated fellow ready to sacrifice his health, his worldly goods and, if necessary, his life to carry the word of God to the benighted heathens. The first American missionaries sent to China were interested only in saving souls, and they suffered greatly from the taunts and actual debris hurled at them by the people they were sent to convert. In those early years, the missionary view of China was a highly subjective and distorted one. Their work was with the poorest and most underprivileged elements of the population. They saw a great deal of China's seamy side, very little of her glory and grandeur. Everything seemed "backward" and therefore cried for change. They went out to slay a dragon and found that in China the dragon, far from being an object of abomination, was a symbol of nearly everything good.

The early missionaries had good reason to complain about the high-handed and contemptuous treatment they received from Manchu officials. Yet the missionaries were themselves often guilty of intolerance, dogmatism, patronizing ways and a self-assumed attitude of superiority. In 1841, an English missionary and naturalist, G. Tradescant Lay, published a book of his experiences in which he volunteered the following anthropological assessment of the Chinese:

> The head of a Chinese is broad behind and narrow in front when compared with the general standard of Europeans. If, according to general opinion, the forepart of the head represent intellectual capability, the advantage is in our favor: a conclusion which is warranted by everything that research brings to light.[1]

Although Mr. Lay was guilty of a lot of similar nonsense, he also dropped a few observations which sound remarkably up-to-date. This one, for instance: "The Government of China is purposely absurd, but the people are reasonable in their views and conceptions." [2]

The missionaries were recruited from all corners of our country. Each one had behind him a large and devoted following. The missionary was not, as a rule, a highly educated person—although as time passed, increasing numbers of doctors and educators made the long, watery crossing. On his return home, after long service in China, he was in heavy demand as a speaker. One of his duties on home leave was to convince his constituents that the work he was doing justified continued and generous financial support. His accounts of life in China, one may be sure, seldom suffered from understatement. What did his people want to know? Well, mostly they wanted to know how the people of China lived, what their customs were, what problems the missionaries faced.

It was the exotic and the odd that most interested Americans about China. The stories people remembered were the stories about opium smoking, female infanticide, long fingernails, women in pants, acrobats, jugglers, pigtails, bound feet, ancestor worship, "thousand-year-old" eggs and the other things and practices that made China so fascinatingly different. Nor have Americans even to this day ceased marveling at the upside-downness of life in China—the fact that Chinese read from right to left, that they write their surname ahead of their given name, that they make

[1] G. Tradescant Lay, *The Chinese as They Are* (London: Wm. Ball and Co., 1841), p. 14.
[2] Same.

soup the last course of a meal, that the Chinese gesture for "come here" is similar to our gesture for "goodbye," and so on *ad infinitum*.

The missionaries had slow going in China for many years, but the more they saw of the tremendous challenge the more impassioned their appeals to the American public became. The movement built up steadily until, near the end of the century, it took on the aspects of a crusade. Important people—even presidents—endorsed it. Speakers moved audiences to tears with their portrayal of teeming masses of humanity shuffling wholesale to perdition. Paul A. Varg, writing on the history of the missionary movement, quotes this passage from a speech by Hudson Taylor, founder of the China Inland Mission, before a meeting in Detroit in 1894:

The gospel must be preached to these people in a very short time, they are passing away. Every day, every day, oh how they sweep over! There is a great Niagara of souls passing into the dark in China. Every day, every week, every month, they are passing away. A million a month in China are dying without God.[3]

Such appeals, in those days, seldom failed to stir the emotions and loosen the pursestrings of God-fearing Americans; although looking back through the smoke and haze of all that has happened, we find it hard to believe. And many millions of Americans had a direct investment and interest in China through the pennies, the dimes and the dollars they contributed to missionary causes. As Professor John K. Fairbank has put it: "Missionary constituencies have been the seed bed of our humanitarianism toward China, a sentiment that has always affected and sometimes almost dominated our policy." [4]

All too often, this humanitarianism has been mixed with self-righteousness, blinding us to the realities of the situation in China and making it almost impossible to see ourselves as the Chinese saw us. To the Chinese, steeped in a tried and proved code of

---

[3] Paul A. Varg, *Missionaries, Chinese and Diplomats* (Princeton: Princeton University Press, 1958), p. 68.

[4] John K. Fairbank, *The United States and China* (Rev. ed.; Cambridge, Mass.: Harvard University Press, 1958), p. 252.

Confucian ethics more than twenty centuries old, the efforts of the missionaries to convert them to a wholly alien religion were puzzling and often unwelcome. Moreover, the missionaries were inevitably linked, in Chinese minds, with the foreign traders and empire makers whose pressures were increasingly felt and increasingly resented. This is scarcely surprising, since the opening of the Chinese interior to missionary enterprise was only made possible through the unequal treaties forced on China by the European powers.

Americans commonly assume that our record in China has been, on the whole, a magnanimous one, characterized by much unselfish giving and very little taking. Many Chinese would dispute this. Our first treaty with China was a treaty of Peace, Amity and Commerce, signed in 1844. Its very first article reads:

There shall be a perfect, permanent and universal peace and a sincere and cordial amity, between the United States of America on the one part, and the Ta Tsing Empire on the other, and between their people respectively, without exception of persons and place.

These fine words, regrettably, were quickly forgotten by both sides. While fair-minded Chinese would concede that in the years that followed we showed more concern for China's territorial integrity than the other powers, they would remind us that from the negotiation of the first treaty throughout the remainder of the nineteenth century we invariably insisted on obtaining from the Chinese the same rights and privileges the British and French had won from them by intimidation and force of arms. True, the unequal treaties were not of our making in the first instance, but we subscribed to them, took full advantage of them, and in the end helped enforce them. It was not until the turn of the century that we became truly independent in our China policy and began giving something more than mere lip service to the high ideals we had constantly espoused.

There are other blemishes on the American record in China of which Americans today are only dimly, if at all, aware. Professor Kwang-Ching Liu, a Chinese-American scholar, points out that in the nineteenth century we played a part in bringing upon China at least two evils—the traffic in opium and the traffic in coolie laborers. Some of the proudest ships of our clipper fleet were engaged in the illegal transport of opium to the beaches of south China. Opium shipped by Americans was perhaps never more than one-tenth of the total quantity imported into China, according to Dr. Liu, but American firms were involved in this traffic for as long as half a century.[5] Missionaries and other men of conscience in the United States denounced this traffic in the strongest possible terms, but it was not until after 1860 that the American participation in it was brought virtually to an end.

The traffic in coolies—some of it to the United States, much of it to Latin America—also provoked notoriety, principally because of the dubious circumstances under which the laborers were recruited and the unspeakable conditions under which they were transported across the Pacific. This was a profitable business for those who were involved in it, and overcrowding was the rule. Dr. Liu cites the case of the American vessel, *Waverley,* in which 260 Chinese laborers died of suffocation during a voyage to South America in 1855.[6]

Although these matters are largely forgotten in the United States today, they were given publicity at the time and in their small way influenced the pattern of our traditional thinking about China. Unfortunately, they have not been forgotten in modern China, where Communist propagandists shrewdly utilize them to provide a basis of fact for their highly exaggerated anti-American outpourings. Nor have the people of China been allowed to forget other examples of American prejudice and abuse, notably the contemptuous mistreatment accorded Chinese laborers brought to the United States to provide muscle for the winning of the West. These coolies—illiterate, but hard-working and thrifty—worked in the mines, cleared forests, grew foodstuffs, laundered, cooked and did dozens of other menial tasks. While it was the Irish who provided much of the labor for the eastern end of the transcontinental railway, it was the Chinese who built the western section. Thus arose the saying that the eastern end was built on whiskey, the western end on tea. The Chinese received poor

[5] Kwang-Ching Liu, *Americans and Chinese* (Cambridge, Mass.: Harvard University Press, 1963), p. 7.
[6] Same, pp. 6–7.

pay and little appreciation. No American of conscience can read without shame the story of calculated persecution to which these virtually helpless people were subjected. Here again, Dr. Liu provides chapter and verse on what the Chinese had to endure:

In the San Francisco area, in 1877–1878, lawless elements committed arson, robbery and murder against the Chinese; in Truckee, in November, 1878, the entire Chinese population of about a thousand was driven out of town. Until the early 1890's, frequent anti-Chinese riots occurred in other states and territories. In Rock Springs, Wyoming, in 1885, 28 Chinese were killed in one day. At Snake River, in Oregon, in 1887, 10 Chinese gold miners were robbed and murdered by men masquerading as cowboys. The incidents reflect the strains in an unstable frontier society; and they are among the darkest stains on the history of liberty in the United States.[7]

These and dozens of other excesses coincided with strong agitation, centering in California, for ever tighter legislation restricting Chinese immigration into the United States. The Exclusion Act of 1882 was followed by a series of extensions until, in 1902, the exclusion of Chinese laborers became permanent. By that time the Chinese population in the United States had reached a figure in excess of 100,000. There was further restrictive legislation in 1924; and it was not until 1943, in the heart of war, that Congress took steps to undo these injustices.

Who can say to what extent the anti-Chinese agitation of the second half of the past century contributed to the lopsided conception many Americans nurture even today of "John Chinaman" and his characteristics?

On balance, our relationship with China during the nineteenth century did us no great credit as a people. Although we were vocally idealistic and not active in the scramble for spheres of influence, our behavior otherwise differed little from that of the British or the French or the Russians. Americans were fascinated by the immense and mysterious complexity of China, its potentialities and the "strangeness" of its people. But it was usual in this country to regard the Chinese as an inferior people who could not hope to achieve real stature in the world until they had abandoned their heathen habits and embraced the ways of Christian

[7] Same, p. 24.

civilization. In those early years few Americans had anything but the most formal contact with the more sophisticated elements of Chinese society. Few had any knowledge of the vast and wonderful world of Chinese art and philosophy. For this situation the rulers of China were in part, at least, responsible. They kept foreigners at arm's length. Their disdain and arrogance matched our own.

There was, to be sure, a great deal of sympathy—quite frequently mixed with exasperation—for the Chinese people in their periods of travail. And it cannot be denied that the missionary effort, if often misguided, was nevertheless based on a spirit of genuine dedication both at home and in the field. By the close of the century American missionary enterprise had spread over a large part of the Chinese hinterland and included, besides churches, an impressive array of hospitals, clinics, schools and colleges. The record is spotted, to be sure, with literally hundreds of anti-Christian disturbances, culminating in the senseless bloodletting of the Boxer Uprising. Yet, as Dr. Fairbank has pointed out, the missionary movement gave a profound stimulus to China's modernization. Indeed it was for this reason more than any other that it was so often violently resisted.

The turn of the century brought a shift both in the policies and attitudes of the United States toward China. A rash of developments contributed to this change. The war with Spain, for one thing, had made us a colonial power in the Far East and given us a new and closer outlook on China. American traders had become increasingly aware of the potentialities of the China market and increasingly disturbed over the obvious ambition of the European powers to partition the country into spheres of influence and trade. It became clear that United States interests could no longer be served by following in the footsteps of the other powers. The time had arrived for a more independent posture. The Hay notes of 1899 and 1900, enunciating the doctrine of the Open Door, not only helped save China from European rapacity but left a permanent imprint on American attitudes toward that country, although there are historians who now question whether the doctrine was as benevolent as it has been made to appear. In any case, the United States was out in the open as the "protector" of China's territorial integrity. This view of China as a ward of the United States grew in intensity in later years and contributed to the emotional attachment of many Americans to China and things Chinese.

By this time, the Manchu dynasty, weakened by foreign pressures, internal decay and popular discontent, was entering upon its final agonies. The Boxer outbreak and the shocking orgy of foreign retribution which it provoked reduced the government to impotence. China lay prostrate and tractable. She abandoned her efforts to dam back the influx of Western ideas. Hostility turned to docility. Or so it seemed until 1905, when Shanghai merchants launched a boycott against American goods in retaliation for the exclusion laws and the maltreatment of Chinese in the United States. The boycott came at a time when Americans were feeling rather self-righteous about their China policy, as a result of the Hay notes; and they greeted the boycott with hurt surprise. Apparently an open door in China was one thing; to demand an open door in the United States was quite another.

The boycott was short lived, and Chinese relations with America and Europe entered upon an era of unprecedented amity and cooperation. Harold Isaacs, in his perceptive study of American attitudes toward China and India, sees the year 1905 as the approximate dividing line between what he calls the Age of Contempt (1840–1905) and the Age of Benevolence (1905–1937).[8] In terms of American attitudes the year represented, in Isaacs' words, a transition from the "exasperated devotion" of the first period to the "devoted exasperation" of the second. Americans responded readily to the new friendliness of the Chinese. Businessmen, journalists and missionaries went to China in increasing numbers, traveled widely and were admitted to circles formerly closed to them. They wrote home about it: The Chinese were, after all, a charming and intelligent people. Peking and Shanghai were great cities. China offered a tremendous market for American manufactures. And so forth.

[8] Harold Isaacs, *Scratches on Our Minds: American Images of China and India* (New York: John Day, 1958), pp. 140–164.

Along the way, the Nationalist Revolution provoked a new upsurge of American interest and sympathy. Dr. Sun Yat-sen, a baptized Christian, seemed to Americans just the man to lead China into a prosperous future in collaboration with the United States and Europe. But Dr. Sun died in 1925, with China still bogged down in disunity and chaos. Americans then found new hope in the rise of a young officer named Chiang Kai-shek, who became even more acceptable to us after his break with the Communists in 1927 and his marriage to a beauteous Wellesley graduate, Mei-ling Soong, in the same year. The fact that the Chiangs were devout Methodists was an additional point in their favor, in American eyes.

It soon became apparent, however, that even with Chiang at the helm the road to unity and stability in China would be long and arduous. The China spectacle, in its turbulence and color, resembled a Shakespearean drama. Regional warlords vied for power and their armies marched and countermarched across the land. Bandits infested the countryside and pirates plagued the neighboring seas. Deep in the interior the Chinese Communists built up an army and plotted their course to power. Chiang, with the national purse strings in his hands, managed to maintain a tenuous equilibrium among the militarists. Although Chiang had troops that looked smart on the parade ground, the mass of the Chinese soldiery was viewed with pity and disdain. The Chinese soldier had yet to prove that he could fight.

Americans had an affectionate and protective feeling for China, yet often despaired of her. It was the mood of the times— a mood that was abruptly jolted one September day in 1931 by a bomb explosion near Mukden, Manchuria, signaling the beginning of the Japanese occupation of Manchuria and, some say, the start of World War II. Americans reacted to the Mukden incident in a curiously mixed way. Critics denounced Japan's action as a cynical violation of the Nine Power Treaty and a brazen challenge to the Open Door Doctrine. Clearly, public opinion was on the side of the long-suffering Chinese and hostile, in this case, to Japan. We had favored Japan a few decades before in her war with Russia, chiefly because she was the underdog. Now Japan had graduated from the role of David to that of Goliath, and American sentiment was preponderantly pro-Chinese.

Yet for all our harsh words, there was little disposition in this country to back up our tough talk with action. The League of Nations, to be sure, had our moral support in its peace-making efforts. And a few newspapers came out for economic sanctions against the Japanese. Outbursts of righteous indignation were commonplace. But isolationism was still a powerful influence in American thinking. The political disunity of the Chinese, their economic disorganization, and their feeble military resistance in Manchuria no doubt contributed to the rather lukewarm public attitude during the period. Moreover, the United States was at that time wallowing in the depths of a depression, and neither the President, nor Congress, nor, for that matter, the people were in the mood for any steps involving the possibility of war.

There was a new eruption of indignation in January 1932, when heavy fighting suddenly broke out between Japanese and Chinese forces at Shanghai. For a few weeks residents of the International Settlement and the French Concession—many of them Americans—watched in fascinated trepidation as bombs exploded and fighting raged in the nearby streets of Chapei and Hongkew. Foreign correspondents had box seats at the flaming spectacle—often covering one side in the morning, the other in the afternoon. Day after day for weeks the Shanghai hostilities commanded large headlines in the American press, with heavy emphasis on the gallant resistance of the Chinese forces under General Tsai Ting-kai. It was the first convincing demonstration of the ability of Chinese troops to stand up against a completely modern military machine—a sign that the comic-opera conception of the Chinese army, then widely prevalent, would have to be revised.

Pessimism over China's prospects, which had sunk to a new low after the ignominious collapse in Manchuria, gave way to a more hopeful outlook after the Shanghai stand. Nevertheless, the disinclination of Americans to become involved in a showdown with Japan was not seriously shaken. There were indeed some influential Americans, including not a few Old China Hands, who felt that the Japanese takeover of Manchuria might be a healthy development for all concerned. Discouraged over the chronic chaos of the Chinese scene (and its inhibiting effect on trade), they hoped that the Japanese might make of Manchuria a showcase of development that would spur the Chinese into more efficient development of China proper. By the same token, the Japanese would have an outlet for their excess population and explosive energies.

As the crisis in Manchuria faded, with Japan in firm and virtually unchallenged control of the situation, agitation in the United States for strong measures against Japan faded with it. Newspapers gave less and less attention to the iniquities of the Japanese army and more and more to the disorganized, disunited, disorderly conditions inside China. Yet the situation offered a challenge and opportunity that many Americans found irresistible. The Tangku Truce of 1933, which gave Japan control over Manchuria, was followed by an upsurge of American interest and activity in China proper. The flow of American capital into the country grew steadily. American missionary and philanthropic institutions greatly expanded their facilities. Mission-sponsored colleges were besieged with Chinese youths eager for an American-style education. More and more Americans took up residence in China and found it good.

Every American who has ever lived in China has felt impelled, sooner or later, to write a book about it. In those years quite a few yielded to the urge. The United States was deluged with literature on China, including Pearl Buck's classic, *The Good Earth*,[9] which gave millions of Americans their first authentic insight into the way of life of China's ordinary people. Various writers produced books purporting to tell the "real truth" about China, but of course none of them agreed on just what the truth was. While the output of literature added greatly to public awareness of the China problem, it added also to public confusion of mind.

[9] Pearl Buck, *The Good Earth* (New York: John Day, 1931).

CHAPTER TWO

American Attitudes
after 1937

In the late 1930s the American people came to a crossroads in their thinking about China. Until then, American attitudes toward China, though sympathetic, had been consistently, even persistently, isolationist. Over the years we had often voiced concern for China's territorial integrity and our rights and interests in that country, but we had not been willing to back up our views with war-risking action. An example was the reaction to the Japanese occupation of Manchuria in 1931–32. Here was a flagrant challenge to the Open Door Doctrine and a violation of the Nine Power Treaty and the Kellogg-Briand Pact; yet except for refusing legal sanction to the newly created situation, we let it pass.

It was our wishful hope that Japan would be content to confine her aggression to Manchuria, where she had long had special influence and interests. But by 1937, the Japanese army had turned its attentions from Manchuria to China proper. Japan's purpose was now crystal clear. She would be satisfied with nothing less than the control of China. This objective put the China situation in a vastly more serious light. The fierce battle for Shanghai, the rape of Nanking and, above all, the sinking of the U.S. gunboat *Panay* shocked and outraged Americans. Chiang's armies, after a strong stand in the lower Yangtze area, were in retreat westward. The best they could do, at this stage, was to slow up the Japanese advance and provide cover for the withdrawal of the National Government into the deep interior, in keeping with the policy of prolonged resistance. Factories, universities and other vital establishments were uprooted and moved piecemeal, with appalling difficulty, into the hinterland. The country presented a picture of deepening tragedy and disarray.

Public-opinion polls of this period showed that the American people were now overwhelmingly sympathetic to the Chinese in their struggle with Japan but were still very reluctant to endorse steps which might involve the United States in the hostilities.[1] However, there was a progressive hardening of the public attitude as reports from China detailed the dismaying story of continuing Japanese excesses and continued Chinese retreat. Black headlines, angry editorials and blood-and-mud newsreels helped build up emotions. Americans were especially outraged by reports of the bombing of helpless civilians from Japanese planes fueled with American gasoline. By this time, the Chinese cause was receiving well-organized support in this country from pro-Chinese action groups, many of them formed under missionary auspices. These organizations publicized Japanese misbehavior, advocated an embargo on war materials to Japan and solicited contributions for medical supplies and other needs for the victims of Japanese bombings.

Step by step public opinion moved away from isolationism. When, in July 1937, the American Institute of Public Opinion (Gallup) asked Americans whether they sympathized with either

---

[1] Except for public opinion polls carried out especially for this survey, most poll results cited in this book were obtained from the voluminous records of the Roper Public Opinion Research Center at Williams College, Williamstown, Massachusetts. Founded in 1957, the Center is a repository for data collected over the past three decades by most recognized public-opinion research organizations throughout the world. In tracing American public opinion on China through recent years, we have drawn heavily on the findings of the American Institute of Public Opinion (Gallup) and the National Opinion Research Center (University of Chicago), and we are grateful to them. Their polling data were made accessible to us through the efficient facilities of the Roper Center. Wherever practical, in this report, references to poll results are accompanied by mention of the polling organization responsible and other pertinent information; hence, footnotes were deemed unnecessary in most instances. It should be noted, however, that in the interest of brevity only partial returns were cited for some polls—which means that the percentages given do not always add up to one hundred.

side, only 44.6 per cent responded in the affirmative. Of those who favored one side or the other, 93.5 per cent said they sympathized with China, and only 6.5 per cent with Japan. At the middle of 1939 a Gallup poll showed that a majority of those with an opinion were in favor of cutting all munitions supplies to Japan. The United States government's decision in July 1939 to abrogate the Japanese-American commercial treaty was widely acclaimed with few dissenting voices. From then on, every move to tighten the noose on Japan and to aid China with money and materials was applauded by the public and the press. As the crisis deepened, public determination rose. Yet as late as September 1940, with Pearl Harbor only months away, only 28 per cent of Americans favored risking war with Japan, if necessary, to prevent Japan from controlling China.

When China and the United States became allies after Pearl Harbor, it was like marriage after an over-long engagement—a shotgun marriage, if you will, but still a happy union. There was a great outpouring of sentiment from both sides but mostly, it must be noted, from the United States. With the cutting off to the Burma road and the relegation of China to lowest priority among the world battle fronts, it had become evident to the Chinese that things were going to get worse for them before they got better. The climax of the Sino-American honeymoon was reached early in 1943 in the triumphal American tour of Madame Chiang Kai-shek. This talented woman received a tremendous ovation in her appearance before Congress, and later 17,000 enthusiastic Americans crowded Madison Square Garden to hear and applaud her.

There was a saying among the cynical that Madame Chiang was worth ten divisions to the Generalissimo. In terms of her influence on American public opinion this was no exaggeration. It can probably be said, in all truth, that Madame Chiang, at that time, commanded more popularity in the United States than in her homeland. This was a fantastic period in Sino-American relations—a period of dreamy unreality, in which the American public seemed prepared to accept and believe anything and everything good and wonderful that was said about the Chinese, their

Generalissimo, the Generalissimo's wife and the heroic Chinese people.

Americans sweating out the war in China had a different view of things. Many had gone to China with the Army or other government services full of romantic notions about fabulous Cathay. Instead they found squalor, filth, inefficiency, corruption, nepotism, runaway inflation and wasteful rivalry between the ruling Kuomintang and the Communists. Some of them had become extremely bitter—so bitter indeed that their perspective on China was distorted out of all relation to the facts. It is hard to say which caused the greater damage in the long run, the uncritically pro-Chiang fervor in the United States or the anti-Chiang, anti-Kuomintang and (in some cases) anti-Chinese hysteria among many Americans in China at this time. Both had serious long-range consequences.

Why did so little information on the "real" situation in China get through to the American public during the first couple of years of the war? Censorship was, of course, partly to blame, but that was not the whole cause. Many of the conditions which newcomers found so scandalous were in reality chronic aspects of the Chinese scene which older residents in China had come to take for granted—perhaps too much so. Moreover, with the world at war and things going badly on most fronts, editors at home were little interested in routine news from China—least of all, stories about corruption, inefficiency and factional bickering. There were those, too, who felt it unsporting to flog an ally while he was down. In these circumstances, the field was wide open to pro-Chinese organizations in the United States to paint the Generalissimo and his government in heroic colors.

One of the more regrettable results of the pro-Chinese euphoria that prevailed in the United States from 1941 to 1944 was that it clouded our understanding of two developing situations which were to have a pronounced impact on American attitudes toward China. One was the deepening personal animosity between Chiang and his American chief of staff, General Joseph W. Stilwell. The other was the growing gravity of the Kuomintang-Communist feud. Some glimmering of the truth about China began to come through in various magazine and newspaper articles in 1943 and 1944.[2] But so strong was the public's compulsion to think the best about our Chinese ally that it was not until General Stilwell's recall in 1944 that the propaganda bubble burst, with explosive force.

The Chinese Communists had never projected a very clear image in the United States. Nor had we taken them as seriously as we ought. We had begun to hear about them in the early 1920s, and by 1926 they had become a thorn in our flesh. Marching north from Canton in alliance with the Kuomintang, in 1926–27, the Communists had been the main instigators of a virulent anti-foreign campaign. Americans and Europeans had sighed with relief when Chiang turned against his Communist collaborators and drove them into the wilderness. For several years the Communists were bottled up in Kiangsi province, in central China, almost forgotten by the outside world. The only news reports reaching us, apart from second-hand accounts from Communist sympathizers like Agnes Smedley and Anna Louise Strong, were Chiang's communiqués on the progress of his seemingly interminable "annihilation" campaigns against the Reds.

It was only when the Communists broke out of the Kiangsi trap and made their way, after a long march, to Shensi province in the high northwest, that they began to loom again as a serious factor in China's political situation. They made headlines in 1936 when they intervened in the sensational "kidnapping" of Chiang Kai-shek, at Sian, and were in the news again in 1937, when they concluded a truce with the Kuomintang for the ostensible purpose of presenting a united front against the Japanese. And in the following year Americans got their first authentic insight into life in the Red areas with the publication of Red Star over China, by Edgar Snow, an American newspaperman.[3] Snow's vivid account of the Long March and his report on personalities and developments in the Communist areas came as a revelation to Americans. After its appearance other reporters visited Yenan, the Communist capital, and a new image of the Chinese Commu-

[2] See, for example, Hanson Baldwin's "Too Much Wishful Thinking about China," Reader's Digest, August 1943, pp. 63–67.
[3] Red Star over China (New York: Random House, 1937).

nists began to take shape in this country. They no longer appeared as creatures with horns, not even as dyed-in-the-wool Communists, but as a people of democratic inclinations, anti-Japanese, friendly to Americans and anxious to get along with Chiang Kai-shek if he would only be "reasonable." The Chinese Communists had graduated from the status of "Red bandits" to "agrarian reformers." And with the onset of the Second World War, they seemed to have become our brothers in arms. They reaped another harvest of generally sympathetic publicity in mid-1944, when a delegation of foreign correspondents, including the representatives of several leading American newspapers, visited Yenan and wired home reams of copy, most of it friendly, on their observations and interviews.

This was a period in China in which the actual situation bore little relation to what Americans at home believed it to be. It was a period in which Americans on the spot were becoming increasingly discouraged and frustrated over the listlessness of the Kuomintang war effort and increasingly interested in the possibility of making more effective use of the underarmed Communist forces. It was a period in which some Americans made statements, drafted policy proposals, or wrote dispatches which, in later years, were exhumed and used as "evidence" of pro-Communist inclinations.

To understand the attitudes that prevailed among Americans in China in those years, it is necessary to know something about the conditions under which they lived and worked. China had been at war with Japan since 1937, and the signs of exhaustion were everywhere apparent in Chungking, the capital. The city had been bombed repeatedly and showed it. Most homes were leaky, shaky and uncomfortable. Rats abounded—lying low during the day, taking over the streets and alleys at night. Climatic conditions were miserable—rain and mud for half the year, oppressively humid heat for the rest. The wartime capital was crowded with underpaid, undernourished government employees (I don't recall seeing any overweight Chinese under the rank of a minister of finance), many of whom found it impossible to support their families without indulging in graft on the side.

Perhaps no one has described wartime Chungking less ele-

gantly but more accurately than General Stilwell,[4] who, in cele-
bration of his sixtieth birthday, wrote an ode to the city which
he included in a letter to his wife. Stilwell's first two verses went
as follows:

> I welcomed the spring in romantic Chungking.
> I walked in her beautiful bowers.
> In the light of the moon, in the sunshine at noon,
> I savored the fragrance of flowers.
>
> (Not to speak of the slush, or the muck and the mush
> That covers the streets and alleys.
> Or the reek of the swill, as it seeps down the hill.—
> Or the odor of pig in the valleys.)

In later verses Stilwell builds up to a profane climax too harsh,
perhaps, for delicate sensibilities. Hence we omit it.

All in all, Chungking was a wonderful place to get away from;
and those American correspondents who could get away did so
whenever the opportunity offered. A favorite excursion, when
feasible, was to Yenan, the cave-pocked Communist capital in
the high, dry loess country of northwestern China. Regardless of
one's politics, stepping off the plane into the dry sunshine of
Yenan after weeks of soupy discomfort in Chungking was invariably a psychologically invigorating experience. In those days
the Chinese Communists were making a play for American cooperation and support, so Americans arriving at Yenan were
given a warm welcome at the airfield. Yenan itself was little more
than a collection of mud huts and caves, but the contrast in
atmosphere to Chungking was very striking. This was the time
of the New Democracy—a transitional phase in the Communist
political program—and to most visitors it seemed that the Communist reforms were mild and that the morale of the people was
high.

No Yenan visit was complete, of course, without interviews
with Mao Tse-tung, Chou En-lai and other dignitaries, and these
were easily arranged. An atmosphere of reasonableness and in-
formality prevailed. The Communists were eager, willing and
anxious to work in close cooperation with the Americans to bring

---

[4] *The Stilwell Papers*, ed. by Theodore H. White (New York: William
Sloane Associates, 1948), p. 199.

the war against Japan to an early and successful conclusion. Or so they said.

In the circumstances there were few if any Americans who did not leave Yenan impressed by what they had seen and heard. If they erred, it was in taking superficial appearances for the real thing, in failing to recognize the real objectives of Chinese communism behind the window dressing of the New Democracy. To know Communist intentions they needed only to read carefully the writings of Mao Tse-tung or, for that matter, to ask Mao a few skillfully leading questions. Probably a good many did. But many could not believe that what they saw in Yenan was not the finished product.

In later years, congressional investigators found it difficult to understand how Americans in China could have been "taken in" by Communist blandishments. As one who was stationed in China during those years, I do not find it surprising. There were many reasons for it—none of them subversive—but back of them lay a central fact. That was the intense distaste, even hatred, which many Americans in China developed in those years for Chiang Kai-shek and the government he headed. Most of these Americans had what they thought were the best interests of China at heart. They wanted democratic reforms, they wanted efficient government, they wanted a united China, they wanted a more serious concentration on the war effort. It seemed to them that Chiang was the major obstruction to these changes. Many of course were influenced by the views of General Stilwell, top-ranking American military officer in the theater, who made no secret of his contempt for the Generalissimo.

This frustration over Chiang and his authoritarian outlook—the conviction that he was hopelessly stubborn and reactionary—made it easier to take a wishful view of the Chinese Communists and to accept appearances for facts. The confusion of thinking on Chinese communism was common among American diplomats, military men, newspapermen, radio commentators, scholars and many important people in public life. All through the fabric of expert opinion in those years ran a thread of wishful thinking as to the real nature of Chinese communism. Yet the harsh facts were there, in the writings of Mao Tse-tung himself.

Dr. Tang Tsou of the University of Chicago brings this point out in his exhaustively researched study, *America's Failure in China, 1941–50:*

In the writings about Chinese politics at this time, one searches in vain for the view that a Communist party based on Leninist principles is a tightly organized and highly disciplined group of professional revolutionaries, aiming at the seizure of power whenever possible, exploiting mass discontent from whatever sources are at hand, and employing a multiplicity of means and a variety of institutional forms to achieve its purpose.[5]

There was at least one person in Chungking at that time who might have described the Chinese Communists in just those terms. His name, ironically, was Chiang Kai-shek. Whatever Chiang's shortcomings—and they were many—he knew the Chinese Communists better than many of those who regarded him with such contempt. For an explanation as to why more Americans could not or would not see the real motivations behind Chinese Communist policy at that time, we turn again to Dr. Tang Tsou:

It is easy to see that the comfortable notion of the Chinese Communists as agrarian reformers, sincere democrats and the like fitted perfectly well with the political and military considerations dominating the mind of American officials and opinion leaders in those years: the desire to utilize the military potential of the Chinese Communists, the hope of avoiding entanglement with Russia over China, and the wish to bring about a unified and democratic China as the stabilizing force in the Far East. These considerations were in harmony with the American aversion to engaging in a rough political and military contest with other powers in continental Asia. The wish was the father to the thought.[6]

The repressed emotions of frustrated American correspondents finally boiled over in October 1944 on the occasion of the recall of General Stilwell to the United States. The recall was an inevitable sequel to the intolerable strains that had developed between General Stilwell and Chiang Kai-shek and of which the American people had little inkling. When Stilwell moved in as

[5] *America's Failure in China, 1941–50* (Chicago: University of Chicago Press, 1963), p. 230.
[6] Same, p. 235.

chief of staff to Chiang and commander of the American ground forces in the China-Burma-India theater, China was already virtually prostrate from more than four years of conflict with Japan. The country had only one overland supply line—through Burma —and even this was soon to be cut. It was China's dubious distinction to enjoy the lowest priority among the major World War II battlefronts, and munitions assigned to Stilwell and his Chinese forces were sometimes snatched away before delivery. Stilwell was sandwiched unenviably between the War Department and Chiang. When the War Department failed in its commitments, Chiang blamed Stilwell. When Chiang reneged on his promises, Stilwell lost face in Washington. If Stilwell became "Vinegar Joe," it was for a reason.

Reading Stilwell's wartime papers one cannot help wondering how Stilwell managed to retain his command—not to mention his sanity—for as long as he did, in light of the countless antagonisms he nurtured. He disliked the "Limeys," who were his allies in Burma. He had little use for Admiral Lord Louis Mountbatten, their supreme commander. He rarely had a good word for Roosevelt or Churchill. He harbored an intensive antipathy for Chennault because of his deference to Chiang and his dreamy views of quick victory in China through airpower—views utterly in conflict with Stilwell's own down-to-earth assessment of the situation.

Stilwell had a foot soldier's view of the war. With only limited resources at his disposal, he stuck to limited objectives. One was blasting a corridor through the Japanese army and the dripping jungle in northern Burma. In the end, what Stilwell accomplished at the cost of so much heartbreak and frustration probably did not notably hasten final victory, if it hastened it at all. Historians may even call it an exercise in futility. But there was a grim satisfaction in it for Stilwell. He had demonstrated for the first time that the Chinese soldier, when properly armed, properly trained and properly led, was the equal of any. Stilwell had a great affection for China's common people and her rank-and-file fighting men, and he managed to pass on some of this feeling to the American public. In his diary, in a moment of frustration, he wrote: "These people are hard to help, I have to keep thinking that there are 399,900,000 of them worth helping or I wouldn't be able to stick it out with the other 100,000." [7]

Stilwell's dislike for Chiang, though at times almost psychotic, is nevertheless not to be taken lightly. There was no American in China at that time, or perhaps ever, who was in a better position to observe the Generalissimo at his best and at his worst. He had scant respect for the Gimo's military judgment and felt constantly blocked by his disregard of suggestions, his failure to keep promises, his political subterfuges, and 101 other derelictions real and supposed. Yet in the thick of the war, in 1943, he was obliged to admit to himself that there was no better leader in sight.

On his side, Chiang returned the ill feeling, complained bitterly about Stilwell to President Roosevelt, and finally requested his recall. It was a cruel comedown for "Vinegar Joe." However, the publicity it generated was more harmful to Chiang's image than to Stilwell's in American eyes; and in this respect the American general had his revenge. The Generalissimo was never again to regain the great prestige he had once enjoyed in this country.

The spate of publicity that followed Stilwell's recall was in the main uncomplimentary to Chiang Kai-shek and the Kuomintang. The regime was labeled as moribund, inefficient and corrupt. It was charged with giving only halfhearted cooperation in the war against Japan. And the Generalissimo was accused of sabotaging all efforts to bring the Communists and the Kuomintang together into a coalition government. Stilwell's side of his bitter feud with the Generalissimo was reported in strong terms.

The disclosures surprised and shocked many Americans and forced them to revise their favorable estimate of the Kuomintang and to take a more pessimistic view of the China situation as a whole. The net effect of this outburst was to stigmatize Chiang and the Kuomintang, make a martyr of Stilwell (in some eyes) and put the Chinese Communists in a relatively more favorable light. Chiang and his government never fully recovered the prestige lost in this onslaught, although it is probable most Americans continued to think of China primarily in terms of Chiang's regime.

The storm passed, Major General Albert C. Wedemeyer replaced Stilwell, and China became, again, a routine story in the

[7] *The Stilwell Papers,* cited, p. 195.

American press. By this time the American public was no longer expecting great things out of China, and, in any case, it had become clear that China's help was no longer needed in bringing about the final downfall of Japan. The question uppermost in American minds was whether civil war could be averted and stability in China preserved as Japan went down to final defeat. Hopes rose and fell repeatedly during those final months of the war and even past V-J day, as Ambassador Patrick Hurley tried stubbornly but unsuccessfully to obtain an accord between Mao Tse-tung and Chiang.

The immediate postwar period in China was one of great turbulence in American attitudes toward that country. There was clearly a chance that in the chaos of civil conflict between the Communists and the Kuomintang we would lose much or all of what we had fought Japan to preserve. However, when Gallup in July 1946 asked a cross section of Americans what they thought the United States should do about the situation in China, 50 per cent answered "Nothing," "Stay out," "Leave them alone," or words to that effect. Few Americans believed at this stage that the Nationalists were in serious danger of overthrow; only 13 per cent of those queried were in favor of giving aid to Chiang in his struggle against the Communists.

It was hardly a time for rapid demobilization of our forces in Asia, yet the voice of the American public came through at this juncture loud, clear and irresistible—"Bring our boys home!" Whether it would have made any difference in the final outcome in China to have retained large American military forces in the area for an extended period is dubious. But that does not alter the irony of the situation. The American public had been willing to go to war to save China and to defend our interests in that country. Now that Japan was humbled, the fate of China was secondary to the need for getting our boys out of uniform and back into civilian life.

This inconsistency was clearly seen by our military leaders at the time, but they were powerless to resist public pressures. General George C. Marshall, in the course of a speech in October 1945, said: "For the moment, in a wide-spread emotional crisis of the American people, demobilization has become in effect, disintegration, not only of the armed forces but apparently of all conception of world responsibility and what it demands of us."⁸

It is true that the American public did not, at first, feel the deep sense of alarm over the postwar situation in China that the actual state of affairs warranted. This is hardly surprising, in light of the questionable assumptions on which our China policy was at the time operating. The public was disarmed, for example, by the administration's persistent faith in coalition government as a workable solution for China. Yet all our experience up to that time had indicated that the prospects were minimal. Secondly, and also mistakenly, there were still those who assumed that the Soviet Union could be trusted to honor the spirit of its pledges to China and to us—that is, to lend its moral and diplomatic support to the stabilization of China under the leadership of Chiang Kai-shek. A third miscalculation was the expectation that in case of all-out civil war the Kuomintang's superiority in manpower and weapons would give it an advantage and that in any case the worst that could happen would be the division of the country into two parts, with the Kuomintang forces retaining the larger share. Fourthly, there was the widely shared assumption (with some believers to be found in the State Department itself) that the Chinese Communists were not in fact dedicated Communists. And the fifth miscalculation, also widely shared, was the view inherited from Franklin Delano Roosevelt that China, under Chiang Kai-shek, would emerge from the war a leading power and, of course, a friendly one.

The appointment of General Marshall, one of the great Americans of the day, to go to China to seek a solution to the problem gave rise to yet another illusion. This was that General Marshall's tremendous prestige could not fail to break down interparty differences. "If Marshall can't do it, nobody can," was the mood of the times.

When he left for China late in 1945, General Marshall had public opinion and, to a large extent, congressional opinion on his side. But some influential Americans were already becoming deeply disturbed over increasing signs of Soviet intransigence

⁸ Speech of October 29, 1945, New York Herald Tribune Forum, *New York Herald Tribune*, October 30, 1945.

and Chinese Communist gains in Manchuria and north China. Marshall had been in China only a few months when their outcries began to be heard. Some concentrated their attack on alleged Soviet violations of the Yalta Agreement and the Sino-Soviet treaty of 1945. Others demanded increased aid for the Nationalists and opposed any cooperation with the Chinese Communists. Prominent Republicans and conservatively oriented newspapers and magazines joined in the clamor. The agitation seriously undermined bipartisan support for President Truman's China policy although it did not reach its peak until after Marshall's return to the United States in early 1947. By then it was clear that Marshall's mission had been a failure and that the Kuomintang and the Communists were engaged in a struggle to the death. Despite the Wedemeyer Report, the Bullitt Report and fresh infusions of American aid,[9] the Nationalists were clearly beyond any hope of rescue at this point. Even the eleventh hour appearance of Madame Chiang in Washington in December 1948 to plead for a three-billion-dollar aid program failed to evoke even an echo of the wild enthusiasm that had greeted her in 1943. Americans could only watch in stunned helplessness as the China they had known fell apart like a house of cards.

The Communist victory on the mainland of China in 1949—dazzling in its speed and decisiveness—set off a furious war of words in the United States. Anger was mixed with confusion and frustration. We had liberated China from the Japanese. We had expended more than two billion dollars since V-J Day to keep her afloat. Now all we stood for had gone down the drain. Who was to blame? Could we have prevented it? Where did we go from here? What to do about Taiwan? The benumbed public had none of the answers. It knew only that it had its fill of China for

[9] Lieutenant General Albert C. Wedemeyer headed an official American "fact-finding" mission to China in July–August 1947. His report to President Truman may be found in *U.S. Relations with China, with Special Reference to the Period 1944–49* (Washington, D.C.: GPO, Department of State Publication 3573, Far Eastern Series 30, August 1949), pp. 764–814. William Bullitt, recently returned from a trip to the Far East, was the author of an unofficial "Report on China" in *Life* magazine, October 13, 1947. Both reports called for large-scale military and economic assistance to the Nationalist regime.

the time being. China had become a prime political issue, with Congress divided pretty much along party lines. All through 1949 and the first half of 1950 the controversy went on, with the so-called China Bloc in Congress making onslaught after onslaught on the administration's China policy. This was the period of Chiang Kai-shek's flight to Taiwan, of the inauguration of a new regime at Peking. Up to the last some Americans believed that the Nationalist collapse on the Chinese mainland could have been reversed by stepped-up infusions of American aid. It was the unpleasant duty of the then Secretary of State, Dean Acheson, to set the record straight in these somber words:

The unfortunate but inescapable fact is that the ominous result of the civil war in China was beyond the control of the Government of the United States. Nothing that this country did or could have done within the reasonable limits of its capabilities could have changed the result; nothing that was left undone by this country has contributed to it. It was the product of internal Chinese forces, forces which this country tried to influence but could not. A decision was arrived at in China, if only a decision by default.[10]

These conclusions were challenged by Republicans in Congress who charged the Democrats with attempting to whitewash their mistakes. Several prominent Republicans, including ex-President Herbert Hoover and Senator Robert A. Taft, advocated use of the United States Navy to prevent a Communist takeover of Taiwan. Others, notably Senator H. Alexander Smith, went so far as to suggest American military occupation of Taiwan. The negative public reaction to these proposals made it clear that the American people were in no mood at this juncture to expend American lives in helping to defend the remains of a regime which (as they saw it) had badly let them down. Moreover, the public was plainly opposed to any line of action that might lead to a new world war. Except in Congress, few protesting voices were heard as the Truman administration went ahead with plans to close out the books on our long relationship with Kuomintang China.

Although the China Bloc in Congress—which included such names as Knowland, Bridges, McCarran, Wherry and Judd—suc-

10 Letter of Transmittal, *United States Relations with China*, cited, p. xvi.

ceeded in obtaining only moderate increases in aid for the de-feated Chiang regime, it did manage to frustrate administration efforts to disentangle the United States completely from the Kuomintang government. Also, with some support from the Democrats, the Republicans effectively discouraged all proposals and suggestions that might have led to recognition of the new Peking regime. Their task was made easier by the attitude of the Chinese Communists, who were missing no opportunity to show their hatred and contempt for the United States both in words and action. The Communists spouted filth, venom and ridicule in our direction. They arrested an American consular officer in Mukden, seized American consular property in Peking. The viru-lence of their hostility surprised and shocked Americans, who still attached importance to the long-standing bonds of friendship between China and the United States and somehow expected that even the Communists would be hesitant to renounce them.

During this period it is clear that most Americans expected an early Communist takeover in Taiwan and obliteration of the Chiang regime. Moreover, they were disinclined to do anything to prevent it. They remained deeply antagonistic, however, to China's new masters. The returns of two polls taken in January 1950, at the lowest ebb in Chiang's political fortunes, illustrate this apparent paradox. A Gallup sounding of public opinion in that month showed only 18 per cent in favor of giving financial aid and war materials to Chiang, while a scant 13 per cent fa-vored using American armed forces to protect and hold the island of Taiwan. Thirty per cent wanted to do nothing, and the re-mainder had other views or no views at all.

At the same time, a representative sampling of Americans showed a strong majority against the recognition of the Chinese Communist regime. When the National Opinion Research Center, a polling organization associated with the University of Chicago, in the same month asked whether the United States should now recognize the Chinese Communists as the legal government of China or should continue to recognize the Chiang Kai-shek gov-ernment, the response was unmistakably favorable to the Na-tionalists: 61 per cent were in favor of continued recognition of Chiang Kai-shek; 11 per cent were in favor of recognizing the

Communists; and 26 per cent did not know what to do. Individual reactions to the NORC questions showed that most of those favoring continued recognition of Chiang's defeated and disgraced government were motivated more by strong anti-Communist convictions than by sympathy for Chiang. Typical views were: "We don't want anything to do with communism anywhere"; "I don't think the Communists should rule any country"; "If we recognize them, they'd soon have the whole works"; and so forth. Only a small percentage expressed faith in Chiang, with such comments as "He has been our ally for so many years," or "We should stick by him because he supports our way of living."

Views on recognition of Communist China during this period were mixed and fluctuating. It is probably correct to say that a majority of opinion leaders in the country expected recognition to follow as a matter of course after Communist occupation of Taiwan—then regarded as inevitable. Some, no doubt, would have welcomed it sooner. But the hostile behavior of the Peking regime, combined with strong opposition from important Republicans and Democrats to hasty action, made the recognitionists understandably cautious. By this time, the "agrarian reformer" myth had given way in many American minds, official and unofficial, to the view that the Chinese Communists were in fact little more than Soviet puppets. This view, too, has since had to be drastically revised.

The reckless irresponsibility shown by the Chinese Communists in their treatment of Americans and American interests failed to goad the American public to a fighting pitch. It would take something bigger. That something turned out to be the North Korean attack on South Korea, in June 1950. Here was a direct and unmistakable challenge to American security and prestige. Once again Americans were outraged. Inhibitions against military action dropped away. The decisions to send troops to the aid of South Korea and to neutralize the Formosa Strait with American naval power were generally applauded in the United States. It was still to be seen, however, what role Communist China would play in the Korean conflict. A large section of "knowledgeable" opinion, including some leading personalities in our military and diplomatic services, was convinced, apparently, that the Chinese would not intervene. The humiliating disaster in the hills of North Korea that followed these miscalculations is today a well-known but tragic episode in our military history.

Peking's intervention in the Korean War did more to "set" American attitudes against the Chinese Communists than anything that had happened up to that time. It now dawned on us that the Chinese were capable of challenging us militarily as well as politically. Even the overwhelming Communist victory over the Kuomintang had failed to prepare us for the possibility that any Chinese army could be the equal of an American fighting force. Now Chinese Communists were killing Americans. Not only had they inflicted heavy casualties on our forces, but they had shown themselves to be devilishly clever in applying their brainwashing techniques to some of their American prisoners. The blow to our pride, the humiliation, could hardly have been more complete. Overnight, our view of the Chinese Communists was changed from patronizing superiority to one of deep anger and apprehension. In all our history we had never felt quite like this about the Chinese. For a parallel we would have to go back to Medieval Europe and the Tartar hordes. It was the rebirth of the "Yellow Peril" specter, and it is still with us.

Having suffered this setback, Americans wanted retribution. So did General Douglas MacArthur. He sought authority to unify Korea and, if necessary, carry the war into China itself so as to "severely cripple and largely neutralize China's capability to wage aggressive war and thus save Asia from the engulfment otherwise facing it." [11] The flood of criticism that descended on President Truman after his dismissal of MacArthur and the tremendous welcome accorded MacArthur on his return to the United States provided convincing evidence of public feeling on the matter. Commenting on these events, one author ascribes the almost hysterical reception of MacArthur to the nation's frustration with the containment policy, "which was psychologically and emo-

[11] General MacArthur's message of December 30, 1950, as summarized in John W. Spanier, *The Truman-MacArthur Controversy and the Korean War* (Cambridge, Mass.: The Belknap Press of Harvard University Press, 1959), pp. 140–141.

tionally in contradiction with American values and experience in foreign affairs." [12] He reminds us that whenever the United States had been drawn into an international arena in the past, its actions had met with success. We had beaten the British, the Mexicans, the Spaniards, the Germans and the Japanese. Failure was an unusual experience, difficult for Americans to explain or comprehend. Hence many Americans were ready and willing to accept the suggestion that treason was behind our political and military failures. And such a charge had already claimed national headlines.

The fear, frustration and anger that had followed the Communist takeover of China had spelled political opportunity for Joseph W. McCarthy, the then junior senator from Wisconsin. It so happened that he had been looking around for a vote-catching issue for his election campaign in 1950, when someone suggested Communist influence in government as a good possibility. On February 9, 1950, the Senator tried it out on an audience at Wheeling, West Virginia. When he dramatically waved before his listeners what was purported to be a list of Communists or fellow travelers in the State Department, it was plain from the excited reaction that he had hit on a sure-fire thing. Almost immediately, McCarthy found himself propelled into the national limelight. And by bluff, bluster and misrepresentation he managed to stay there until, finally, censure, sickness and overexposure to the public gaze brought him down.

The McCarthy period represented a distinct break—an interregnum—in American thinking on China. Reason abdicated to emotion. McCarthy's timing, if largely accidental, was perfect. The inflamed public was baffled and angry over the "loss" of China and the inability of the United States to check the spread of communism abroad and at home. The Hiss trial and other security cases just completed had planted disturbing uncertainties in the public mind about Communist influence within the government itself. These were real and serious problems requiring further investigation and clarification through responsible agencies. It was a situation in which a bungled job could do incalcu-

[12] John W. Spanier, *American Foreign Policy Since World War II* (New York: Frederick A. Praeger, 1960), p. 92.

lable harm. Yet the public wanted some answers, and McCarthy, a demagogue, claimed he had them. When he came charging out of the wings with his stories of Communist conspiracy in the State Department, he found a ready audience.

McCarthy had plenty of company. He was not a lone comet flashing across the troubled sky. There were millions in the country and not a few in Congress itself to agree with him and encourage him. He was the personification of a mood shared by a very large sector of the public at that time. McCarthy was not concerned alone, or even primarily, with the Chinese issues, nor was he the first to suggest publicly the possibility of pro-Communist plotting among American foreign service officers. The idea had originated more than four years before with the then Ambassador to China, Patrick J. Hurley. The dapper Hurley had gone to China confident that he could bring about unity between the Kuomintang regime and the Communists. When he left, empty-handed and frustrated like others before him, he pinned the blame for his failure on his diplomatic colleagues. In his letter of resignation to President Truman, in November 1945, Hurley wrote: "Our professional diplomats continuously advised the Communists that my efforts in preventing the collapse of the National government did not represent the policy of the United States. These same professionals openly advised the Communist armed party to decline unification of the Chinese Communist Army with the National Army unless the Chinese Communists were given control." In a later passage he charged that "a considerable section of our State Department is endeavoring to support communism generally as well as specifically in China." [13]

Hurley's charges made something of a stir but were weak on details. They were not taken too seriously; nor was Hurley himself. His erratic behavior in China had made him a tragi-comic figure. And in any case the outlook in China was not considered, even at that date, acutely serious. The Chinese Nationalists still had the upper hand, and there was a general expectation they would retain it.

By the time McCarthy came along, however, the crisis was ripe for exploitation. Although many informed and responsible

[13] *United States Relations with China*, cited, p. 582.

people deplored McCarthy's methods, almost from the beginning, the mood of the public was that where there was so much smoke there must be some fire. Wherever he went, "Tailgunner Joe" attracted large and, in the main, enthusiastic audiences. They cheered his extravagant and usually unproved accusations of pro-communism, betrayal and even treason against people in high places. Shouts of "Give 'em hell, Joe!" came from his audiences as he dragged reputation after reputation through the muck of his oratory.

McCarthy was reputed to have had close ties with Alfred Kohlberg and other members of the so-called China Lobby and presumably drew heavily on them for "background" information for his attacks on Owen Lattimore and members of the China service in the State Department. He recklessly smeared or wrecked dozens of reputations. While it is quite possible, even probable, that in his scattergun attacks he hit some fellow travelers or Communists, the reasonable assumption is that an overwhelming majority of those attacked were loyal Americans. Unfortunately for the innocent, there was no way of replying to McCarthy's charges that would undo the damage done. In those times of fear and suspicion the public was all too ready to listen to the witch-hunters, however unconvincing their accusations. Some families are still paying off the toll of embarrassment, shame and financial difficulty inflicted on them for no proved cause.

McCarthy's popularity with a large section of the public gave him a powerful club with which to intimidate his critics. And he used it at the slightest provocation. For a time McCarthy was probably the most feared man in the United States. To attack him was to invite a counter-charge of "Communist stooge." Even his Senate colleagues feared him. The press, which had built him up, was for the most part critical of him. Yet in the early months of the McCarthy era there were few individuals with the courage to challenge him openly. One who did was Senator Millard Tydings of Maryland. It cost him his Senate seat in his next time up for election. But in time, McCarthy's increasing recklessness and irresponsibility brought about his downfall. Censured by the Senate, ridiculed by a large part of the press, he died a discredited man.

Among those specialists on China who took exception to McCarthy's methods—and that means most of them—the period is recalled as a kind of bad dream. The effects were mostly seriously felt in the academic and diplomatic fields. Interest in China studies dropped off. There was some shrinkage in funds available for study and research.

"It was almost a lost generation," the head of an Asian studies program in a west coast university said recently. "We are only now beginning to get some good people."

In the State Department, meanwhile, the results were devastating. Men who had spent the better part of their adult lives acquiring knowledge and experience in China and fluency in the Chinese language now found themselves under attack. As a leading member of the China service put it:

Our China service was politically castrated during the McCarthy era, and it has not yet recovered. Because of the casualties of that period there is no fully experienced leadership level today. Nowadays, our China specialists tend to have a conditioned reflex on questions that arise.

This was perhaps the gravest consequence of the McCarthy era. In and out of the State Department, experts on China were so hamstrung and intimidated that their usefulness was seriously impaired—and at a time when their expertise was sorely needed. Under the circumstances, new and original suggestions for dealing with the China question were not encouraged. "Why stick my neck out?" became the mood. In such an atmosphere, wise decisions all too often became more a matter of luck than of careful reasoning. The question asks itself: But for these inhibitions would our China policy be different today?

This is not to say that either the State Department or the liberal community, which were principal targets of the McCarthy attacks, were beyond reproach. It was not difficult to find genuine instances of misjudgment and miscalculation in the State Department's handling of the China situation. There were some proved instances of indiscretion and worse. And the passion of many liberals in those days for left-wing causes, particularly their penchant for joining "front" organizations, was certainly revealing of a naive credulity with respect to communism and its methods. Yet despite the sound and fury expended, McCarthy himself was able to produce no proof of Communist party membership by any person not already known to be a Communist.

If the McCarthy era showed a few useful results—for example, in alerting the public decisively to the dangers and techniques of Communist penetration—the damage it caused was incalculable. Many self-styled liberals discreetly buttoned their lips on the China question. Some State Department personnel stopped suggesting new and original approaches. Our China policy went into the deep freeze. For several years free and open discussion of China and our China policy was severely inhibited. And evidences of caution on the subject are still plentiful today.

CHAPTER THREE

Chiang Kai-shek, Taiwan and the Old China Hands

For almost forty years, Chiang Kai-shek has been the controversial symbol of American successes and failures in China. The United States has backed Chiang with fluctuating enthusiasm, but withal with remarkable steadfastness, since he took charge of the Chinese Nationalist revolution in 1926 and marched his armies triumphantly from the south of China to the Great Wall in the north. We retain significant commitments to him today.

Although Chiang has continuously enjoyed the support of the United States government throughout this prolonged period of alternating triumph and travail, Americans as individuals have been deeply, often bitterly, divided in their sympathies. It would be difficult to find a better illustration of our conflicting emotions on China than the controversy that has swirled around the Generalissimo during the past two decades.

Chiang won popularity with Americans through his prolonged record of resistance to Japanese aggression and his stubborn anti-Communism, although he was often ineffective in both. He had other assets, not the least of which were his Methodism and his astute wife. Long before he reached the peak of his prestige, however, in the early part of World War II, contradictory views about him had begun to develop among Americans with a knowledge of China. Those who admired Chiang usually did so with concentrated loyalty. Those who disliked him often did so with an intensity bordering on hatred. Although there was no uniformity of view in any group, Chiang's sharpest critics were to be found among the following categories of Americans: military men and civilians attached to the staff of General Joseph W. Stilwell; young liberals attached to the American Embassy and various advisory and aid missions in China; academic people and other intellectuals; newspaper correspondents.

The motivations of these critics were varied. Frustration was a predominant emotion, which General Stilwell epitomized as none other. Stilwell's caustic and often profane views on Chiang deeply influenced many Americans in China, including newspapermen, and through them thousands of others in the United States. Yet these same Americans needed only to go to the headquarters of another high-ranking American, Major General Claire Chennault, commander of the Fourteenth Air Force, to hear Chiang described in terms so different you wondered whether Chennault and Stilwell were talking about the same man. Such were the contradictions that made China such an exasperating yet tantalizing country to understand.

Other American officers who tried to work with Chiang during and after the Stilwell period also had their moments of intense frustration. But unlike Vinegar Joe, they managed, for the most part, to keep their emotions under control and seemed to get better cooperation by so doing. One of them, a general, told me he has in his files copies of more than one thousand memoranda sent to the Generalissimo. "They were usually ignored," he said, "and occasionally I would call Chiang's attention to the many that had not been acted on. He was tolerant and kind about it. But he thought I was naive." This officer described Chiang as a man with a deep sense of loyalty to his friends—"in fact he has them loaded around his neck."

Among academic people, American or Chinese, Chiang had few friends or admirers. No intellectual himself, he distrusted the breed. They were always getting in his way or coming up with reformist notions which did not conform to his basically Confucian outlook on life. American intellectuals had hoped that the liberal tradition would ultimately triumph in China, but they saw little chance for it while Chiang was in charge. They disliked his authoritarian methods. He was constantly putting pressure on the academic community to conform. He saw the universities in China as hotbeds of pro-Communist agitation, as indeed they quite often were. His dilemma was that he knew of no answer for this condition but repression.

An American professor of mildly conservative inclinations who worked in China during the war told the writer that the wishful thinking then so widely prevalent among American liberals with regard to the Chinese Communists was in large part a reflex reaction to their hatred of Chiang. "Some American intellectuals identified Chiang with the bad demons who pushed professors around," he said. "These people were fighting for liberalism in the Kuomintang and not recognizing the dangers. Many other foreigners in China, including some businessmen, made the same error. They were angry with Chiang for betraying the Chinese people. This made them willing listeners to the Communist sweet talk about New Democracy."

Like other liberal-thinking Americans in China at that time, a number of the newspaper correspondents became emotionally involved in China's internal problems and were critical, in conversation and in their writings, of Chiang's unwillingness to institute bold rural reforms in order to counter the Communist challenge and mobilize public opinion on his side. In the earlier years of Chiang's leadership such a program might indeed have been feasible and effective. But by 1944 it was probably already too late. Chiang was not only at war with the Japanese; the Chinese Communists were also working continuously to undermine his position. The Generalissimo's authority was by then so heavily dependent on landlord support that any serious move to undercut it would have been an invitation to political suicide. As an old-time China resident put it: "You cannot carry out reforms when you are hanging on the ropes."

Newspapermen are a skeptical lot, and trying to squeeze hard news out of Chiang's headquarters made them more so. Chiang's speeches and statements were usually devoid of color and studded with pompous abstractions. Interviews with him rarely contained enough red meat to justify large headlines. Chinese communiqués on the military situation were uninformative and unreliable. American correspondents depended heavily on Stilwell's office for inside information. Another place where they could always count on picking up a delectable morsel or two was at the Chungking headquarters of the Communist delegation. Chou En-lai, when in town, was a gold mine of gossip on the Generalissimo and the Kuomintang. Affable, smooth and convincing, Chou was always prepared to explain in great detail just how Chiang's armies were sabotaging national unity by squeezing the Communists out of this or that area. The impression grew—and it was communicated to the American public—that it was the Communists who were doing most of the fighting against the Japanese while Chiang seemed more concerned with blockading the Communists.

This was a warped view of the situation that did Chiang an injustice. While it is undeniable that both Chinese camps wasted a great deal of their wartime effort watching and fighting each other instead of the Japanese, the suggestion that the Communists were the aggrieved party was both dubious and misleading. If it was not clear then, it is certainly clear now that the Sino-Japanese war was a godsend to the Chinese Communists. They welcomed it. It was their key to power in China. They saw with cold-blooded foresight and realism that war with Japan would not only divert Chiang from anti-Communist suppression, it would also steadily undermine his strength while opening up countless opportunities for expansion of Communist influence and control. Chiang's armies, pinned down in the cities, would have to take the main blows of the enemy, while the Communists, completely mobile, could afford the luxury of fighting only when the odds were in their favor. For the Communists, attainment of national power in China was the primary goal, the Sino-Japanese war but a convenient tool for achieving it.

By the time Chiang and his followers had lost their last battle on the mainland and fled to Taiwan, they were so discredited in the United States that public opinion was fully prepared for the imminent loss of the island stronghold and Chiang's final surrender. Polls of the period show this shift clearly. In 1947, the National Opinion Research Center (NORC) asked this question of Americans: "In general, do you have a favorable or unfavorable impression of the present government of China headed by Chiang Kai-shek?" The replies showed 31 per cent who were favorable, 25 per cent who were unfavorable and 38 per cent who did not know. In 1948, the same question was asked, under the same auspices. This time, only 26 per cent had a favorable impression of Chiang's government and 33 an unfavorable impression, with 40 per cent saying they did not know. In 1949, the year of Communist victory on the Chinese mainland, Chiang's prospects were considered so hopeless that 50 per cent of the Americans responding to a Gallup poll said that the United States was right in withholding further aid from the Nationalist government. Only 20 per cent said it was doing wrong.

But we had underestimated Chiang's guardian angel. A look at the record would have shown that at least twice previously Chiang had been on the brink of oblivion only to be saved by wholly unexpected circumstances. In 1936, Communist intervention had delivered him whole after his "kidnapping" at Sian. Later, he was to snatch victory out of defeat in his war with Japan, after the Japanese sneak attack on Pearl Harbor brought the United States into the war on his side. And now, providentially for the Generalissimo, the surprise onset of war in Korea again brought Uncle Sam to the rescue, this time to ensure his security in Taiwan. Once again, Chiang's friends in this country were able to raise their heads—and their voices. Chiang might be finished in the eyes of much of the rest of the world. He still carried political weight in the United States.

The reversal of sentiment produced by the traumatic Korean outbreak was again reflected in the opinion polls. Suddenly Americans were willing to support to the hilt a regime they had all but abandoned a few months before. In 1951, at the height of the Korean conflict, NORC asked a nationwide sampling of Americans if they would approve or disapprove of the United States government's giving the Nationalist government under Chiang Kai-shek the help it needed to attack the Communists on the Chinese mainland, and a topheavy 58 per cent said they would approve. Only 24 per cent disapproved and the remainder said they did not know.

Even in 1955, when the Korean conflict was past history, the deep residue of hostility and distrust it had left in American attitudes toward Communist China was plainly revealed in public opinion polls of the period. An NORC poll showed that 73 per cent of those interviewed approved of the action of Congress in authorizing President Eisenhower to use American armed forces to help defend Taiwan in case of a Chinese Communist attack. Only 18 per cent disapproved. Meanwhile, Chiang's prestige in this country had rebounded from its 1949–1950 low. In a check, in 1955, on the popularity of various world leaders, NORC found that 54 per cent of Americans had a favorable impression of Chiang and only 20 per cent an unfavorable impression. The remainder of those interviewed had no opinion. The popularity poll showed Chiang slightly behind Anthony Eden but ahead of such world figures as Konrad Adenauer and Jawaharlal Nehru.

While Chiang has now recovered some of his lost prestige in this country, his image is but a shadow of what it was before the collapse of his mainland rule. This is clearly reflected in the comments of persons recently interviewed in widely scattered cities throughout the United States. The ignominy of the Kuomintang's collapse made a deep and unhappy impression on Americans, although there is evident confusion and disagreement as to the causes and responsibility. There are those who contend that the United States is to blame for the "loss" of China by reason of its failure to back the Chiang regime to the hilt against the Communists. More often, one is told that what happened was the inevitable consequence of the sins, errors, omissions and decadence of the Nationalist government as it was then constituted.

It is interesting to note in passing that although many of those interviewed volunteered a good word for the Generalissimo—and a few spoke of him with admiration—it was rare to hear the Kuomintang mentioned except in terms of lack of interest, distaste or disdain. The label of corruption, for example, simply will not rub off, even though there is no longer much meaning to it. Nobody has produced evidence to show that the present regime in Taiwan is any more corrupt than dozens of other governments with which we are doing business, yet to this day the Kuomintang and corruption seem inextricably linked in the public mind. Some speak of them in the same breath as if they were indivisible. It may also come as a surprise to note that an astonishing percentage of Americans is not even aware of the Nationalist government's existence.

The poll on China conducted in 1964 by the Survey Research Center of the University of Michigan (see Appendix A) actually showed that for only a relatively small portion of the American public—"probably under 50 per cent"—is the existence of the Nationalist government a salient reality.

Nevertheless, as was many times impressed on me, Chiang still has devoted supporters in important places in the United States. A former diplomat who knew him well, said:

Chiang's experience was not of great breadth, but he did have considerable understanding of the Japanese. Up to 1945 he did an extraordinary job. He was constantly on the defensive, and he had people like Stilwell to deal with on one side, Hurley on the other. His estimates of the future were more farseeing than those of Roosevelt and Churchill. The worst part of his record was from 1945 on. And don't forget that at the time the Communists were doing everything possible to obstruct economic development and wreck the government.

Chiang's strongest American support today comes from the military and naval brass, active and retired, and the two major veterans' organizations which are less concerned with his past record than with his present potential as the leader of a powerful little army on a tight little island on the fringe of a hostile China. Among Americans generally, however, the consensus on Chiang is lukewarm, at most. But whether they like Chiang or not, Americans are overwhelmingly agreed that we are honor-bound to stand by our commitments to him. It is not only a question of international morality; with some it is also a question of fulfilling our obligations to the Taiwanese people or of denying to the Communists the use of a strategically valuable piece of real estate.

A United States senator echoed a popular view of Chiang when he described him as "a moral responsibility whom we must continue to support as long as he lives." Another person used the term "cumulative responsibility," another, "unique responsibility." The senator ended his comment with the suggestion that Chiang's death or retirement might open up opportunities for a new approach to a China settlement. This theory that Chiang's demise will give us more flexibility in dealing with Communist China has gained surprisingly wide currency among those who favor modification of our policy. I encountered it on numerous occasions in my cross-country travels. It is premised on views like the following: (1) that our moral responsibility is primarily to Chiang rather than to the government he heads; (2) that our entire China policy is in a blind alley because we are "stuck" with Chiang; (3) that Chiang's withdrawal from the scene will be followed by drastic changes in the Taiwanese political structure, possibly even an upheaval of the Taiwanese people, leading to a modification or elimination of mainlander rule.

The internal imponderable in Taiwan is not whether the native-born Taiwanese would like self-government—they would hardly be human if they did not—but rather the intensity of their feeling on the matter. Tens of thousands of them have benefited economically from the reforms of the past fifteen years. Do they feel strongly enough about self-government to fight for it? Most Americans interviewed had no strong views on the subject. But a few did.

A Yale professor said: "When Chiang goes there will be a big crisis." A retired Navy captain in Idaho said: "When Chiang dies, the whole thing will collapse." And this from a college teacher in California who recently did a tour of study in Taiwan: "I don't think the Kuomintang regime will ever survive Chiang's death. Either the Taiwanese will revolt or there will be complete suppression. The army itself could take over. Some day we may have to make a very grave decision in Formosa. We may have to decide between letting it go or going in there to suppress a rebellion."

A Protestant mission official had another slant, based on reports he has received from missionaries in Taiwan:

Today more than three-fourths of the Christians in Formosa are native-born Taiwanese. Almost to a man they are anti-Chiang. They do not feel they are free. Yet they are strongly anti-Communist. Many fear that the Chiang regime will eventually disintegrate and come to terms with the Communists.

Chiang's sympathizers in this country discount such views as alarmist or "based on guesswork." Or they attribute them to the propaganda of exiled Taiwanese nationalists. What is the truth of the matter? The American public has no way of knowing. It is uninformed and confused. The reporting on the internal political situation in Taiwan has been less than adequate. A common complaint is that "we are not getting the information." But if they were offered the facts, would Americans be interested enough to read them? I have found a rather obvious lack of interest in the subject. To be sure those I talked with who had visited Taiwan within the past two years were almost uniformly impressed with the progress made. What they saw suggests the probability that the Kuomintang would have had more friends on the mainland had it shown a more genuine concern for the public interest in its early years of power. Having once been misled in their estimate of Chiang and his government, however, many Americans now are inclined to be apathetic or skeptical with respect to developments on Taiwan. They would rather not have to think about it.

Several of those interviewed, while agreeing that we could not abandon Taiwan, suggested that we seek a solution for the problem through the United Nations.

"In Formosa we have got our neck out a mile," said an importer in Portland, Oregon. "We cannot go on pretending that Chiang is China or maintaining the fiction that he is going to get back the mainland. Eventually the solution will have to come through the UN, with an international tribunal taking the onus of responsibility. I would hope that we could get an independent Taiwan as a *quid pro quo* for withdrawal of American military installations from the island."

In the main, American thinking on Taiwan is fluid, confused and uncertain, except on such basic propositions as the following: (1) We cannot abandon Taiwan; (2) We must honor our treaty obligations to the Chiang regime; (3) We must give full consideration to the wishes of the Taiwanese people in any discussion of their political future. On these matters we have found wide agreement and very little dissent among Americans.

Few Americans in leadership categories take seriously, nowadays, Chiang's periodic pledges to fight his way back to the mainland. With each passing year, the prospect of a mainland invasion from Taiwan has become dimmer until today it has assumed in most minds the status of a myth or an illusion. Consider, for instance, this rather cynical view from a senator from a far-western state: "The Formosa government has never been based on the free consent of the Formosan people. We can hide a lot of sins under the blanket of anti-communism. We have supported an army three times bigger than necessary to defend the island and one-tenth big enough to invade the mainland—all for the sake of satisfying an old man's dreams."

Even those who once were foremost in urging that Chiang be "unleashed" so that he would be free to invade the mainland are notably more cautious in their estimates of Chiang's prospects. Some say we have missed the boat, others that it is simply a matter of waiting until conditions in China and the world make invasion prospects more propitious. But the fading invasion outlook has not shaken the faith of these people in Chiang and his army as an indispensable bulwark in the free world's defenses against Communist expansion. The growing crisis in Southeast Asia, with its implication of possible conflict with Communist China, has intensified this feeling. If Chiang enthusiasts in this country are relatively few in number, they are, nevertheless, vociferous in their enthusiasm.

The era of Chiang, in China, was also the era of the Old China Hands, whose impact on American public opinion has been too significant to be overlooked in this report. A China Hand may be defined, for the purposes of this study, as any American who has lived in China—that is, been a part of it to some small or large extent. The species includes businessmen, diplomats, military men, missionaries, newspapermen, teachers, scholars and people of other occupations or no occupation at all. They make up a highly variegated lot, with highly variegated views.

It is doubtful whether any other country of the world has made as deep an impression on Americans who have lived in it as has China. China Hands are inclined to disagree violently on what is right or what is wrong about the country. Some will emphasize the agreeable, unhurried way of life as it used to be, the exotic sights and sounds, the good food. Others will discourse on the wonders of Peking, the overwhelming sense of a rich culture and history all around. Some find their fascination in the ever-cheerful, ever-toiling, often exasperating people, others in the unique and enormous challenges that the country offers. Certainly most would agree that the months or years they spent in China were among the most exciting and rewarding in their lives.

The war and the Communist takeover brought disillusionment and bitterness into many of these lives and put an end to the China they had known. But it did not destroy their fascination with the subject. Although the China Hands make up only an infinitesimal fraction of the population of this country, their influence on public attitudes toward China has been far out of proportion to their numbers. For the most part, they are articulate people who get around. The number of contacts made by a returned missionary, for instance, is likely to be numbered in the hundreds, or even thousands. Over the years the China Hands have had a lot to do with shaping the sentimental attachment of a large part of the American public to China and the Chinese people.

Perhaps we should here exempt from the China Hand category a majority of those young Americans who went to China as servicemen in our armed forces during the war. They were in China, but not many of them were a part of it, or wanted to be. They saw the country at its abysmal worst. From them, easily evoked, comes the other side of the story—all about the squalor, the dysentery, the lice, the corruption, the boredom of life in Chungking, or Kunming, or Kweilin or some little back country airport. Not many of these G.I.s ever saw the glories of Peking or ever got to know a Chinese with more than a grade-school education. Theirs was a dreary existence on the forgotten fringe of World War II. They can hardly be blamed for the aversion to China that many of them developed.

In my interviews across the country I came in contact with many China Hands and, of course, with many more who were not. Some of the latter admitted they had been influenced in their thinking by friends who had lived in China. For example: "I don't know much about China, but so-and-so, who was there, tells me the Chinese are a wonderful people." Or, "So-and-so has told us about his life in China. Sounds great."

On the west coast I met a well-known educator—a specialist in Asian studies—who felt strongly that the missionaries were primarily responsible for the emotional buildup on China and Chiang Kai-shek in this country. "I was born in Europe," he explained, "and therefore have no complex or sacred cow fixation about China. Here in the United States there is an emotional aura on China which I do not share. Americans feel a responsibility for China which they do not feel for other countries. This attitude started with the missionaries. I can only explain it on a basis of missionary activity. I don't know how much impact the missionaries made on China, but they certainly made an impact on the United States."

PART TWO

Recent American Attitudes — Interviews, Polls and Pressure Groups

CHAPTER FOUR

New Illusions for Old

Traditional American attitudes toward China lie shattered and disordered in the trail of the tempestuous events of the past thirty years. The Communist revolution has confronted us with a China so different from the China we once knew that we are still groping to comprehend it. It is plain to see that some of our fondest assumptions about the celestial land are no longer valid. The shock of disillusionment, the haunting fear of the unknown, the specter of 700 million Chinese regimented into "Hate America" campaigns, the memories of Korea, with its "human waves," its brainwashing and its American dead—these and many other unexpected developments have left grievous wounds in our emotions and our thinking.

Yet we are reluctant to part with our comfortable old notions. We do not want to believe that China—and more particularly the people of China—have changed as much as surface appearances indicate. Is it possible that a country which once seemed so friendly and "for which we have done so much" could be as implacably unfriendly as the People's Republic of China today appears to be? We say we want the truth; but when stories conflict we often prefer to believe the version that fits best with our traditional thinking. We are confused, frustrated and resentful over a situation which it is no longer within our power to control.

Among our souvenirs are the broken pieces of many fond illusions. One such was that the best service we could do China was to make her over into our own image. It seems unthinkable now, in the light of our knowledge and experience, that we could have imagined such a metamorphosis possible or even desirable. Yet it was long fashionable among Americans to regard Christianity and democracy as the twin cures for China's troubles. Both, to be sure, left their mark, but we know now that our brand of Christian civilization is not so easily transplantable. Indeed experience in China and elsewhere indicates that the effort to transplant it can sometimes lead to disruptive consequences.

Akin to that illusion was the belief that we were linked to China by rather special bonds of mutual affection capable of surviving any change of government. Undeniably, there was a love affair of sorts and, on our side, at least, a protectively sentimental attachment. It is now apparent that the relationship was not as reciprocal as we had imagined. It is not that we lacked friends in China. Undoubtedly large numbers of Chinese developed a warm regard for Americans during the years when our two countries were cooperating closely; and they perhaps even found Americans more like-minded and compatible than foreigners of other nationalities. But the China we knew—or that knew us—was only a small part of the whole. The great mass of the Chinese people was largely untouched by American influences and must be presumed wholly vulnerable, therefore, to Peking's anti-American propaganda, as is the new generation growing up in complete isolation from the Western world. Do we still have friends on mainland China? Judging from the unbroken torrent of abuse directed at us from Peking, we would have to answer "no." Common sense points to a different answer. It seems unbelievable that even Communist brainwashing could have succeeded in erasing completely the friendly feelings of many of those who had personal contact with Americans.

The trail of fractured illusions winds endlessly through the recent history of Sino-American relations. Here are some more examples: the belief that China could not survive without our economic help; the notion that Chinese communism was a milder brand than the Russian variety; the supposition that the Chinese Communists and the Kuomintang could somehow be spliced into a workable coalition; the conviction that a people as "individualistic" as the Chinese could never be regimented; the notion that the Chinese could never be made into good soldiers.

These and many other misconceptions have contributed to American confusion and misunderstanding about China.

Against this background, let us take a look at what Americans are thinking today. Are we more realistic? Do we see China more clearly? In some respects, perhaps. Yet on the basis of more than 200 interviews with individual Americans in scattered parts of the country the writer is forced to the conclusion that not only do many of the old myths still persist but new ones have sprouted like weeds in the seed-bed of our insufficient knowledge. If the reader discovers as much contradiction and disagreement in the views cited as he finds uniformity, it is because that is the way we found it. It may be noted, for example, that those with a special knowledge of China not only differ, at times, with the prevailing viewpoint but sometimes, indeed, among themselves. Communist China is only dimly seen by most Americans. It is a subject on which Americans are still groping for the truth—a subject, therefore, on which all points of view, any and all fresh ideas, need to be taken into consideration.

Most of those interviewed could be described as opinion leaders. They are representative of the better-educated, better-read, better-informed elements of the population and occupy responsible positions in their respective communities. Many are persons of wide influence, a few of national prominence. Some have a special interest in and knowledge of China. What follows is a representative selection from the author's notebooks of excerpts from interviews with these people, intended primarily to outline the shape and dimensions of China's image as Americans see it. Attitudes toward United States policy will be discussed in a later chapter.

The Once-Friendly Giant Becomes a Threatening Colossus

"I am afraid," said a Congressman, "that Americans do not have any real visceral realization of the immense size of China—the inescapable immensity of it."

But they do. There is probably no single fact about modern China that impresses Americans more than her enormous manpower. It is this swarming bigness combined with Peking's implacable hatred for the United States which gives the China problem such nightmarish proportions to most Americans. Few of those interviewed failed to mention China's huge population as a matter of great concern; but having mentioned it, many seemed puzzled as to what significance they should attach to it.

There was a time when China's vast numbers raised the entrancing prospect for Americans of 400 million customers. Carl Crow wrote a book about it.[1] But that pleasing vision has given way to the apparition of 700 million potential adversaries. Today, China's expanding population, her nationalist ambitions, her rivalry with the Soviet Union, her racial opportunism, and her small but growing nuclear "punch" are seen as constituting a grave danger to the peace and stability of the world for a very long time. Yet few of those interviewed saw China as an immediate or direct threat to American security. Few saw her as a top-ranking power, as yet, in the industrial and economic sense. For the present, it was widely felt, the danger from China lies mainly in the influence and pressure she can exert on her neighbors (Viet-Nam, Laos, Cambodia) and on the countries of Africa, Latin America and the Middle East. In her capacity, in short, for upsetting the international balance.

These considerations might be less upsetting if we had a clearer picture of Communist China's strength and intentions. Instead, our exasperation, our frustrations, and certainly our suspicions are intensified by our inability to look behind the bamboo fence to see what is going on there.

Hence we get views like the following:

A west coast editor: "Here is a big, hostile country, going ahead, developing, without our knowing very much about what is going on. It is frightening to think about."

An east coast editor: "China is the greatest, the most portentous danger in the world."

[1] Carl Crow, *Four Hundred Million Customers* (New York: Harper, 1937).

A senator: "I think China is the real danger, not only to the rest of Asia, but to the Soviet Union as well."

And this from a California businessman, formerly associated with General Claire Chennault, of "Flying Tigers" fame: "I am forty-eight years old. I am absolutely certain that before I die we will be at war with Communist China; and I don't believe that Soviet Russia will intervene."

In another section of this report we summarize the returns from a number of questionnaires sent out to newspaper editors and TV-radio executives. Both groups were asked which country they regarded as the greater long-range danger to the United States—Soviet Russia or China. An overwhelming majority picked China. Some of their comments were arresting:

"Communist China. Infinite manpower, backward but growing industry, a hotter Marxist fanaticism than the Soviets."

"For the long term, China directly; for the short term, still China, but indirectly."

"Red China. Right now, they're tougher—and they breed a hell of a lot faster."

There are, of course, many variations to this theme and occasional sharp dissents. An author-diplomat said: "I cannot conceive of any situation in which there would be a Chinese attack on the United States. After all, they cannot even mount an attack on Quemoy and Matsu."

An east coast professor agreed. "I cannot regard Communist China as a military threat to us," he said. "They have a nuisance value, but that's all. Moreover, they are not keeping pace militarily. Generally speaking, China is good for us. It keeps us alert. Our resentment of China has made it possible for our government to pour millions into India, Southeast Asia, etc., and justify it."

An American military man of high rank, formerly in China, felt that China's immense population would prove a "terrible liability" in the long run. And he added: "Here is a mass of human beings without commensurate facilities of food and shelter. I say to you that the Soviet Union would be happy to be rid of them as allies."

From a former military attaché with a deep knowledge of China and a fluent command of the Chinese language came this contribution: "The Chinese are a ruthless, chauvinistic force, intoxicated with the idea of power. They despise all of us. They believe we are barbarians. China is more dangerous than the Soviet Union because of this Messianic pride, this chauvinism. Moreover, they need land."

This presumed land hunger of the Chinese, based partly on an expansionist tradition, partly on the necessity of finding more space for China's exploding population, cropped up with regularity in the interviews. "Let's face it," said a China specialist in the State Department, "Peking is in the real-estate business." A number spoke of Chinese expansionism as an urge the Communists have inherited from previous dynasties. A United States senator said: "History shows that China is traditionally an expansionist nation. The Chinese are an intelligent people with long memories, a great potential and an increasing population. They have got to explode somewhere. That somewhere is going to be the Asiatic continent."

While it was the consensus that Southeast Asia is China's primary target for expansion, a few argued that the thinly populated steppes of Siberia and Mongolia would exert an irresistible lure in the long run. India, overcrowded and poor, was considered to have a low priority in Chinese thinking.

China's Magnetic Influence

A California professor who has traveled much in and around China over the past twenty years stated the basic situation, as he saw it, in these terms: "The Chinese importance in the Far East is a magnetic importance. Anyone living within 1,000 miles of China feels it—Japan, Viet-Nam, all the surrounding countries. No matter how many missiles you put in Okinawa, this feeling of China's nearness and importance will remain. You will find that even a Japanese who talked to you about being afraid of Chinese communism is likely to have more respect for Communist China than he has for the United States."

A State Department official added another brush stroke to the background picture: "In the political sense," he said, "China is the central problem in the Far East. It has a quarter of the world's population. The key to the whole area is whether China is going to behave. There is no question but that the Long March veterans who rule China are aiming at hegemony over the Far East. In the face of determined deterrence, they are behaving with extreme caution. But they are very aggressive in the political sense."

Another State Department employee, who has spent half his life in China, put it this way: "The Chinese consider Asia their world. They are the Middle Kingdom. They see themselves as leaders of the slant-eyed peoples. A few years ago, I believed China was on her way to becoming a world power. But Chinese behavior since then has made me wonder. They have made so many blunders."

And yet another: "Population alone is not a source of strength, as the Chinese themselves are beginning to realize. Yet, whereas Russia, in terms of nuclear capacity, is by far the greater threat to the world if it becomes aggressive, the Chinese presence, over a period of time, may be more disturbing and more crucially felt. Why? Because the Chinese regard themselves not only as Marxist-Leninists but also as spokesmen for the lesser, underprivileged countries, which are being ignored both by the West and the more advanced Communist countries."

A political scientist at Stanford University summed up the popular view. "Communist China," he said, "is slowly becoming the nucleus for those countries that identify themselves with a different set of values and goals than those with more affluent societies."

Some emphasized the racial factor, noting Communist China's incessant efforts—though with very mixed results—to enlist the collaboration and support of the non-white peoples of the world. A Los Angeles judge said: "The Chinese are trying to incite a racial conflict, the colored races against the white race. Many people have a phobia on this subject."

China and Southeast Asia

— "I don't think we can assume that the Chinese will accept any boundaries as inviolate," an Oregon wheat exporter commented. "They are going to bust out somewhere. There is no question that if the United States were not standing in the way, the Chinese would move right on down to Singapore."

Would the Chinese Communists welcome war, as the tone of their propaganda sometimes seems to suggest? I think many of those I talked with would agree with the Chicago professor—a specialist on China—who said: "My view is that the Chinese Communists want war but not atomic war. They favor national liberation wars. They will pose a serious threat to the United States, but more on the lines of 'surrounding the city with the countryside' on a global scale. Viet-Nam is the testing ground for Mao Tse-tung's strategy and for American policy."

A doctor in St. Louis expressed a similar thought, with a different twist. "If you eliminate the 'domino effect,'" he said, "I don't think China presents any real problem to us. It is not strong enough economically, it is not strong enough in the military sense. It presents no danger in the ideological sense. But we keep being told by our military people that we are likely to lose Southeast Asia, indeed the whole world, by the domino effect. This is the danger."

A Washington, D.C., economist, who has made China a specialty, offered this grim observation: "The mainland Chinese are isolated, embittered, full of feeling that the world has misunderstood them. Consequently, they are arrogant and very difficult to deal with. I consider Communist China already a great military power under conditions where it does not have to cross water and where its opponents are unable or unwilling to use nuclear weapons. If the Chinese wanted to occupy all of Viet-Nam they could do so. In a Korea-type war, the Chinese would win unless their opponents were prepared to escalate it into a nuclear war."

A Chinese-American doing business in Los Angeles felt that patience was the answer. "Red China is spreading out," he noted.

"She will become increasingly involved in Southeast Asia, Cuba and elsewhere. The explosion of one firecracker leads to the explosion of a whole string. The Chinese Communists will spread themselves too thin. This is the thing we await."

China's Pull on Japan

Several persons, including two of outstanding reputation for their knowledge of Far Eastern affairs, felt that in the long run United States security might be more directly threatened by Chinese influence on Japan than by developments in Southeast Asia. One of them—a leading New York lawyer—emphasized China's historical "pull" on her insular neighbor.

"China," he said, "is a magnet to Japan. For a century or more Japan looked on China as a big but easily handled neighbor. Conditions have changed, but the fascination remains. Today it is translated into desire to trade. The Chinese understand this. Mao has articulated this view to people I know. The Chinese want to see Japan sever itself from U.S. influence as a prerequisite to trading on a large scale. The implications of this would be very serious if we should get, in Japan, a government less interested in the free world's interests than the present one and which confuses communism with socialism."

A distinguished former member of the Truman administration saw things in much the same light. "The Chinese are going to cause a lot of trouble in Asia," he said, "and in that respect they probably are a threat to our security. They may be troublesome in Southeast Asia and India, but I would be bothered more about Japan, insofar as our security is concerned. We may be headed for trouble if China overawes Japan. The natural pull in Japan is toward Asia."

A former general living in Portland, Oregon, felt it would be "a natural" for Japan and China to join up and saw grave dangers for the United States in this combination of technical skill and manpower.

These were not majority opinions. In general, people interviewed took a more sanguine view of Japan's future orientation, and some had not thought at all of Japan as a possible adversary. The sanguine view was that Japan is a dependable ally, that she cannot prosper without American trade, that she can be expected to increase her commercial contacts with mainland China but not to the extent of seriously straining her relations with the United States. More than one suggested that Japan might in time serve as a bridge to improved relations between the United States and Communist China.

A completely different impression of Communist China's expansionist aims came from a woman of national reputation living in New York.

"If geography is the mother of foreign policy, it must follow that China's foreign policy is more concerned with Soviet Russia than any other country," she said. "If I try to pour one full glass of water into another, there's going to be a proper mess. You just cannot pour more people into India. India is already full of bodies. There is not much in Viet-Nam. Burma has oil. But the only place where the Chinese could go in number is where they went before. They could walk into Siberia. . . . My feeling is that if the Chinese are left to their own devices they will do one of two things. When they are faced with starvation, the breakdown of their system, and the failure to industrialize at any tempo commensurate with their population growth, Mao will be forced to make war on Russia or face an internal revolution."

On Prospects for Internal Change in Communist China

A majority of those interviewed doubted whether the Chinese mainland has an economic potential capable of supporting the grandiose ambitions of its leaders. The extreme difficulty of building a powerful industrial base on a "vegetable" economy—that is, an economy dependent largely on agricultural production—was often mentioned. A State Department official who has made a specialty of this subject said: "In their efforts to transform China into a great power the Communists are in deep trouble. There is no likelihood of their getting out of it unless they get a lot of help. As far ahead as we can see, the Communists will have to put major emphasis on agriculture. The only way out is a massive effort in agriculture, and this could only be achieved by giving a freer hand to the peasantry and by providing more incentives with consumer goods."

I found that this skepticism over Communist China's economic future was widely shared. It obviously is a factor in the very widespread belief that in China, as in Russia, time will have a moderating effect on Peking's policies.

"I am perfectly certain," said a New York lawyer, "that China will not be communistic twenty or thirty years from now. Internal absorption and internal change will transform the situation. You can never breed out of the Chinese their basic philosophy. The changes could come about by evolution, revolution or progressive undermining."

A businessman in the same city said that he did not think the Chinese would remain long under a Communist regime. "In my book," he went on, "socialism never succeeds except to the extent that it fails. It is inevitable that the situation in China will change. The Chinese people are people of good sense; and intelligence always asserts itself."

A Hollywood radio commentator: "What's going to happen when the Long March people go? That's the big imponderable. But I think we can learn something from the Russians. The third generation will want to hold on to what it has got. You have to wait until a few of the old timers die off. You cannot be sure that there are no moderates. I would say there are."

A banker with long experience in the Far East felt sure the Chinese Communists would mellow over the years. As he put it, they are in one of their dynastic cycles. A west coast trader, who did a lot of business in China in the pre-Communist years, felt that the Chinese people ultimately would react against Communist regimentation. "The Chinese Reds have got railways running on time, good roads and improved housing," he said. "But the basic nature of the Chinaman is that he is an entrepreneur. He is the Jew of the East. Put him under too much regimentation, and he will kick over the traces."

One of the more colorful appraisals of Communist China's prospects came from a nationally known columnist: "China will always be a menace, because the Chinese are the most talented and industrious race in the world. But the present regime in China will not endure, first, because the problem it is seeking to solve is forty times more difficult than the problem faced by Stalin, and second, because it runs counter to the natural bent of the Chinese people. There would have been greater progress in China without the Communists. The Chinese have a genius for capital formation. Look at Hong Kong. Nine-tenths of the refugee capital in Hong Kong has gone into building. There is no reason why this couldn't have happened on the mainland on an infinitely larger scale. Moreover, you would have had an agricultural system not entirely dependent on human manure."

A more somber view came from a former army officer, with a long China experience, who said: "Chinese communism will not become diluted with the passage of time, as so many believe. It is more likely to become explosive as a result of China's efforts to reach sources of raw materials needed for her expanding population."

Peking's Hymn of Hate

The face that Communist China now turns in our direction—a face that is harsh, rigid, scornful and implacable—has chilled in many American hearts the warm sentiments that once motivated American attitudes toward China. As a foundation official in Boston put it: "Americans have come to regard Red China as some kind of an evil thing that is not going to go away." Another spoke of the Communist "ogre." People were obviously perplexed by the intensely vicious tone of Peking's anti-American propaganda. The instinctive disposition of many was to return malevolence for malevolence. But behind their indignation was frequently discernible a readiness to be "understanding" should the Chinese adopt a more agreeable demeanor. This feeling came through in such comments as: "If they would only drop their hostile manner"; "Why can't they behave like human beings?"

The belief persists that it is not the people of China who hate us; it is the Communist leadership. Or, as a former missionary stated it: "It is not a case of 700 million people; it is a handful of people who control 700 million."

A high-ranking labor leader, talking to me in his Washington, D.C., office, made much the same point but in quite a different way. "It is necessary to make a distinction," he said, "between the Communist regime and the Chinese people. The Communists are reaching the people in some ways, but it would be silly to say that these contacts are having a profound effect. We just feel that human nature being what it is, the people of China are not happy with the Communist regime."

Views like this are of course based on intuition and deduction rather than on any inside information on the state of mind of the Chinese people. Even the experts have very diverse views on such questions as the popularity or unpopularity of the Communist regime and the "real" attitude of the Chinese people toward the United States. There is nothing on which the specialists are more unsure.

Peking's unceasing anti-American pyrotechnics are widely attributed to the continuous need for strengthening China's home-front morale. The United States serves admirably as a bogey man big enough and powerful enough to take the minds of the Chinese off some of their domestic troubles. A retired diplomat, with long service in the Far Eastern division of the State Department, put it this way: "Revolutionary people have to have an enemy. Someone they are dead against. Someone they can scream about. It is politically advantageous to have an enemy, preferably one you cannot do much about. Manuel Quezon, the Filipino nationalist, was a good example of this psychology. Privately he used to say he hoped we would not give the Philippines their independence immediately. . . ."

Seeing Ourselves as the Chinese See Us

How much validity is there in Chinese hostility toward us? How much truth is there in the arguments Peking employs in its efforts to sway Chinese and world opinion against us? Except in scholarly circles, I found little evidence that Americans have bothered to study and weigh these arguments, or that they are particularly interested in doing so. It is easier (and less controversial) to write them off as propaganda. Not infrequently, however, I encountered signs of uneasiness on this score among those interviewed. It was evidenced by remarks like: "Of course, the Communists have a case, too," or, "There's something to be said for the Chinese point of view," but few seemed to have a clear idea of what that point of view was.

There has been some soul-searching, to be sure, among Americans who once lived and worked in China—an attempt to pinpoint mistakes made and to profit from them. Protestant missionaries, now barred from mainland China, have done quite a lot of agonizing on the subject. After the Communist takeover in China, a committee of the Division of Foreign Missions of the National Council of Churches made a study of the lessons to be learned from the experience of Protestant missions there.[2] Questionnaires sent to returned missionaries evoked a flood of replies from which the following reactions are picked, not because they are necessarily typical but because they touch on points which might have had a particular impact on Chinese attitudes toward us.

Many missionaries formerly stationed in China felt there had been too wide a gap between their way of life and the living conditions of their Chinese followers. It had been a mistake, for instance, always to emphasize the American way of doing things and to live in American-style houses. One offered this advice on the basis of lessons learned: "Live a simpler, more friendly, less remote life, more on a plane of native colleagues." Another observed: "Do not suggest the idea of a 'foreign' religion by emphasis on foreign buildings and foreign methods. Stick to native architecture in places of worship and even for missionary homes."

[2] Harold S. Matthews, comp., *Lessons to Be Learned from the Experiences of Christian Missions in China: A Study Made under the Auspices of the Research Committee of the Division of Foreign Missions Serving Simultaneously as the Standing Committee on Research in Foreign Missions of the Central Department of Research and Survey with the Cooperation of the China Committee of the Division of Foreign Missions, the National Council of the Churches of Christ in the United States of America* (n.p.: National Council of the Churches of Christ in the United States of America, August 31, 1951).

Another commonly mentioned point of self-criticism was that the missions had been too land-hungry, had acquired too much real estate. This, of course, is no longer a problem insofar as China is concerned, as all church properties have been confiscated. But it was felt that the criticism might also be valid elsewhere.

One of the returned missionaries complained about "too much denominational emphasis." Recounting his experiences before leaving China, he said: "Over and over again I was asked by the people what was basically the difference between the denominations and between Catholicism and Protestantism. After all, said they, didn't we all believe in Jesus?"

"Most missionaries," wrote another of them, "are not well enough educated to meet the complex situation they have to face today. They should be not only well trained in their own field but should have a background of the history and culture of the people they serve." Anyone who has traveled much in China will recognize the validity of this comment. While a minority of the Protestant missionaries were persons of extensive education and a deep knowledge and appreciation of China's cultural background, too many viewed the great civilization around them as a cultural desert. Traveling about China before and during the war, this writer visited dozens of missionary homes, some of them buried deep in the interior. Invariably they were populated by God-fearing, hospitable people, but they usually showed little sign of cultural adaptation to the environment. Most of these homes were faithful imitations of the homes these people had lived in back in Iowa, or Pennsylvania, or California. In some living rooms one looked in vain for anything Chinese, even a piece of Chinese bric-a-brac. The illusion of being completely out of China while in it was perfect—but hardly a matter for congratulation.

This inability to appreciate China's cultural riches—her art, her philosophy—was not confined to missionaries. It was common to many other Americans living in China. It is probably common to Americans generally today. Yet the reason for it is less a lack of interest than a lack of contact. An American woman of letters with a long interest in China expressed feelingly her view that an understanding of the Chinese is impossible without some understanding of their cultural achievements and their historical background. She said: "The Chinese have much to contribute culturally to the world. When a Chinese exhibition comes to the Metropolitan Museum of Art people stand in line to see it. It is an unknown world to them, an extraordinarily advanced culture. If art is any criterion of civilization, the Chinese may well be a people capable of the utmost refinement. All my contacts with Chinese art I find enormously seductive. My feeling for China is one of envy and admiration culturally. It is not difficult to imagine that they might think of us as barbarians. We do not understand, in this country, the extent to which the Chinese consider themselves the Central Flowery Kingdom, the heartland of the world. The Chinese do not question their deeply historic central importance. They have this profound sense that they don't have to prove their ancient, noble and extraordinary lineage." An observation that perhaps helps to explain why the Chinese Communists confidently believe that they are destined for world leadership.

China and "The Bomb"

Prior to the first nuclear detonation in China, there was evident concern in Washington over the supposed unpreparedness of American and international opinion for the long-predicted blast. It was feared that many smaller countries and perhaps also the American public would be caught off guard and take an unjustifiably alarmist view. Hence preparing the public for a nuclear "surprise" became one of the public relations tasks of the administration.

Perhaps the preparatory job was too well done. There was of course no panic. On the contrary there was an element of complacency in the public's reaction—a feeling that without Soviet assistance the Chinese Communists would require a prolonged period (usually reckoned at between ten and twenty years) to develop their nuclear capacity to the point where it would constitute a real threat to American security. Some, to be sure, noting our old habit of underestimating the Chinese Communists and their totalitarian capabilities, were less sanguine. None doubted, in any case, that Communist China would continue to be aggressive and belligerent for the predictable future and that the situation in East Asia would grow considerably more serious, from our viewpoint, before any improvement could be expected.

If American impressions of Communist China differ greatly from person to person, there are good reasons for it. Like the blind men in the familiar story of the blind men and the elephant, we are groping for comprehension of a behemoth we cannot see.

CHAPTER FIVE

Currents and Crosscurrents
of Leadership Opinion

Among Americans, as we have seen, there are innumerable variations of opinion on China—on its strength, on its intentions, on its capabilities and on its prospects. Turning now to the question of American policy toward that country, we find a similar diversity and perplexity in public attitudes. A State Department official, in an interview, summed up the position aptly (if wryly) in the following words: "First, there is an almost total inability to agree on the facts; secondly, there is an inability to agree on what the goals are."

Traveling about the country, talking informally with Americans in business, professional, editorial, political, governmental, religious and other responsible occupations, I was often struck by the large element of truth in this observation. Yet despite the many and various differences of opinion as to what is right and what is wrong with our China policy, there are clearly discernible currents and crosscurrents of which we must take note. Before doing so, however, it may be advantageous to take a quick tour—from right to left as it were—through the whole wide sweep of opinion on this subject. We start with the view of a former national chairman of the American Legion: "Our China policy is a do-nothing policy that is getting us nowhere. We've missed the bus on a number of occasions. We should have turned Chiang Kai-shek loose during the Korean involvement. I feel it is too late now. We are taking a licking in Viet-Nam; we may be sorry that we did not act sooner." And this from the spokesman for another veterans' organization: "It would be a catastrophe if we appeased Red China. The only rock on which the people of Asia can stand in opposition to communism is American power. The slightest indication of appeasement would start a chain reaction."

A Chicago business executive, who also believes that toughness is the best policy, said: "We are the world's most powerful nation, yet we seem unable to make effective use of our power potential in our foreign policy. Brinkmanship—that is the thing. It worked at Quemoy and Matsu."

"Here we are," said a former congressman, who is from the Midwest, "in a war and in danger of losing it because it is the war called Peace. Some people have never got it through their heads that communism has a dogma which requires world control. You cannot get a settlement until the Communists abandon their doctrine. People do not seem to realize the religious zeal behind those people. I would keep on the present course."

A retired naval captain, now living a landlubber's life in Idaho, agrees. "Communist China," he remarked, "is like an annoying mother-in-law. We have never learned to live with her. The people who run Communist China hate our government. There's nothing we can do about that. We have been a thorn in their flesh. If we had weakened earlier they might now be sitting on top of the heap. We'll get nowhere by giving up now."

But a middle-of-the-road senator from a northern state looked at it a little differently: "I don't know whether a more flexible policy toward Red China would get us anywhere. What I deplore is that we don't have the guts to face up to this situation. It is this reluctance to raise the flap of the tent to see what is there that is so aggravating. What would it cost us? Let's have a look and see what the price tags are."

The following from a newspaper editor in Massachusetts: "I don't think we have any alternative to a policy of containment and deterrence. But we must make it work or pull out of Asia. It must be an intelligent policy of restraint. We must work both sides of the fence, using every opening, doing everything in our power to soften them up, just as we did in Russia. Our policy toward China lacks many of the openings that were available in our relations with the Soviet Union, but who can say that the Chinese Communists will not eventually change?"

A "middle" view came from a Seattle, Washington, lawyer. "I am opposed to extremes," he said. "It is premature to go in and recognize Red China, but on the other hand it is foolish to say 'never.' Let's make a fresh new statement of our intentions. Let's recognize the fact that there are 700 million people in China and that they have a government. Let's be positive, not negative; let it be known that we will recognize if our conditions are met."

This theory that the United States can improve its positions by accenting the positive in its relations with Communist China has some prominent disciples. A former government official turned author and lecturer put it this way: "Instead of saying 'no' to everything, let us say 'yes' we will come to terms if certain conditions are met—for example, (1) that Red China makes legal peace with the United Nations, (2) that Peking agrees to unification, on mutually acceptable terms, of Korea and Viet-Nam, (3) that the Chinese Communists agree not to use force against Formosa, and (4) that there be two Chinas in the UN. Peking would not agree to these conditions, but by advocating them we would put our policy on a positive footing."

Many hammered on the need for a more mobile, day-to-day approach to the ever-changing problem—in short, more flexibility. Here is a sample of that line of thinking, from a west coast university professor: "The biggest issue of the twentieth century is whether or not we are going to be able to bring China into the field of world opinion and to some accommodation on outstanding questions. If we don't do this we are condemned to a more or less continuous cold war that could become hot when China attains nuclear power. We are feeding a military outlook in China through our policy of isolation and containment. We are, therefore, making very difficult any sustained movement toward moderation in China. I think it is time to put the kind of pressure on Peking that will mean something—that is, American flexibility versus Chinese rigidity. We should make it clear that any time the dogmatists in Peking are ready, we are ready to talk. Unfortunately, American politicians see no political pay dirt in a new

China policy. And the last thing the Chinese want us to do is to change our policy, because their whole argument is based on the intransigence and implacability of the United States."

Moving on to those who see almost nothing sensible about our China policy as it stands, we quote a New York editor: "The sense of the country is a desire for peace; from the Presidency down there is a total sense of unreality on our China policy." And this from a China specialist in a California university: "Our political and military presence in the Far East is an abnormality. It is abnormal for us, and it is certainly an abnormality for Asians. Sooner or later, we must face up to this. We should reconsider the assumptions of our containment policy. We should contemplate a situation under which we could withdraw. Of course, disengagement is opposed by the American public. Even to raise the question of the legitimacy of our containment policy is considered almost treasonable. I have almost abandoned hope of a rational decision on China based on reasonable discussion."

The Basic Viewpoints

Notwithstanding the diversity of the above opinions, American attitudes on China policy do tend to polarize around certain specific viewpoints. It is tempting to use the labels "conservative" and "liberal" in describing the predominant points of view; and for reasons of convenience these terms have been employed occasionally in this report. But talking to large numbers of people about China one soon discovers that such expressions as "hard" and "soft," "rigid" and "flexible," "liberal" and "conservative," mean different things to different persons. There has been so much crisscrossing of ideological boundaries on the China question that it is not easy to say where the conservative viewpoint ends and the liberal viewpoint begins. To attempt to draw a line of demarcation would be a profitless, even meaningless exercise. There is, nevertheless, a vast gap between the two poles of the China controversy, represented, on the one hand, by the no-compromise "fundamentalist" school and, on the other, by those who believe that coexistence with Communist China offers the best hope in the long run.

Each of these viewpoints has the dedicated support of a hard-core minority of Americans, though it seems clear from the results of this study and of other surveys that the great majority of the people has no firm attachment to either camp and tends, rather, to hold intermediate, varying and often indecisive views. An interesting thing about the two basic and mutually antagonistic schools of opinion is that each claims its position is based on the "realities" of the situation.

The foundations of the fundamentalist position were bluntly stated by Admiral Arthur W. Radford in his foreword to a recent book: [1]

Anyone who is in doubt as to the wisdom of the policy developed by the late Secretary of State John Foster Dulles should keep in mind three points that are largely ignored by the new revisionists and the old "agrarians": (1) except for Taiwan and the Pescadores, China is an occupied country, like the Ukraine, and the people captives of an alien regime; (2) as far as the Moscow-Peking axis is concerned, World War III began some time ago (and here 'war' should be understood in its broadest application—the struggle for victory by all available means, political, economic, and subversive, as well as military); (3) Red China intends to rule the western Pacific and subjugate all of the Asias outside the Soviet empire.

There is a fourth point that should never be overlooked: the ultimate aim of the axis is the isolation and eventual defeat of the United States.

Thus, the fundamentalist view is that we are in fact at war with the Communist world and that no gestures of conciliation on our part can be justified unless the Communists renounce their policy of promoting world revolution. If one looks at China in this light, any change in our policy becomes appeasement, any concession becomes surrender, any withdrawal of aid to Chiang Kai-shek becomes betrayal.

The opposing position is more difficult to define; it shows up in so many different manifestations. A typical expression of it might be summarized something like this:

[1] Forrest Davis and Robert A. Hunter, *The Red China Lobby* (New York: Fleet Publishing Co., 1963), p. vii.

You cannot ignore 700 million Chinese. You cannot ignore the probability that the Chinese Communists will be in control of the mainland for a very long time. In the interests of world peace and our own security we should be in contact with them, even if they are our sworn enemies. Our policy of containment and isolation is out of date. By isolating the Chinese Communists we make them more rather than less truculent, more rather than less irresponsible, more rather than less prone to reckless adventurism. We must face up to China's traditional position in Asia and recognize that she can no more be expected to welcome unfriendly influences in territories adjacent to her borders than we welcome them in Cuba or would welcome them in Mexico or Canada. Realistically, we can never hope for a final solution in Korea, Taiwan, or Southeast Asia unless China is in some way a party to it. We are fighting a futile war in Viet-Nam and should settle for neutralization on the best terms possible.

Taiwan is a major political problem. We must accept the fact that the Chiang Kai-shek regime no longer commands the support of the Chinese people and that his hopes of fighting his way back to the mainland are unrealizable. We have no choice, however, but to honor our commitments to Chiang and our obligations to the Taiwanese people. Both Peking and Taipei oppose a two-China solution, but perhaps they will come around to it in time. If not, another alternative must be found. Meanwhile, let us re-evaluate our policy and drop our rigidity. Let us take steps to communicate with Communist China, trade with her, bring her into the United Nations and, in the long run, recognize her—insisting, of course, on a suitable *quid pro quo*. This is the approach that offers the best hope of undercutting extremism and encouraging moderation in Communist China.

A large section of the public tends to go along with present United States policy, but often with doubts and reservations. Relatively few are as rigidly uncompromising in their approach as Admiral Radford, although doubtless a very large number of those who voted for Barry Goldwater in the recent presidential election, as well as others, would agree with the basic premise that we are, in effect, at war with the Communist world and should implement our policy accordingly. By the same token, there are many persons who consider themselves liberals who would argue that the moderate credo outlined above goes too far in accommodating Peking at this stage; and there are a few who would say that it does not go far enough.

Frustration, one finds, is a predominant emotion in the present situation. Communist China is such an enigma, the future is so full of imponderables, that it was a rare person indeed who spoke with complete confidence and conviction about the rights and wrongs of United States policy. Frustration was expressed in many different ways, but it was epitomized in the comment: "I don't like our present policy, but I see no alternative as long as China refuses to change her attitude." This "no alternative" theme was a recurrent one.

Though variegated, the viewpoints expressed do tend to fall into rather clearly defined patterns. They show a geographical pattern, for example, that is quite pronounced. The outspoken liberalism of San Francisco, where there is much sentiment in favor of improved relations and trade with Communist China, stands in marked contrast to the predominantly rigid views of, say, Dallas. In general, I found the west coast more flexible on China policy than the east coast, the east coast more elastic than the Midwest, and the Midwest less conservative than the Southern and Mountain states.

An occupational pattern is also apparent in the interviews. Academic people, in the main, find our present policy too rigid and, to a greatly varying degree, favor change. Newspaper editors tend to be less flexible than the scholars but more so than the general public, although this flexibility does not always show up in their editorial columns. Attitudes of business and professional people toward China policy are mixed, ranging from extreme to extreme, but usually tilted toward prudent moderation. In Washington, the inwardly elastic but outwardly controlled attitudes of the State Department contrast with the inflexibility (on China) of most members of Congress. Yet politicians who stand publicly for the *status quo* on China policy sometimes display surprising flexibility of viewpoint in private conversation. Not surprisingly, Republicans tend to take a harder line on China than Democrats, though large numbers of both parties are to be found milling about on middle ground.

Policy Considerations on Which Attitudes
Are Preponderantly Negative

The preponderance of opinion among those interviewed was clearly opposed to either or both of the following propositions, at least for the time being:

1. Diplomatic recognition of Communist China.
2. Admission of Communist China to the United Nations.

There are no policy matters on which it is more difficult for an American to take an affirmative public position. To support either is to invite criticism or ridicule on grounds of being "soft" on communism. Yet the familiar arguments that "you cannot ignore 700 million people," or "recognition does not necessarily mean approval," or "you have to talk to the guy who holds the keys to the jail," do have a ring of realism that appeals even to some conservatives.

The pros and cons of recognition and admission have been endlessly reiterated and belabored since the twin problems were deposited on our doorstep after the birth of the People's Republic of China in 1949. Little purpose would be served by parading the whole array of tired arguments through these pages, since neither of the problems is really a live issue for the time being. As a former Secretary of State told the writer: "They are symbols, not issues."

It was the consensus of Americans interviewed by this writer that the ruthless and irresponsible behavior of the Peking regime at home and abroad, and its consistently hostile attitude toward this country, made talk of recognition rather meaningless for the present, especially since the Chinese themselves had shown no recent interest in it. There was a time, just after the Communist takeover of the Chinese mainland, when the idea of recognition had widespread support, but the Korean War put a stop to that. After Korea, a new upsurge of recognition talk was again effectively squelched by Chinese misbehavior. The fact is that from 1949 up to the present day the Chinese Communists have, by their own acts, made it almost impossible for Americans to consider the recognition question dispassionately. The brutal repression in Tibet, the cynical show of force on the Indo-Tibetan frontier, the Quemoy-Matsu crisis, and, more recently, the worsening situation in Viet-Nam—all have served, one after the other, to keep American nerves raw and antagonisms alive. And never for a day, an hour or a minute has there been any letup in the torrent of anti-American abuse emanating from Peking.

Interviews disclosed that a fair number of those persons who once favored recognition are now either opposed to it or are disinterested in it except as a pawn to be used for bargaining purposes. Some said that whereas recognition might have produced useful results at a time when Peking was receptive to the idea, the benefits under present conditions would be negligible. They pointed to Britain's diplomatic experiences in Peking as an example of the thin pickings to be expected. Some felt that while recognition is probably inevitable, in the long run, pushing it now would be an exercise in futility. As they see it, recognition is out of the question until the Chinese Communists show a profound change of attitude, of which there is presently no sign. Here is a Boston editor's comment: "In principle, I believe in the doctrine of recognition. I feel that recognition would be in our national interest, although it is problematical whether we would get anything out of it. But for the present it is almost impossible for the American public to accept recognition. There are simply no dynamics in the situation to support it. Also, there is the question whether Peking would agree to it."

The question of admission to the United Nations is, of course, beyond ultimate U.S. control. All our soundings of public opinion show that while a majority of Americans is opposed to admitting the Peking regime to the UN, an even larger majority is against withdrawing from the UN if Peking is voted in over U.S. objection or abstinence.

Although advocates of immediate recognition and admission were distinctly in the minority among those interviewed, most of them were firm in their view that theirs was the counsel of peace, realism and good sense. A few were self-conscious about the stand they had taken. There was the California editor, for instance, who made this forthright statement: "My personal opinion is that we should reappraise our whole policy. For the sake of world tranquility, *de facto* recognition of Red China is certainly called for." Having said this, he paused and asked nervously: "Does that make me sound like a Communist?"

Undoubtedly the antipathy for recognition and admission which showed up in many interviews was as much emotional as intellectual in content. The feeling was inescapable that Americans would respond readily to a friendlier posture on the Chinese side.

Policy Considerations on Which Opinion Is Deeply Divided

Two issues of importance belong in this category: (1) the issue of Viet-Nam, and (2) the question of trade with Communist China.

Viet-Nam lies outside the scope of this survey. Events in that tragic country are, in any case, in such flux at this writing that any attempt at detailed analysis of public attitudes toward them would almost certainly be out of date by the time these words are printed. The subject did, of course, come up spontaneously and with great frequency in interviews with opinion leaders. Clearly the public is coming to regard the Viet-Nam conflict as less and less a dirty little local war, more and more as the arena in which the issue of peace or war between Communist China and the United States may be decided. One side-effect of our involvement in Viet-Nam has been to revive isolationist sentiment among some Americans.

Among those interviewed who favored a relaxation of the American embargo on trade with Communist China, the argument most often advanced was that trade would provide the most effective means of establishing communication with the mainland Chinese. However, the element of self-interest, though usually played down, is undoubtedly also a motivation of great importance, especially with American businessmen. Certainly it is more than coincidence that much of the active support for trade with Communist China comes from areas and from groups in the

United States which stand to benefit economically from such commerce. Very frequently, however, individuals are torn by conflicting emotions on the subject. American farmers, for example, are among those most likely to gain economic benefit from the sale of grain to China. Yet many of them would consider such trade a betrayal of their traditional conservatism and anticommunism. An official of the powerful American Farm Bureau Federation stated the position of his constituents as follows: "The question of trade with Communist countries has been a hot issue with us since 1956. If it came to a vote it is probable that trade with Red China would be opposed, as would an extension of Public Law 480 (surplus grain) assistance to that country. Nevertheless, we have not objected to Japan or Canada doing business with Peking. Our feeling toward China is based on our general feeling toward communism. Farmers might go along with traffic in nonstrategic items. But, if it became an issue affecting U.S. security there would be trouble."

This conflict between the question of what would help the individual and what was best for the country showed up frequently in interviews, although it was of course no problem with those who believe that the best interests of the United States lie in a policy of coexistence and conciliation toward Communist China.

Nowhere in the United States is the sentiment for modification of the existing trade embargo stronger than in the San Francisco area where such diverse institutions as the *San Francisco Chronicle*, the World Trade Association of the San Francisco Chamber of Commerce, the International Longshoremen's Union, the California Young Democrats and the Committee for a Review of Our China Policy have all taken stands in favor of trade with Communist China. San Francisco takes great pride in its traditional predominance in transpacific commerce and yearns nostalgically for a resumption of its former shipping and trading contacts with the Chinese mainland. There is a disposition to be doggedly optimistic over trading prospects, once barriers have been removed, and to minimize the political obstacles. Views popular in San Francisco trading circles are: (1) that the easiest way to break down barriers between us and Communist China would be through trade, and (2) that private businessmen with past experience in the China trade are best qualified to make the initial contacts. The San Francisco area is well supplied with traders of long experience in Chinese-American commerce. Among some of them there is a strong dissatisfaction with the American embargo on trade with the Chinese mainland and a feeling that Pacific Coast interests have been neglected. Criticism of the State Department is often heard in the West, but I encountered more of it in San Francisco than elsewhere.

"We are being naive about China," said a businessman formerly resident in China. "We are beating out heads against a wall. In this matter the West Coast is more realistic than the rest of the country. We don't see why we should sit next to Canada and watch them sell wheat to Communist China, while we do nothing. We are handcuffed. We can do nothing until we educate the United States government. There are plenty of people around who know the situation and could be of help. But they are Old China Hands. The thinking in Washington is that businessmen of this type cannot be helpful because they have ulterior motives."

A similar lament came from the head of another big import-export concern. "Ten years ago," he recalled, "I felt that we had made a great mistake in not opening up unlimited trade with China. Had we done so, the quality of our goods would have been much better known to the Chinese today. The more time that passes, the less the Chinese know about our products and the less they care. I don't believe we could do much volume—maybe a few one-shot deals. Maybe some trade in wheat, cotton, Douglas fir, apples and so forth. The point is that without contact you have no potential. Trade would promote contact. I am not advocating recognition. Even without recognition, traders should be allowed to do what they can on their own. We might have to sacrifice a lot of face to do a little trade. But from the standpoint of the national interest it would be worthwhile."

Not all San Franciscans, of course, share these sentiments. A stronghold of dissent is to be found, for instance, in the affluent and conservative Commonwealth Club. Early in 1963, members of the club were polled by mail on their views about our China policy. By a margin of 1935 to 730 they opposed establishment

of trade relations with Communist China. It was in the Commonwealth Club, incidentally, that Roger Hilsman, former Assistant
Secretary of State for Far Eastern Affairs delivered, in December
1963, a widely publicized speech interpreting American policy
toward China in more liberal terms than had been heard from
any State Department official in more than a decade.[2]

Elsewhere on the Pacific coast, I found attitudes toward
trading with Communist China more mixed. This from an official
of the Los Angeles Chamber of Commerce: "We have not gone
along with San Francisco on trade with China because we don't
think we should feed the regime that seeks to destroy us. People
here will acquiesce with official United States policy, whatever
it may be." He complained, as others had on the coast, about
the failure of the federal government to keep businessmen adequately informed on economic developments in Communist
China. "I feel lost," he said. "We are getting so little information,
and there is so little continuity in what we are getting."

In the Pacific Northwest, where the booming trade with Japan
is keeping the principal ports busier than they have ever been,
there is also an underlying interest in the reopening of trade with
China proper, if and when Washington gives the word. The
Northwest was once a heavy shipper of timber, grain and apples
to China (in 1939, 16.4 per cent of all exports from the Oregon
customs district went to China), and traders see Communist China
as a possible market for timber and wheat, at least. Businessmen
in the Northwest, however, are less optimistic and less aggressive
in the matter than their brethren in San Francisco. While probably the majority would like to see the embargo lifted on nonstrategic goods, there is a disposition to be nervous about adverse
public opinion and to be guided by the federal government's
views on the matter.

Here are some random observations from persons interviewed
in the states of Washington and Oregon. A Seattle businessman:
"Feeling here is mixed on trade. The consensus lies somewhere
between a feeling that we have something to gain and that it is

[2] For the text of this speech, see *Department of State Bulletin*, v. 49,
January 6, 1964, pp. 11–17.

not morally right." A Portland lawyer: "At present there is no real movement here for trade with Red China. From the political standpoint it is dangerous to raise the issue." A wheat exporter in Portland: "Personally, I think it is ridiculous for us to sit here while people in Canada sell wheat to Communist China, but some of my colleagues don't agree with me. They consider China our most dangerous enemy." A retired general in Portland: "In this part of the country people are against any dealings with Red China. Any such relationship would give a boost to the greatest enemy of the white race." A Seattle export-import executive: "Trade would be an opening wedge for something bigger—for example economic aid. The consensus here is against trade with Red China." A Protestant minister in Portland: "Trade would be a step in the right direction. It would break the ice."

In inland areas, the total embargo on trade with Communist China enjoys widespread support, although this attitude is being noticeably eroded in cities with international trading contacts. The Far East no longer seems remote from Chicago, which has developed important commercial relations with Japan and sees mainland China as a potential market for a part of the prodigious volume of raw materials and manufactured goods pouring out of its tributary territory. Chicago attitudes toward trade with Communist China are quite similar to those in the Northwest. Some businessmen are ready, some eager, to trade with Communist China if the United States government would give the "go-ahead" signal. The general public, on the other hand, is inclined to be hostile or apathetic to the idea. I quote below the views of three prominent Chicago business executives.

Executive One: "We are not as isolationist here as we used to be. Our international trade is mushrooming and our businessmen get around as never before. I feel we should trade with Red China in nonstrategic goods. Trade breaks down barriers. The only way we are ever going to get understanding is through trade."

Executive Two: "Trade with China is kind of an enigma. There are no great passions here one way or the other. On the wheat deal with Russia, it was the consensus that it was a good thing to do—just keep them poor buying wheat. On trade with

China, the State Department knows much more than we do about the best line to follow."

Executive Three: "The business community here would not object to trade with Communist China. But public opinion might look at it differently. So would the *Chicago Tribune*."

A prominent merchant in Memphis, Tennessee, had this comment: "I don't see how you are going to find out anything about your enemies unless you talk with them, deal with them and trade with them." But he added ruefully, "My friends think I'm nuts."

Even in Kansas, the wheat state, which would almost certainly stand to benefit economically from trade with Communist China, relatively few spoke up strongly in favor of such trade in face of the deep underlying conservatism and anti-Communist sentiments of the region.

On the Eastern seaboard I found a lively interest in East-West trade insofar as it concerns the Soviet bloc but little public interest in commerce with Communist China. Reactions in New York were generally passive, with a disposition to go along with official policy, although a few spoke up in favor of modifying the existing embargo. "If the trade is not of a strategic nature, we should have no objection to it," a New York banker said. "A little trade would give us a little contact. Unfortunately, we have lost so much contact that the situation may be irretrievable. Many of our business people have strong feelings against trading with the Chinese Communists. Most just don't think about it."

The United States Chamber of Commerce, which has often taken a bellwether role in promoting the views of American business on matters of national policy, recently completed a study of East-West trade and went so far as to recommend a re-examination and re-evaluation of export controls governing trade with the Soviet bloc. It had little to say, however, on the total embargo against Communist China and certain other countries beyond observing that "no change in these embargo provisions is contemplated by the National Chamber." Later, at its annual convention, the Chamber went on record, cautiously, in favor of opening up channels of communication with the *people* of mainland China, while at the same time specifically opposing recognition of the Peking regime or admission of Communist China to the United Nations.[3] Although the resolution made no suggestion of trade, critical columnists and editorialists were quick to read commercial implications into it. In a typical comment, the *Tucson Daily Citizen* [4] noted that "some Americans will interpret the resolution . . . as proof that greedy businessmen want to extend the chase after the almighty dollar onto mainland China, despite the fact that the Red Chinese are stepping up their aggression in Viet-Nam and other countries which the United States is obligated to defend."

Not many businessmen feel strongly enough about trade with Communist China to advocate it publicly at the risk of being denounced as avaricious and unpatriotic. Yet it is apparent from the mixed views quoted in this chapter that a large number of Americans have serious doubts about the sense and logic of the strict controls in light of the fact that most of our friends and allies are trading freely with Peking in nonstrategic products and, to some extent, in goods of a strategic nature. Among businessmen, in particular, there is evident concern that the embargo, as it now stands, has largely failed of its purpose and serves only to deprive them of an opportunity to compete with the rest of the world for the China trade. These views are shared by others outside the business community who are impressed also by the argument that trade might provide an effective means of establishing informal contact with the mainland Chinese.

I have the distinct impression that such attitudes are more widely prevalent among Americans in leadership positions than public statements would indicate. There is an evident reluctance, however, to take issue openly with the established policy of the United States. Fear of criticism is a factor. Mixed with it is an element of uncertainty as to the rights and wrongs of the matter. On the other hand, supporters of the *status quo* in our embargo policy are highly vocal and have the sympathy of many influen-

---

[3] U. S. Chamber of Commerce, *Challenge to Free Enterprise in World Trade: Communist Economic Offensive as It Affects American Business* (Washington, D.C.: Author, June 1964); *The New York Times*, April 25, 1965.

[4] April 29, 1965.

tial persons in labor, farm and veterans organizations and in the Republican and (to a lesser extent) Democratic parties. They can contend, as they do, that it is not only economically wrong, it is also morally wrong to trade with the Chinese Communists. They can argue, as they do, that trade is used by the Communists as a political weapon, that to trade with them is to help them, and that the amount of trade to be gained would not be significant enough to compensate for the prestige lost by engaging in it.

The cautious approach of most American businessmen to this touchy question is exemplified by the experiences of the organization known as the Committee for a Review of Our China Policy, which has been making strenuous but so far unsuccessful efforts to promote a dialogue between mainland Chinese and our businessmen on trade possibilities. While in California, I talked with Ernest Nash, one of the cochairmen of this small group. He said that while the Committee has had considerable private encouragement from businessmen and others, particularly on the west coast, many of its sympathizers have shied away from becoming members or contributing funds. This reluctance is attributed, in some instances, to the fact that many businessmen do not wish to be identified publicly with a movement that might be construed to be in opposition to the existing policy of the United States government. In the case of academic people, it is often a matter of not wanting to be publicly committed on a controversial policy. Other presumed reasons for timidity include: apprehension over the possibility of being criticized as "soft" on communism; unwillingness to jeopardize business connections in Taiwan; a feeling of futility over the prospects of change; a feeling that trade with Communist China probably would not amount to much, anyway.

Clearly the issue of trade with Communist China is one on which the public looks to the nation's capital for guidance. Many of those interviewed gave the impression that they were going along with the embargo policy less because they believed in it than because of their assumption that the United States government, in its wisdom, must have good reasons for persisting in it. Yet the government, too, has its doubters, some in high places.

Policy Considerations on Which Attitudes
Are Predominantly Favorable

There are several aspects of our policy, present and proposed, on which there was quite general concurrence among those interviewed. They include:

1. The desirability of more contact and communication between the American and Chinese peoples.

2. The necessity of standing by our treaty commitments to the Nationalist regime under Chiang Kai-shek.

Nearly all persons interviewed were agreed on the need for more communication; and time after time the absence of such communication was cited as a prime reason for our misunderstanding of the Chinese and their misunderstanding of us. Improved communication, it was felt, would (a) enable us to obtain better information on conditions inside Communist China, (b) give the Chinese government and people some access, however slight, to real attitudes and real conditions in the United States, (c) help dissuade Peking from reckless behavior to which she might otherwise be driven through isolation.

With few exceptions, even those of a pronounced conservative outlook favored increased contact, although they often differed as to the extent to which they would carry it. Here, for example, is the view of an Idaho businessman who greatly admires Chiang Kai-shek and believes the United States should assist Chiang in an invasion of the Chinese mainland: "Generally, I would favor improved communications with Red China 'so that we would know what is going on inside the country. When you have an adversary, you are better off knowing what he is doing. Even if it is necessary to admit a few Chinese to this country in exchange, it wouldn't matter."

A retired general, also extremely conservative in his views, came to the same conclusion but for somewhat different reasons. "If I were President," he said, "I would want to maintain contact at all times, commercial, scientific, cultural and psychological, with Communist China. It is futile to hope for a breakthrough unless we establish this contact. Force is no answer. To attain this contact I would make quite a few 'concessions.' At least, they would sound like concessions to the John Birch Society, but they wouldn't be."

Almost to a man—and woman—the persons interviewed were agreed on the desirability of getting American newspaper correspondents into Communist China, although a few felt such direct coverage would be useful only if the "right kind" of correspondents were sent. On the question of exchanges of scholars, scientists, businessmen and plain tourists, reactions, though mainly favorable, were much more mixed and, in a few instances, emphatically negative. I would judge, however, from the responses received, that a great many, and possibly a majority, of those we class as opinion leaders would go along with the view expressed by a professor of political science in a California university. "I feel strongly the necessity for Americans to visit China," this professor said. "The long see-saw over newsmen—to say nothing of scholars—is unfortunate. It was stupid to restrict travel to China when we had an option. Bad communications aggravate bad relations and could mean the difference between peace and war. If communications are blocked between man and man, he becomes more and more pathological. I rather dread the idea of a China isolated. There are some risks in open communications, but a world with open communications is better than a world with closed or partially closed communications. And by communications I do not mean just stepped up intelligence. I am thinking of an interchange of engineers, scholars and newsmen. I would like to see top Chinese leadership invited on a real tour of the United States. Unquestionably, Khrushchev was influenced by his visit to this country."

This interest in improved communication as a key to better understanding of or with China is to be found right up into the highest circles of our government. A specialist in Asian affairs in President Kennedy's Executive Offices put it this way: "Travel is the first step. You get people traveling and coming back and telling their story. That is the sure way to stir public interest."

We have seen that Americans differ radically on some aspects of our policy toward the Nationalist government; a conspicuous example is the question of what we should or should not do in event of a Chinese Communist assault on the offshore islands of Quemoy and Matsu. But it is generally agreed that we are legally and morally bound to honor the commitments we have made to Chiang Kai-shek and his government with respect to the mutual defense of Taiwan, even if it means war with Communist China. It should be noted, however, that the many persons reaching this conclusion are often motivated by opposite lines of reasoning. One school sees Taiwan as a vital outpost in the world struggle against communism—a bastion essential to the eventual "liberation" of the Chinese mainland; another views the island as an undesirable but unavoidable responsibility forced on us by circumstances.

CHAPTER SIX

Boundaries of Public Tolerance: The Public Opinion Polls

It is apparent from the foregoing that American opinions on China are not only extremely diverse but also subject to much shifting and adjustment to conform to changing situations. They are tied, however, to certain underlying attitudes—for example, anticommunism—which change much more slowly, or not at all.

The volatility of public opinion on some issues is illustrated by the fluctuating views on Viet-Nam. Many people who formerly regarded the Viet-Nam war as little more than a civil conflict between Vietnamese factions later came to view it in a more serious light as the testing ground for United States ability to halt the spread of Chinese Communist influence into Southeast Asia. The effect was to strengthen public support for American policy in this area.

This illustration raises the question of the approximate limits of public consent in the matter of American policy toward China. In other words, how far could the United States government go toward easing or stiffening its policy without provoking strong opposition from the American public? The immobility of many of our national leaders and legislators on the China question is based on the assumption that public opinion is solidly behind our policy as it stands and that any attempt to modify or even re-examine it would provoke devastating political reactions from the voting public. Is this true?

It goes without saying that the limits of public tolerance on such a problem cannot be fixed with anything like scientific accuracy. But it is possible, through public opinion polls, to determine how strongly opinions on China are held, which way the winds of change are blowing and the approximate limits of elasticity in public thinking at a given time. In exploring these matters in this study, reliance has been placed mainly, but not exclusively, on two public opinion polls undertaken on our behalf. One was the nationwide sampling conducted by the Survey Research Center (SRC) of the University of Michigan (see Appendix). Carried out in May and June 1964, it involved interviews with a representative sample of 1,501 persons across the country. The other survey, made in 1963 by Samuel Lubell Associates, based its findings on 169 "man-in-the-street" interviews in Eastern, Midwestern and Southern towns. The Lubell report, though not published for general circulation, produced some revealing information on the contrasting images of China and Russia in American eyes and on major trends in American thinking on the China question. It was supplemented, in 1965, by a few additional findings.

The Survey Research Center's poll revealed a disturbing lack of knowledge among the general public on even the most elementary facts of the China situation: more than one-fourth (28 per cent) of the public was not aware that China is now ruled by a Communist government; and 39 per cent of those who did know of the Communist government could not think of any other Chinese government. In evaluating the SRC's findings it needs to be borne in mind that on some questions of policy the polling organization excluded from its questioning those who were apparently unaware of either of the two regimes. It was felt that to invite opinions about a foreign regime from people who did not know of its existence might lead to serious distortions in the findings. Nevertheless, one cannot ignore the probability that in a crisis situation many of these people would be stimulated into having an opinion and taking sides and, therefore, would have to be counted.

For the purposes of this study it was decided that perhaps the best way to get a rough measure of the flexibility of public opinion on China policy would be to determine public reactions to various hypothetical initiatives by the President of the United States. This approach was based on the fact that it is usually the President who initiates legislation relating to China and that it is his influence that is most persuasive for or against any measure. Thus, public response for or against his recommendations would tend to indicate the amount of "give," if any, in public attitudes. Therefore, when interviewers of the Survey Research Center went to the people with a series of questions on China, they led into the difficult area of China policy with this statement:

Now the President of the United States might decide that it was in our best interests to take certain new actions with regard to Communist China. For each thing I mention, would you tell me how you would feel about it if the President suggested that action?

This statement was followed by a series of five questions, each relating to a particular phase of U.S. policy. In the returns on these questions, the respondents were divided into those who *definitely* favored and *probably* favored each proposition and those who definitely *opposed* and *probably* opposed each one. This subdivision of categories is worth noting, since it provides a clue to the intensity, or lack of it, with which opinions are held. We can assume that those with strongly held opinions are more likely to persist in them and to fight for them than those whose views are lightly held. By the same token, we can assume that those whose views are not strongly held are more likely to alter them with changing circumstances. Translated into political terms, this means that a view held by an intensely and actively committed minority can often prevail over the view of an indifferent majority.

The Survey Research Center's findings are discussed below. The commentaries on these findings are based on material from various sources, including the Lubell survey.

There are no surprises here. As has been pointed out, if there is any question of China policy on which there is overwhelming agreement in all of our public opinion samplings, it is on the desirability of increased communication between the American and Chinese peoples. As far back as 1957, when the Chinese Communists seemed receptive to the idea of an exchange of news-

On the Question of Communication

QUESTION: Suppose the President suggested visits between Americans and people from Communist China—like newspapermen from each country visiting each other?

ANSWERS:

Definitely favor following his suggestion on this	41%	
		73%
Probably favor following his suggestion on this	32%	
Probably be against following his suggestion on this	6%	
		16%
Definitely be against following his suggestion on this	10%	
No idea whether I'd favor or be against it	10%	
Not ascertained	1%	
Total	100%	

paper correspondents and our State Department was being negative about it, the National Opinion Research Center (NORC) asked the American public the following question: "Do you think our government should allow American reporters to visit Communist China or not?" The replies even then were emphatically favorable: Should, 65 per cent; Should not, 23 per cent; Don't know, 12 per cent.

The response to this question is consistent with the generally favorable attitude of the public toward increased communication with Communist China and the negotiation of high-level differences. However, we must avoid reading too much meaning into the answers. An exchange of ambassadors involves diplomatic recognition, but it is doubtful whether all persons responding to the question understood its full meaning. From the establishment

On Willingness to Exchange Ambassadors
with Communist China

QUESTION: Suppose the President suggested that we exchange ambassadors with Communist China the way we do with other countries?

ANSWERS:

Definitely favor following his suggestion on this	24%	⎫
Probably favor following his suggestion on this	27%	⎬ 51%
Probably be against following his suggestion on this	11%	⎫
Definitely be against following his suggestion on this	23%	⎬ 34%
No idea whether I'd favor or be against it	14%	
Not ascertained	1%	
Total	100%	

of the Peking regime, in October 1949, public opinion polls have shown a generally consistent but variable opposition to diplomatic recognition of the Communist government. A Gallup poll in October 1949 showed only 25 per cent of the public in favor of recognition; an NORC poll in January 1950, only 11 per cent. In November 1954, just after the Korean War, an NORC poll found 55 per cent of the public favorable to recognizing the Communist regime (with 30 per cent opposed and 15 undecided). But a Gallup poll in October 1964 indicated that there had been a stiffening of attitude on this question in the intervening decade. In 1964, Gallup asked this question: "Do you think it would be in the interests of the United States to establish diplomatic relations with Communist China within the next five years or not?" The returns were as follows: Would be, 36 per cent; Would not be, 39 per cent; Don't know, 25 per cent.

On Negotiation with China on Asian Problems

QUESTION: Suppose the President suggested that we talk over problems of Asia with Communist China and try to come to some agreement with them?

ANSWERS:

Definitely favor following his suggestion on this	37%	⎫
Probably favor following his suggestion on this	34%	⎬ 71%
Probably be against following his suggestion on this	7%	⎫
Definitely be against following his suggestion on this	12%	⎬ 19%
No idea whether I'd favor or be against it	9%	
Not ascertained	1%	
Total	100%	

It is interesting that the consistently antagonistic attitude of the American public toward the Chinese Communists has been accompanied by an equally consistent desire for peace and harmony through negotiation of our differences. The overwhelmingly favorable response to the suggestion of negotiation with Communist China, above, follows a pattern of opinion that has remained virtually unchanged for a decade. In April 1955, NORC asked a nationwide sampling: "Do you think it would be a good idea or a bad idea for U.S. representatives to meet with Chinese Communist leaders to try to reach an agreement on some of the problems of Asia?" The replies were: Approve, 70 per cent; Disapprove, 21 per cent; Qualified, 3 per cent; Don't know, 4 per cent. Substantially the same question has been put to the American public on three or four occasions since then, always with substantially the same results. Leadership opinion, I found in interviews around the country, does not share the optimism of the general public on this subject. It tends to take a more serious view of obstacles standing in the way of agreement—notably the presently irreconcilable position of the two sides on Taiwan.

On the Question of Trade with Communist China

QUESTION: Suppose the President suggested selling things like wheat to Communist China?

ANSWERS:

Definitely favor following his suggestion on this	19%	⎫
Probably favor following his suggestion on this	24%	⎬ 43%
Probably be against following his suggestion on this	14%	⎫
Definitely be against following his suggestion on this	33%	⎬ 47%
No idea whether I'd favor or be against it	9%	
Not ascertained	1%	
Total	100%	

The public mood has been tested repeatedly on the nettlesome question of trade since the Communist takeover of the mainland, with generally inconclusive results. A Gallup poll in October 1949 showed a majority of those with opinions as being opposed to trade. Yet a sounding in January 1950 showed a slightly favorable sentiment. Views on trade were hostile, of course, during the Korean War and remained so for some months afterward. But a favorable trend developed in 1955, and an NORC poll in September of that year showed 55 per cent of those interviewed as favorable to trade in nonstrategic goods. Polling records indicate a predominantly disapproving attitude in 1956–57, but a poll in

February 1961 showed the weight of opinion as favorable to the idea of the United States and Communist China buying and selling goods to each other. The src poll, tabulated above, shows that there was slightly more sentiment against selling "things like wheat" to Communist China than in favor of it. Throughout these pollings, the margin of difference between the pros and cons on trade has generally been too narrow to show a clear pattern of preference. And the mixed reaction is consistent with the divided views of opinion leaders quoted in the previous chapter. A point to be noted in the src poll, however, is that while only 19 per cent of those questioned were *definitely* favorable to selling things like wheat to Communist China, no less than 33 per cent were *definitely* opposed. Here is a rather clear indication that those opposed to such trade hold their views more strongly than those who favor it and would probably put up a strong fight against any serious attempt to modify the existing embargo.

On Admitting Communist China to the United Nations

QUESTION: Suppose the President suggested that we let Communist China join the United Nations?

ANSWERS:

Definitely favor following his suggestion on this	13%	} 31%
Probably favor following his suggestion on this	18%	
Probably be against following his suggestion on this	13%	} 53%
Definitely be against following his suggestion on this	40%	
No idea whether I'd favor or be against it	15%	
Not ascertained	1%	
Total	100%	

This is the one Presidential initiative of the five suggested that met with opposition from a clear majority of those questioned. The negative response fits into a pattern of opinion which has prevailed consistently since the question of Communist China's entry into the United Nations was first raised and no doubt is influenced by our government's firm, continued and well-publicized opposition to such entry. There has been a slow decline, however, in the percentage of the public opposing admission. The opposition was once overwhelming. In November 1953, for example, a NORC poll showed 74 per cent opposed to admission and only 12 per cent favorable.

There are those on the far right, in this country, who advocate U.S. withdrawal from the United Nations if Communist China is voted in over American objections. Is this view shared by the general public? Emphatically not. When SRC sought public reactions to this question, 75 per cent of those questioned said the United States should remain in the UN even if Communist China is admitted. Only 5 per cent favored withdrawal.

Lubell, in his 1963 sampling, also found public opinion strongly opposed to admission of Communist China to the United Nations. In later soundings (1965), following the nuclear explosions in China and the worsening of the situation in Viet-Nam, opposition remained strong, but there were some signs of uncertainty linked mainly to the deterioration in Viet-Nam. "Up to this point," Lubell informed this writer, "Viet-Nam had not been on people's minds. It was only after the Viet-Nam blow-up that the public realized the gravity of the situation and began to give more thought to China policy. Some people became less rigid in their outlook. There was a growing feeling that we should 'do something.' People who wanted to pull out of Viet-Nam tended to think we should admit Communist China to the UN. Those who wanted to fight on in Viet-Nam were against it. Public opinion on admission and recognition could be influenced either way by developments in Viet-Nam."

Lubell said that the most frequently mentioned reasons for opposing UN admission were that it would increase Communist power in the United Nations and that China, as an aggressor, had no place in an organization devoted to peace. Our commitment to Nationalist China was also cited fairly often as a reason for opposing UN admittance. Other typical quotes: "We should stick by our friends"; "They (the Communists) would have one more platform from which to disrupt things"; "They have nothing to offer—they are anti-everything"; "It would be like giving them a stamp of approval."

Arguments most used by the minority favoring Communist China's entry were (1) that mainland China is a world power, here to stay, and that we can no longer ignore her and (2) that bringing her into the UN may restrain or soften her. "How can you expect to develop friendship in isolation?" a New Jersey lawyer asked.

The Lubell interviews indicated that some of the opposition to admission would melt away if China showed herself less belligerent and more cooperative. A retail salesman in New Jersey said we should hold back UN admission "until they're more flexible and more peaceful." Other comments in the same vein: "They've got to calm down"; "They won't listen to anyone"; "Their minds are made up"; "You can't deal with them." Several suggested resolving this dilemma by recognizing Communist China but not admitting her into the UN, on the theory that admission implies approval but recognition does not.

Younger People More Flexible

Analyzing its findings, the Survey Research Center found that willingness to follow the Presidential initiatives was greater among younger age groups than among older groups and that people of higher education were somewhat more likely than those with less education to favor Presidential initiatives to improve relations with Communist China. However, those with more knowledge of China did not always take the same line as those of greater education. The better informed were more likely to favor visits between the two countries and somewhat more likely to oppose an exchange of ambassadors with Communist China and to oppose letting Communist China into the UN. No differences of outlook were observed between the sexes.

Why do persons past middle age tend to favor a hard line toward the Communist regime, while those below middle age tend to favor a more conciliatory approach? One can only speculate, but a probable reason comes quickly to mind: those longer in years are also longer in memory and have stronger recollections of the *status quo ante* in mainland China, when the "old" regime, for all its faults, was nevertheless friendly and cooperative. Another factor, no doubt, is the deeper emotional involvement of the older generation in the China problem. The fact that the older age group is less well educated than the younger could also be a consideration. Whatever the reason, there are indications that opposition to dealing with the Chinese Communists has been slowly fading with time.

Attitudes toward War and Peace in Asia

Among the broad conclusions that can be drawn from these samplings of American opinion is that a majority of the American people would favor a peaceful solution of outstanding differences with Communist China if it could be had on just and honorable terms. This is indicated by the overwhelming endorsement of the suggestion of negotiation with Peking on Asian problems. It shows up again in the response to src questions about Viet-Nam in which 46 per cent (61 per cent of those with opinions) said they would like to see a compromise settlement in that embattled land, even at the price of neutralization. And the strong sentiment against supporting the Nationalist Chinese in any attack against the Chinese mainland reflects a desire to avoid precipitating a war with China.

While the American people clearly are against aggressive action which would invite war with China, they have also demonstrated that they are willing to accept heavy risks in support of U.S. commitments for the mutual defense of Taiwan and Viet-Nam. On the question of risking outright war, opinion has tended to vacillate with the changing situation and with our government's attitude of the moment. In 1955, to be sure, the public approved overwhelmingly when Congress authorized President Eisenhower to use U.S. armed forces, if necessary, to defend Taiwan. But in

1958, Gallup put this question to the public: "There's been much discussion whether this country should get into an all-out war with Red China over the Quemoy and Matsu Islands and over Formosa itself. How do you feel? Should the U.S. go to war for Quemoy and Matsu . . . should the U.S. go to war for Formosa?" Only 28 per cent said we should go to war for Taiwan, 32 per cent said we should not, and 40 per cent were undecided. Incidentally, only 18 per cent were willing at that time to get into on all-out war for Quemoy and Matsu, although a 1955 question about "defending" Quemoy and Matsu had won approval from a majority of those with opinions.

The American public time and again has shown a reluctance to endorse war-risking action. But once the die is cast and the country embroiled, the people are sometimes prepared to take even bigger risks than their leaders are willing to approve. Such was the case during the Korean conflict when an NORC poll (June 1952) showed 61 per cent of the public in favor of bombing Communist supply bases inside China.

Changing Attitudes toward Taiwan

Responses to other questions indicate that the public is becoming more and more realistic in its appraisal of the relative strength of the Communist and Nationalist governments in China. Chiang Kai-shek's much-advertised ambition of invading the mainland is no longer taken seriously by most Americans. This represents a marked change of attitude since the Korean War. We have earlier noted that in 1951 nearly six out of ten (58 per cent) of those responding to an NORC survey said they would approve of the United States' helping the Nationalists in an attack on the Communist-held mainland. In our 1964 survey, the Survey Research Center asked the following question:

Some people say we should give the Nationalists all the help they need to attack the Communists on the mainland of China. Other people say we should protect the Nationalists from Communist attack but should not help them to attack the Communists. Do you have an opinion about this or not?

In reply, only one person in ten (10 per cent) favored U.S. assistance for a Nationalist attack, while more than six times that proportion (62 per cent) felt we should protect the Nationalists but not assist them in attacking the mainland. Giving reasons for their attitudes, 45 per cent of those responding indicated that they were opposed to action that might involve the United States unnecessarily in a war with China or with both China and the Soviet Union.

Clearly the Nationalist government on Taiwan, which U.S. policy recognizes as the only legitimate government of all China, is today regarded by most Americans as no more than a local regime. Nowadays, when Americans speak of China they usually mean Communist China.

The Changing Sino-Soviet Image

All our public opinion soundings agree that the American people are becoming increasingly concerned over Communist China's growing strength and menacing aspect and have tended to revise their thinking on the respective roles of China and the Soviet Union. Communist China has succeeded Soviet Russia in American eyes as our "most dangerous enemy." This is a development of quite recent years and has far-reaching implications. In 1961, a Gallup survey asked: "Looking ahead to 1970, which country do you think will be the greater threat to world peace: Russia or Communist China?" Almost half (49 per cent) of those interviewed named Russia; only 32 per cent picked China. But when, in October 1964, Gallup asked a somewhat similar question: "Which do you think will turn out to be the greater threat to the U.S.—Soviet Russia or Communist China?" China led with 55 per cent.

Lubell's polling showed a similar opinion shift. In 1961, Lubell asked this question: "Which country would you say is the bigger threat to the United States, Soviet Russia or Communist China?" The replies were: Russia, 45 per cent; China, 40 per cent. By 1963, when the same question was asked again, the percentage picking China had risen to 60 per cent. Elsewhere in this report we have noted that a parallel view of Communist China as the more menacing of the two Communist giants is shared by newspaper editors and other relatively well-informed Americans interviewed by this writer.

The Lubell organization explored public opinion on this subject in considerable depth and came up with some rather surprising findings. Although only 169 persons (in twenty states) were asked questions about China in the 1963 Lubell survey—and not always the same questions—it should be noted that responses on pivotal questions paralleled those of other surveys involving a much larger sampling of the population. Lubell also probed issues seldom touched upon in the larger polls. For instance, in a 1961 survey he had found that fewer than one in twenty persons interviewed described the threat posed by China in either racial terms or as a conflict of Eastern and Western civilizations, but now two years later, nearly one in five of those questioned talked of a coming conflict between the yellow people and other races. Asked by the Lubell interviewers what they saw as the main differences between the Soviet Union and Communist China, many Americans pinned on China all the barbaric, warlike, irrational traits they abhor and attributed to Russia the main features of Western culture. Supposed characteristics mentioned (in order of frequency) were: overpopulation or starvation; low value on human life; more warlike or wanting war; yellow people hostile to West; more aggressive, hostile, inflexible; not as civilized; fanatical; irrational leadership; nothing to lose, have-nots; immature, less responsible.

Lubell points out that only a few years ago the Soviet system was being denounced in much the same terms as those now popularly applied to the Chinese Communists. But the Russians are looked at quite differently today. A regional industrial manager from Rochester thought "the Russians are somewhat like us in their thinking. Russia is changing. The people are becoming aware of another way—the Western way. But China is completely separated, closed up, tight as a clam. It's impossible to communicate with her." Some people who, not long ago, were criticizing the Soviet system as atheistic, with a low value on human life and run by ruthless dictators, saw Russia's Christian background as a moderating influence. A Lexington, Kentucky, businessman said: "The Russian way is more like the Christian way, so Russians are easier to deal with." A city employee in New York predicted: "The Russians will have to ask our help against the Chinese eventually."

Some even saw the Soviet Union and the United States joining forces eventually against the Chinese Communists. One thought the shift in alignment would come "when China starts applying her land-grabbing policy to Russia." Those who talk of moving closer to the Russians believe that Soviet and American interests can be reconciled but see no meeting ground in the future with China.

The conception of Communist China as the more dangerous of the two Comunist giants, though widely shared, is by no means universal among Americans. At the time of the Lubell poll, 31 per cent of those questioned still saw Soviet Russia as the greater danger and close to half voiced distrust of both countries with such remarks as: "We and the Communists can never agree." Republicans, as it turned out, were considerably more distrustful of the Soviet Union than were the Democrats. Among persons who voted for Richard Nixon in the 1960 election, 42 per cent still saw Russia as the greater threat, while 56 per cent picked China. Among Kennedy voters, only 12 per cent chose Russia as the main villain, 80 per cent China. People hostile to civil rights legislation tend also to have strong views on China, the Lubell findings show. In the South, six out of every seven persons interviewed picked China as the bigger threat.

As for the Peking-Moscow split, most Americans were more inclined to circle around it watchfully than to interfere. Lubell asked: "Should the United States try to capitalize on the Russian-Chinese split by playing off one country against the other?" More than half the respondents rejected the suggestion as out of hand. Some thought the United States is not suited to such devious tactics. "You can't start playing off one country against another," said a New Jersey housewife. "That just breeds distrust all around." But a more common view was that such a stratagem might boomerang. Russia and China, both being Communist, it was argued, "are closer to each other than to us and would patch things up if we stepped into their quarrel." The Kentucky businessman insisted that "they're both our enemies and will remain so as long as they are communistic. They'll always be closer to each other than to us." Of those who did think we could capitalize on the Sino-Soviet differences, nearly all wanted to move closer to Russia, not China.

There were a few—but very few—in the Lubell sample who had a kind word for the Chinese Communists. A mathematician from Baton Rouge repeated the oft-expressed, "China has nothing to lose in a war," but he went on to say, "She has been downtrodden, oppressed and exploited for years. England never did anything but exploit her and neither did we. It's not the wealthy man but the man without any money in his pocket who steals." A photographer from New York City thought China would be less cantankerous "if her insides were in better shape." He felt that the Sino-Soviet split "puts China all by herself, with her back against the wall, and makes her more desperate."

The Lubell report suggests the possibility that Nikita Khrushchev, while Soviet premier, played a bigger part in shaping recent changes in American attitudes toward China and the Soviet Union than Americans realize. Lubell says that Khrushchev, by his actions, "touched off powerful currents of feeling which are moving much of the American electorate in the direction of conciliation with Russia." To many, the threat of China seemed to create a common interest which we and the Soviets shared. Americans became ready listeners to Soviet propaganda against the Peking regime. It confirmed and intensified what we were already strongly disposed to believe.

The issue of wheat sales to Communist countries was in the news at the time of the Lubell survey. Returns from interviews on the question of whether or not we should sell wheat to the Soviet Union and Communist China showed that seven out of ten were prepared to sell to Russia, only four out of ten to China —an indicator of the sharp distinction many Americans draw between the two Communist powers.

Three out of ten were unwilling to sell wheat to either country. These were representative of the hard-core resistance to any relaxation of U.S. policy toward Soviet Russia, Communist China or any other Communist country. Only one of this group favored admitting Communist China to the United Nations. Six to one of this group had voted Republican in the 1960 elections. Here are some quotations representing the deep distrust of Soviet Russia and the even deeper hostility to Communist China that actuates the thinking of these ultra-conservatives:

"We may fight them tomorrow. They are still our enemies."

"You don't nourish a baby rattlesnake."

"I'd rather burn the wheat. You don't sell to those you are at war with."

"I don't think Communism and Christian ethics can ever cooperate."

Within this group there was considerable skepticism as to the depth of Sino-Soviet differences. Two dismissed the split as a "fake," a third as "some minor difference of opinion," while seven doubted whether the quarrel would prove lasting. "It's just that China is impatient and wants to act faster than Russia," said one. An Army staff sergeant maintained that "sooner or later Russia will give China something she wants and then they'll be happy together again." All in this group either wanted to hold to our present policy or to move to a tougher line. But only two envisioned Chiang Kai-shek's return to the mainland.

Among the persons who were willing to sell wheat to Russia but not to China, the reasons most often cited were that China is too warlike and that her huge population constitutes a threat that can be better dealt with by withholding food than giving it. "There are too many of them," said a salesman in Pennsylvania. A dental technician in New York state felt we should sell wheat to Russia because it might keep the Russians from resorting to violence. But on China he felt that "starvation would weaken China and weaken the government there." In short, the same people who are willing to gamble that a strengthened Russian economy will make Moscow more tractable also think that a weakened China will contribute more to peace.

"When a country is content," said a New York housewife, "the people don't want trouble. They want things to stay as they are." But she opposed selling wheat to China or admitting China to the UN and said: "Wait until they're more peaceful and less land-hungry." She continued: "China is overpopulated and filled with starving people. That makes them an angry mob. The Chinese are illiterate and so they just blindly follow any leaders. They're fanatical." A window-cleaner, among those interviewed, also showed some inconsistency. On wheat sales to the Soviet Union he said, "Give starving people food; it's the human thing to do." Asked about wheat to China, he replied, "Starve 'em out."

The group that would sell wheat to both Russia and China was made up of two divergent elements—(1) those who favored wheat sales primarily for economic reasons and were cool to closer relations with Russia; (2) those who favored wheat sales largely to improve relations and were strong for admission of China to the UN and for a general relaxation of our policies toward China and the Soviet Union.

The first group, containing a high percentage of Republicans, advanced arguments like the following: We should sell wheat "only for cash" and to help our balance of payments; if we don't sell to them, they'll get it from other countries; we have a tremendous surplus which is costing us a great deal of money; if China wants it, let her buy it.

And those who wanted better relations with the Communist bloc said: If a country is starving, we should help them, even if they are unfriendly to us; we must open up channels of communication with Communist China, and trade is a way of doing it; trade with Communist China would not only improve our relations with that country but also improve our international standing generally.

In the South, the dovetailing of attitudes toward Communist China and civil rights was again demonstrated on the wheat question. Those who would sell wheat to both China and Russia favored the public accommodations section of the civil rights law by two to one, according to the Lubell report. Those who opposed selling wheat to either country were six to one against the accommodations section.

CHAPTER SEVEN

Pressure Groups and
Other Influential Organizations

For a decade and a half, pressures opposed to modification of our China policy have been predominant—reaching a high point during the heyday of the so-called China Lobby and continuing, in diverse forms, up to the present. Pressures for flexibility and change have been cautious and inconspicuous during most of this period and have never regained the large measure of support they enjoyed prior to the Korean War.

The term "China Lobby" is usually applied rather loosely to that disparate collection of organizations and individuals which, in the 1940s and 1950s, attempted to influence the United States government and the American public in favor of supporting the Chinese Nationalists and opposing compromise with the Chinese Communists. The Lobby attained prominence—or, more accurately, notoriety—in April 1952, when *The Reporter* magazine devoted the better part of two issues to a critical survey of its activities.[1] The magazine painted an unsavory picture of chicanery and influence-peddling, centering in the Chinese Embassy in Washington, during and after the inglorious months of the Nationalist collapse on the Chinese mainland.

It was a story, as *The Reporter* told it, of a defeated and demoralized regime desperately pulling political strings and squandering dollars in its attempts to persuade the United States government not to abandon it in its hour of extremity. In late

[1] *The Reporter*, April 15, 1952, pp. 4–24; April 29, 1952, pp. 5–24.

1948 Madame Chiang Kai-shek had come to America for a year to help direct the propagandist effort, while her clever and wealthy brother, T. V. Soong, exerted his considerable charm in high places. High-salaried Americans in Chinese employ did what they could to persuade congressmen, government officials and others of the merits of the Nationalist viewpoint. At least one of them, according to the magazine, had contact with Senator McCarthy and helped pass the ammunition for McCarthy's scatter-gun charges against "left-wingers" in government.

The objectives of the China Lobby at the time were to prevent the cutting off of American economic assistance, which seemed imminent, and to forestall United States recognition of the Chinese Communist regime. These aims were compatible with those of influential elements in the Republican Party, which had discovered a powerful political issue in the China question and were making the most of it. Because both objectives were realized, it is easy to assume, erroneously, that the combined influence of the China Lobby and certain Republican leaders was decisive. The truth is that the Truman administration was determined to disengage the United States from its involvement with the defeated Chiang government and probably would have realized its intention but for the wholly unforeseen developments in Korea. Both President Truman and Secretary of State Acheson stated flatly in 1950 that we would not defend Taiwan.[2] The China Lobby, in fact, had little or nothing to do with rescuing the Nationalists from oblivion. What did it was the Communist attack in Korea.

The China Lobby was never as highly organized or as integrated as some of its critics imagined it to be. Max Ascoli, publisher of *The Reporter*, stated the situation accurately when he remarked in a summing-up editorial, "One of the astonishing things about the China Lobby is that, as far as one can find out, it has no leaders, only mouthpieces."[3]

The main strength of the China Lobby lay not with the paid agents of the Chiang government but in the traditional concern of the American people for China and their deep-seated antipathy

[2] See *Department of State Bulletin*, v. 22, January 16, 1950, pp. 79–81.
[3] *The Reporter*: April 29, 1952.

for international communism. Let us not make the facile error, however, of equating hostility toward the Chinese Communists with affection for Chiang, or of equating dislike for Chiang with being soft on communism. Doubtless there have been times over the years when large sections of the public were confused as to just what and whom we were fighting for. But today this much, at least, is self-evident. The primary problem in the public's mind is not Chiang and his fate, but communism. Chiang, to be sure, still has ardent admirers in this country, but it is my impression, based on a large number of interviews, that most Americans today have lost interest in Chiang except as the commander of a strategically important bastion off the coast of China and as a symbol of Chinese resistance to communism. There are not many who still consider him a decisive factor in the future of the Chinese mainland.

Our apprehensions of communism were not, of course, born yesterday. Nearly half a century ago a British visitor to our shores made this observation:

No one who was in the United States, as I chanced to be in the autumn of 1919, will forget the feverish condition of the public mind at that time. It was hagridden by the spectre of Bolshevism. . . . Property was in an agony of fear, and the horrid name, 'Radical,' covered the most innocent departure from conventional thought with a suspicion of desperate purpose.[4]

To Americans who remembered those times, the subsequent McCarthy era must have had familiar undertones.

Origins of the China Lobby

Long before the term "China Lobby" had become a part of our language, various citizen groups had been working actively in this country to influence public opinion in favor of Nationalist China and to raise funds for China causes. These groups became particularly numerous during the early years of the Sino-Japa-

[4] Quoted from A. G. Gardiner, *Portraits and Portents* (New York: Harper Bros., 1926), p. 13, as cited in Roger Burlingame, *The Sixth Column* (New York: Lippincott, 1962), p. 31.

nese war. The multiplicity of causes and appeals made some coordination of fund-raising essential and led to the formation, in 1941, of United China Relief (UCR). After an initial financial transfusion from Henry Luce, the publisher, UCR went on to raise an impressive total of about $40 million in the next four years. It should be noted, however, that during the latter part of the war as much as 90 per cent of UCR's income was coming from the National War Fund, which represented a joint effort by a large number of fund-raising organizations.

United China Relief was primarily interested in raising money for humanitarian causes. It was not a pressure group *per se*. Yet it became one in effect. A person who was prominently involved in the management of the UCR financial campaigns told me in 1964 that he now realized that his organization had played no small part in building up the Chiang Kai-shek image in this country.

"We did a lot to sell China to the United States as an ally," he said. "We overdid it. We did it through high-powered salesmen in connection with our fund-raising efforts. Most people who had been in China recognized this. Chiang Kai-shek, for example, was built up to outlandish proportions. Then, along about 1943, our machinery began to creak. In both Washington and Chungking we began hearing more and more talk about agrarian reformers. A dichotomy developed. Some of the members of our board became noticeably cool toward the Chiang regime and more interested in aid to the Chinese Communists. We managed to hang together until the end of the war; then a real strain developed. A number of our member groups which had been working in the Communist areas of China dropped out. Meanwhile, with the waning of public interest, our finances began to go downhill. The UCR struggled along until 1950, when it was completely deactivated. Its work was taken over by the United Service to China."

A similar conflict of opinion was becoming apparent, on a vastly wider scale, in the country at large. In the final months of World War II, the China question had become the vortex of deepening controversy in the United States. China seemed headed for full-scale civil conflict. American newspapers were showing increasing disenchantment with the once greatly admired Chiang Kai-shek and a growing curiosity about the Chinese Communists. The rising sympathy for the Communists and the declining prestige of the Nationalists alarmed many Americans. Some decided the time had come to combat actively the intensifying pressures from the left.

Early in 1944, Christopher Emmet, a New York lecturer and writer, organized a small meeting at the home of Emily Hahn, the writer. Emmet, who claims wryly to be the "father" of the China Lobby, told the writer that the purpose of the gathering was to discuss illusions about the Chinese Communists "then so widespread in the U.S. press, radio, magazines, book publishing and book review fields." "You will remember," he said, "that at that time the prevailing image of the Chinese Communists was of austere agrarian reformers who had done the only effective fighting against the Japanese, while Chiang and his government were often pictured as reactionary, cruel and corrupt. This meeting, as far as I know, was the first gathering of private citizens concerned with the problem of the Chinese Communists. You might say that it was the genesis of the so-called China Lobby." When Emmet and his group met again, in 1945, they organized the American China Policy Association, with J. B. Powell, former editor of the *China Weekly Review*, as president and Alfred Kohlberg, an importer of textiles from China, as treasurer. It was not long before the Association came under Kohlberg's domination, and several of the founding members, including Emmet, withdrew.

Many of those who were active in those early days of the China Lobby were liberals—or at least so considered themselves. The impression, widely propagated at the time, that the China Lobby was an exclusive preserve of hard-shell reactionaries, is resented by people like Emmet, who is himself a registered member of the Liberal Party. As Emmet sees it, there were really two lobbies working on China's behalf in those years—a Lend-Lease lobby and an anti-Communist lobby—and much confusion and injustice has resulted from the efforts of some critics to treat the two as if they were one and the same thing. Of his own group,

Emmet says, "We were not conservatives; we were liberal anti-Communists." Some of Emmet's associates had been active supporters of Wendell Willkie. Even Kohlberg was, in those days, a person of relatively moderate political outlook, though he became increasingly emotional in his anti-Communist and pro-Chiang views as time went on.

It pleased Kohlberg to be described as the "big wheel" of the China Lobby. Making effective use of a mailing service which he financed, in large part from his own pocket, he tore into his opponents with what at times seemed reckless abandon. Early in the war, Kohlberg had strongly supported the Institute of Pacific Relations, of which he was a member. Later, he helped wreck the IPR after becoming convinced that it was promoting the Communist line through its publication, *Pacific Affairs,* and in other ways. This was a view later supported, in part, by the McCarran Committee. Kohlberg struck up an association with Senator McCarthy and is reputed to have fed him a great deal of information—some say misinformation—for McCarthy's campaign against Communist influences, real and supposed, in the government.

Former associates of Kohlberg tend to be critical of his methods but convinced of his sincerity. Emmet, who knew him well, had this to say of him.

"I did not, of course, agree with Mr. Kohlberg's later activities. He became a zealot and a fanatic, sometimes attacking people's motives without sufficient evidence. He was intellectually limited, and he became emotionally obsessed. But I am wholly convinced that unlike Senator McCarthy, who apparently did not care whether what he said was true or not, Kohlberg sincerely believed everything he said. I am also convinced that his motives were not financial." This view of Kohlberg was, of course, charitable compared to the opinions (some unprintable) of those who were the targets of his charges and insinuations.

Kohlberg's American China Policy Association was but one of a number of pro-Chiang groups which became active politically in the United States during the postwar years and which, sooner or later, found themselves included in the "China Lobby" category. Some of those who quit the ACPA after becoming disenchanted with Kohlberg's methods later drifted into another pro-Nationalist group organized under the rather pretentious title of Committee to Defend America by Aiding Anti-Communist China. This body, too, had its financial angel—a casket-manufacturer from Pittsburgh named Frederick C. McKee. McKee, like Kohlberg, was a wealthy man with deep anti-Communist convictions who drew freely on his private resources to help finance his cause. Unlike Kohlberg, he was usually restrained in his public statements and avoided involvement with Senator McCarthy.

This was a period of bitter nationwide controversy over China policy, in which smear tactics were freely employed on both sides. But increasing disillusionment with the Chinese Communists, intensified by the Korean War, transformed the situation. Now Chinese Communists were killing Americans. Now disillusionment with the Communists matched disillusionment with Chiang's regime. The crystallization of American policy that followed the Korean outbreak left the China Lobby with very little to fight for. Its dream of American intervention in the Taiwan Straits had come true but from reasons quite beyond its control. The Lobby as then constituted—or at least its leadership—faded into obscurity.

A sidelight on the China Lobby is provided by a California scholar, Ross Y. Koen, whose book, *The China Lobby in American Politics,* was withdrawn abruptly from circulation just as it was about to be put on general sale in 1960. Koen told me that he had worked on the book for six years, while a teacher at the University of Florida. It contained some serious allegations regarding the origin of funds used to finance the China Lobby. Koen explained that the publishers, Macmillan, decided to withdraw the book, for revision, after attorneys for the Chinese Embassy had threatened legal action if the disputed passage was not modified. Meanwhile, review copies had gone out and other copies had reached bookstores. Some were never recovered and became collectors' items. Koen said he had agreed to make certain revisions and still hoped to see the book published.

Successors to the China Lobby: The Committee of One Million

As the old China Lobby faded away, other influences employing a more sophisticated assortment of techniques took over. Today, organizations and individuals supporting an uncompromising policy toward Communist China fall into several categories. They include groups like the Committee of One Million, certain professional anti-Communist groups, and various organizations concerned with China in only a secondary way.

We have indicated that the China Lobby and its successors have owed much of their influence to the plain fact that most Americans are anti-Communist. They have had the sympathy and, at times, active support of the lobbies of dozens of old-line national organizations, among them highly influential groups like the American Legion, the Veterans of Foreign Wars, the AFL-CIO, the Farm Bureau Federation, the United States Chamber of Commerce and a host of others. Though highly diverse in their main interests, these organizations have at least this much in common—they are all alert to the Communist danger and tend to agree, either tacitly or by assertion, on the need for firm policies to combat the advance of international communism, including the need for a firm China policy.

Members of Congress are of course well aware of this powerful body of opinion and of the hardened attitude of a large and influential section of the popular press. They consciously or subconsciously take it into consideration in weighing any legislation that involves a change in our relations with Communist countries. Taken altogether, these influences provide a solid basis of active support, or sympathy, for any movement that opposes concessions to international communism in general and the Chinese brand in particular. To comment on individual pressure groups in isolation from this context would be to mislead the reader by giving such groups more importance than they deserve. What makes them effective is the relatively favorable milieu in which they operate. If Congress gives ear to the China lobbyists it is because the tune they play is in harmony with the background noises.

The main pressure on Congress in opposition to any change in our China policy comes from the Committee of One Million (Against the Admission of Communist China to the United Nations). The Committee of One Million operates with a small staff, on a modest budget, from unpretentious offices in downtown Manhattan. But despite its lack of opulence and glitter, it is not to be taken lightly. Its firm-handed technique of political persuasion has been remarkably effective in keeping Congress in line on the question of China policy. Born only two months after the conclusion of the Korean War, at a time when virtually all Americans were still hotly indignant over the actions and attitudes of the Chinese Communists, the Committee has, from the beginning, enjoyed the sponsorship of a large number of influential Americans, including a strong bi-partisan representation from Congress. The letterhead of the organization carries the names of six senators—Thomas J. Dodd (D., Connecticut), Peter H. Dominick (R., Colorado), Paul H. Douglas (D., Illinois), Bourke B. Hickenlooper (R., Iowa), William Proxmire (D., Wisconsin) and Thomas E. Morgan (D., Pennsylvania)—and such other well-known personages as Charles Edison and Dr. Walter H. Judd. H. Alexander Smith, a former senator, serves as honorary chairman. Senator Hickenlooper is, of course, the ranking Republican member of the Senate Foreign Relations Committee, while Congressman Morgan heads the Foreign Affairs Committee of the House. Generals and admirals are plentiful among the Committee's adherents.

Some of the prominent liberals who lent their names to the Committee during the period of intense anti-Peking emotion that followed the Korean War have lately become increasingly uncomfortable with the organization's policies. A number of them— for example, Vice President Hubert H. Humphrey—have withdrawn. But the continued participation of Senator Paul H. Douglas and other well-known liberals in the same cause with former Senator Barry Goldwater and Senator Everett M. Dirksen does indeed demonstrate a wide spectrum of support for the *status quo* in our China policy.

In its methods, the Committee of One Million shrewdly concentrates its attention on groups and individuals capable of influencing China policy—for example, the Congress, the administration, the political parties. Its use of petitions and declarations has been effective in persuading the majority of our national legislators to commit themselves in black and white to a "hard" position on China. Although the steering committee makes all policy decisions, day-to-day management is in the hands of Marvin Liebman, the executive secretary. Liebman, forty-two, learned about organization and discipline as a youthful member of the American Communist Party. He saw the light in 1945, quit the Party, and has since been involved in anti-Communist causes.

The conception of a committee of one million to oppose Communist China's entry into the United Nations originated with Nicholas de Rochefort, Russian-born university lecturer. Dr. Walter H. Judd, the former Congressman and medical missionary, well known for his determined advocacy of a firm policy toward the Chinese Communists, liked the idea and helped get the ball rolling. Started in 1953 as the Committee *for* One Million, the group succeeded during the first ten months in obtaining more than one million signatures on petitions to the President of the United States opposing Communist China's admission to the United Nations. With this mission accomplished, the Committee suspended its activities in 1954. It was revived in the following year as the Committee *of* One Million.

In 1961, the Committee circulated a second petition much stronger than the first. It opposed not only admission of Communist China to the United Nations but also diplomatic recognition and any other steps which would build the power and prestige of the Peking regime. Again, more than one million signatures were obtained. Members of Congress were also invited to put their signatures on this declaration. To do so meant that they were committing themselves unequivocally to the support of an inflexible policy toward Communist China. As of July 1964, a total of 345 members of Congress had been persuaded to endorse this cleverly phrased document; but 78 of them were casualties of the Democratic landslide in November of the same year.

Jarred but undismayed, the Committee of One Million decided that this was a good time to revise the text of the declaration and to go out again for a million signatures. The new declaration, launched early in 1965, concentrates on the theme of bi-partisan support of our China policy, opposes "any steps which would build the power and prestige of Communist China to the detriment of our friends and allies in Asia and of our national security," and concludes:

> . . . We are opposed to the admission of Communist China to the United Nations.
> We are opposed to granting United States diplomatic recognition to the Peiping regime.
> We are opposed to trade relations between the United States and Communist China.
> We are opposed to any policy of accommodation which might be interpreted as US acquiescence in, or approval of, Communist China's aggression, direct or indirect, against her neighbors.
> In endorsing the above, we earnestly believe we are acting in our national interest and the interest of freedom throughout the world and that this statement represents the thinking of the great majority of the American people.

By August 1, 1965, the Committee had obtained 312 congressional signatures, representing a majority of both houses, on the new declaration. Representation was quite evenly divided between the two parties.

The Committee of One Million makes no secret of the pressures it is prepared to apply on those congressmen and senators who do not collaborate. In a memorandum to "members and friends" outlining its "offensive" plans for 1964 the Committee reported: "We will endeavor to exert constituent pressure on all members of Congress who do not join in endorsing the Committee's statement." The memorandum then went on to explain how this "grassroots" pressure would be put into effect—for example, through letter-writing campaigns, through enlisting the cooperation of friendly organizations, through paid advertisements in local newspapers, and through organized visits from constituents to obstinate legislators.

The mere threat of pressure from constituencies is the sort of thing that sends prickles along congressional backbones. Most members of Congress, as we have previously noted, are convinced that the general public favors a tough line toward Communist China and expects its representatives in Congress to feel likewise. And most of them, undoubtedly, are themselves convinced of the need for firmness. But some resent being pushed into signing the Committee's declaration which, in effect, puts them in a strait jacket by committing them to a fixed position. Liberal members of Congress are particularly sensitive on the subject. They are reluctant to risk voter displeasure, yet they dislike, equally, the possibility of being labeled "captive" liberals.

Leaders of the Committee of One Million deny that it is right-wing or extremist in orientation and point out that they have deliberately refrained from soliciting funds from millionaire supporters of Far Right causes. The Committee's primary aim, they claim, is simply to ensure the effective implementation of the existing policy of the United States government toward China. Of this policy the Commitee says that "there is no other single issue of foreign or domestic policy which enjoys such over-whelming unanimity of opinion." The Committee notes that "every major American veterans', fraternal and civic organiza-tion has adopted resolutions expressing their opposition to the admission of Communist China to the United Nations, American diplomatic recognition and any other steps which would build the power and prestige of the Peiping regime." [5] Lacking a strong grassroots organization of its own, the Committee seeks the co-operation of such groups in applying pressure on members of Congress and others. The Committee's general program for 1964 includes the following paragraph:

The key to the entire program . . . will be local community action. Because of increased pressures this year, we will have to mobilize and enlist greater grassroots action than ever before. We can count on the active cooperation of a number of national veteran, youth, fra-ternal and civic organizations toward this end.

The Committee of One Million operates on an annual budget of about $60,000, representing contributions from about 10,000

[5] *Statement Commenting on American China Policy with Reference to Address Made by Assistant Secretary of State Roger Hilsman in San Francisco on December 13, 1963* (New York: Author, n.d.).

persons, Mr. Liebman said in an interview. Besides its administrative outlays, the Committee puts money into pamphlets and full-page advertisements in important newspapers read by influential people. It sponsored and has shown widely a 30-minute black and white documentary film, "Red China—Outlaw," with Lowell Thomas as narrator and in 1965 issued a new documentary titled "Appeasement—Ally of Red China." The Committee is quick to launch a counterattack against any significant threat to its point of view. For example, it mailed out an eight-page, point-by-point rebuttal of the important speech on China policy by Roger Hilsman, former Assistant Secretary of State, in December 1963. The Committee interpreted Hilsman's remarks as an attempt to promote the "two-China" formula, which it opposes.

Most members of Congress continue to treat the Committee with nervous respect, though some are showing increasing resistance to its pressures. The Committee's capacity to apply pressure varies considerably from region to region and from issue to issue. But Liebman maintains that it could mobilize powerful opposition from like-minded organizations against any serious move by the administration toward recognition of the Peking regime or its admission to the United Nations. "In a sense," Liebman observed to this writer, "the function of our Committee is to serve as a watchdog for the public on China policy."

There are skeptics who view the Committee of One Million more as a paper tiger than a watchdog. But the fact that the Committee is able to obtain a majority of congressional signatures on its petitions and that no effective counter-pressure has developed against it would seem to indicate that the organization is still a force to be reckoned with. One of the keys to the Committee's success is its talent for making any suggestion of modification in our China policy seem unpatriotic and contemptible. The following excerpt from a mimeographed circular letter sent out by Liebman in March 1965 and addressed to "Fellow American," is typical:

Each day we read about young Americans being slaughtered in Viet Nam. They are killed by Communist bullets; they are burned while they sleep in their barracks by Communist mortars; they are shot down from the air by Communist anti-aircraft guns. And yet, in spite of all this, there are still all too many American individuals, organizations and publications *who continue to urge concessions to these same Communists who are killing Americans:* admission to the United Nations; diplomatic recognition; trade; and even "cultural" exchanges. How despicable!

In the light of this and similar appeals it is hardly surprising that so many of our national legislators feel it necessary to sign the Committee's petitions.

The Hamilton Wright Matter

Considering the notoriety the Chinese Nationalists received from their lobbying efforts in the late forties and early fifties, one would expect them to be extremely wary about embarking on any showy new attempt to influence American opinion—especially at a time when things were going their way. Not so. When an American public relations firm, the Hamilton Wright Organization, proposed in 1957 a prettily packaged plan for a publicity campaign for Nationalist China, the Taiwan regime accepted it. Details of the four-year relationship which ensued were exposed to public view when the Foreign Relations Committee of the United States took an interest in the matter and later made public documents and testimony offered during a hearing before the Committee in March, 1963.[6]

The record shows that Hamilton Wright, head of the firm bearing his name, wrote Dr. Tsiang Ting-fu, Chinese Ambassador to the United Nations, on May 2, 1957, and offered to do all possible to arouse public opinion in the United States, Canada, South America and Europe and "to create a sympathetic understanding of Free China that would have dramatic impact on members of the United Nations and prevent the seating of Red China in the United Nations and the lifting of trade sanctions against Red

---

[6] *Activities of Non-Diplomatic Representatives of Foreign Principals in the United States,* Report on a Hearing before the Committee on Foreign Relations, U.S. Senate, 86th Cong., 1st sess., March 25, 1963 (Washington: GPO, 1963).

China." The proposal went on to say that this campaign would "bring vociferous moral support from the American people when the day comes for a 'return to the mainland.' " [7]

The Chinese government accepted this proposal and agreed to pay a fee of $300,000 annually for the services of the Hamilton Wright Organization. Attached to the agreement was a guarantee from the company that Nationalist China would receive at least $2,500,000 worth of publicity in newspapers, magazines, television and other media. The secret of success, said the letter of proposal, was to gather the material from the American point of view and to tell the story with human interest. American editors, the letter added, "will publish the stories and pictures free of charge if they are interesting enough for their readers." And the letter clinched the matter as follows: "I have never known of an opportunity that is so natural. Everything is in its favor. It is long overdue. It should have been started years ago." [8]

The efforts of the Hamilton Wright Organization on behalf of the Chinese Nationalists apparently resulted in the planting of a great deal of well-disguised propaganda in the mass media of this country. What if any effect this publicity had on American attitudes toward China is, to say the least, highly problematical. The Senate hearing did, however, reveal rather clearly the vulnerability of the American press to this kind of penetration. The fact that there was nothing novel about the practices mentioned did not make them any less disturbing. The testimony showed that stories written by a Wright employee, Don Frifield, were being used by well-known syndicates, including the *New York Herald Tribune* syndicate and the North American Newspaper Alliance.

In one instance an article prepared by Frifield, and citing arguments against United States recognition of Communist China, was passed on to Marvin Liebman, the executive secretary of the Committee of One Million, who, in turn, persuaded Senator Douglas to put it over his name. When the Senate Committee queried Senator Douglas on his matter, he replied, by letter, that

[7] Same, p. 685.
[8] Same, pp. 684–685.

he had found himself in general agreement with the sentiments and arguments contained in the article and, after making some changes, he authorized its distribution over his signature. The Senator said he knew the manuscript had been prepared by the Hamilton Wright Organization but did not know that the firm was receiving money from the Nationalist government. "I have been very careful myself to keep aloof from the Chinese Nationalist government itself and have insisted that the Committee of One Million should not receive any direct or indirect subvention from it," Senator Douglas wrote. He went on to say that he had remained on the Committee's executive committee only on the assurance that no direct or indirect financing came from the Chinese government and that the Committee was independently financed.[9]

The contract between the Chinese Nationalist government and the Hamilton Wright Organization was terminated, on an unhappy note, after four years. The Nationalists were displeased, among other things, with the fact that the Hamilton Wright Organization had taken on the Union of South Africa as a customer. After this experience, the Chinese Nationalists dropped, or at least greatly curtailed, their expensive efforts to build up their image in the United States.

In fairness to the Chinese, and for the information of those readers who may not be completely familiar with the sometimes mysterious workings of the nation's capital, it should be noted that Washington swarms with paid lobbyists and public relations representatives, many of whom are in the employ of foreign governments. The Chinese were not unique in employing an American firm to handle their publicity in this country. The practice is common, and the Senate Committee's hearings were concerned not alone with the Chinese and their use of American publicists, but with the whole question as it applied to other foreign governments as well.

9 Same, p. 825.

The Far Right and China

The proliferation of right-wing organizations in the United States since the late 1950s is one of the phenomena of our time. These shrill-voiced, ultraconservative groups are the by-products of a whole medley of widely shared frustrations—big government, high taxes, "creeping socialism," civil rights agitation, declining United States influence in the United Nations, the foreign aid "giveaway" and our seemingly insoluble foreign policy problems in China, Korea, the Caribbean and Southeast Asia. Each has its pet cause or pet antipathy, but if there is anything these organizations have in common, it is their resistance to any compromise with the Red governments in Moscow and Peking. Although China is of secondary interest to most of them, it is a subject on which they are easily aroused when big issues are at stake. They are, in effect, a pressure front supporting a firm, no-compromise attitude toward Communist China.

The Far Right includes, of course, many shadings of viewpoint, ranging from those whose views are based on the logic of events, as they see it, and who attribute our errors of policy simply to stupidity and soft-headedness, to others on the radical fringe who see all our national policies with which they disagree as evidence of a Communist conspiracy in government. In discussing China there is a tendency to belabor the familiar themes: that Nationalist China was betrayed by Communists and Communist sympathizers working through the State Department and the Institute of Pacific Relations; that we sacrificed victory in Korea by accepting compromise instead of listening to General Douglas MacArthur; that any *modus vivendi* with Communist China now or in the future would amount to appeasement and betrayal and cannot be tolerated; that Chiang Kai-shek deserves our fullest support and should be encouraged to stand firm in Quemoy and Matsu and reject a "two-China" policy.

Virtually all the spokesmen of the right have expressed themselves strongly at one time or another on China, but among them are a number who have a special interest in China through experience or association. The better known of these include General Albert C. Wedemeyer (retired), former Commander of U.S. forces in China; Major General Charles A. Willoughby (retired), former intelligence chief for General MacArthur in the Far East; Edward Hunter, author of *Brain-Washing in Red China*,[10] who directs a liaison group coordinating the policies of anti-Communist organizations; and Dr. George S. Benson, who spent ten years in China as a missionary and claims that his film, "Communism on the Map," has been viewed by ten million people. The John Birch Society claims a special tie with the China question because of the "martyrdom" at the hands of Chinese Communists of Georgia-born John Birch, a former missionary, from whom the organization took its name. Birchers call Birch the first American casualty in "a war that is still being waged."

The Far Right looked considerably more formidable before November 1964 than after. Yet the inclination of some observers, particularly in the East, to write off the right wing as a negligible influence on public and congressional attitudes reflects a misapprehension of the situation. Organizations of the Far Right are numbered in the hundreds. They have enlisted the support of many influential business and professional men and retired officers from the armed services. Several of their leaders are men of great wealth. With strong financial backing and a tremendous output of propaganda via TV, radio and the written word, the Far Right constitutes a minority of more than negligible significance. Aggressive in its approach, it exercises influence not only through the active promotion of its causes but by inhibiting—in some cases intimidating—those who hold contradictory views. This has undoubtedly been a factor in discouraging open discussion of touchy issues like China policy in communities where the right is strongly entrenched.

The disciples of the right, like the followers of many other causes, are prolific writers of letters to newspapers and members of Congress. Much of this is normal "gripe mail" from citizens with sincere and well-reasoned grievances. But a great deal of it is "organized" and dictated. A part of it, from the hysterical fringes, is abusive or threatening. Senators and congressmen will tell you that they do not read extremist mail—or at least that

10 *Brain-Washing in Red China* (New York: Vanguard, 1951).

they pay it no mind—but there is little doubt that it carries more weight with them than they care to admit.

A few members of Congress—among them Senator Thomas H. Kuchel of California and Representative Edith M. Green of Oregon—have spoken out boldly against the so-called fright peddlers. Senator Kuchel (who, incidentally, is a supporter of the Committee of One Million and a regular signer of its declarations opposing concessions to Communist China), remarked in a Senate speech recently [11] that of the 60,000 letters he receives each month, about 10 per cent belong to the "fright mail" category. Some of the reports relayed to the Senator are so fantastic as to make one wonder whether there are any limits to human credulity—for example, the story that 35,000 Chinese Communist troops, carrying arms and wearing powder blue uniforms, were poised on the Mexican border, about to invade southern California.

Pressures for a Modification of China Policy

The Korean War for some years thwarted the activities of organizations favorable to a modification of our policies toward Communist China. Since then, Peking's continued truculence, the festering hostilities in Viet-Nam, and the intensified activity of anti-Communist organizations in this country have continued to make talk of conciliation unpopular and, at times, risky. It is only in the past few years that moderates have again begun to speak up audibly in favor of change. Such expressions have been cautious—seldom advocating immediate recognition of the Peking regime or its admission to the United Nations, but, more often, urging improved communication and a rational, step-by-step approach to other issues. So far these efforts have been largely ineffective, although our survey shows that public opinion is gradually becoming more flexible on the subject of China policy.

Among pressure groups favorable to change none has stood out more temptingly as a target for critics than Americans for

[11] Speech of May 2, 1963. For the full text, see the *Congressional Record,* v. 109, pt. 6, pp. 7636–7641.

Democratic Action (ADA). This is a loosely knit body (some call it a state of mind rather than an organization) with a high content of intellectuals and with little grassroots following. Its sweet-sour saga has been the story of American liberalism since 1947. Of China policy its statement of principles says in part:

ADA urges immediate initiation, together with our allies, of negotiations toward diplomatic recognition of the Peiping regime and its accreditation to the United Nations as the government of China, not as gestures of moral approval of its past actions but as means of establishing the normal channels of international communication.[12]

China has always figured high in ADA's thinking, but it has been more often a jinx than an asset. In 1950, just after the Communist takeover of mainland China, ADA inserted a plank in its platform to the following effect: "We believe that sooner or later we will be compelled to establish diplomatic relations with the Mao Tse-tung regime as the effective government of China, however much we detest its devotion to totalitarianism." [13] A few months later, the United States was at war with China in Korea, and the platform plank became meaningless, except as a weapon for McCarthy and others to beat ADA with.

ADA's present position in support of diplomatic recognition of Communist China and its accreditation to the United Nations is qualified by a recommendation that the people of Taiwan should be allowed to decide for themselves whether to join the United Nations as an independent nation or to rejoin mainland China. In the meantime, according to the ADA formula, the United States would abide by its treaty commitments to the Taiwan regime, but with the explicit understanding that these commitments do not include the defense of Quemoy and Matsu.[14]

After McCarthy, little was heard about ADA until John F. Kennedy became President, when newspapermen discovered an extraordinary number of ADA alumni in influential posts in the administration. Estimates ranged from thirty-five to forty-five,

[12] Americans for Democratic Action, *A Program for Americans* (Washington, D.C.: Author, n.d.).
[13] Clifton Brock, *Americans for Democratic Action* (Washington, D.C.: Public Affairs Press, 1962), p. 144.
[14] *A Program for Americans,* cited.

of whom three were in the Cabinet. On the China question Kennedy had come into office apparently predisposed to take a more flexible position. How much and what kind of advice he got from his associates on this subject is a moot point, but, in any case, he found his hands tied. China went on the shelf.

The ADA brand on the administration faded after President Johnson assumed office. Arthur Schlesinger, Jr., and Ted Sorensen, for example, withdrew from the President's inner circle. Talks of ADA influence in administration circles revived with the election to the Vice Presidency of Hubert H. Humphrey, perhaps the biggest "ADAer" of them all. But Humphrey has quite clearly demonstrated that he does not let the ADA do his thinking for him. While in the Senate and until shortly before his election to the Vice Presidency, he was not only active in ADA but also a supporter of the Committee of One Million—surely a feat of elasticity.

The National Council of Churches (NCC), which, through its member denominations, represents about two-thirds (35 million) of the Protestants in the United States, has long had an active interest in China. Most of the member churches have a background of missionary activity in China, and many former missionaries occupy positions of prominence and influence on the Council's executive staff. Hence the future of Chinese-American relations and, more particularly, the future of the Christian faith in China are matters of great concern to the National Council and its leadership.

Although the National Council has put itself on record as being "unalterably" opposed to communism and has taken no *official* position with respect to a modification of U.S. policy toward China, it is no secret that many of its lay followers and certain of its influential leaders feel that the time is past due for a reconsideration of our China policy. One official of the NCC put it in the following way during the course of an interview: "I think that the bulk of the opinion of our leadership would favor the kind of relationship with Communist China that Canada has. We think it is best to know what the Chinese are thinking. You have got to have coexistence. The alternative is co-destruction."

This type of sentiment came into the open at the Fifth World Order Study Conference, convened under NCC auspices, at Cleveland, Ohio, in November 1958. A principal product of that meeting was the now famous Cleveland message, embodying (among other things) the following resolution on China:

With reference to China, Christians should urge reconsideration by our government of its policy in regard to the People's Republic of China. While the rights of the people of Taiwan and of Korea should be safeguarded, steps should be taken toward the inclusion of the People's Republic of China in the United Nations and for its recognition by our government. Such recognition does not imply approval.

These diplomatic relations should constitute a part of a much wider relationship between our peoples. The exclusion of the effective government on the mainland of China, currently the People's Republic of China, from the international community is in many ways a disadvantage to that community. It helps to preserve a false image of the United States, and of other nations, in the minds of the Chinese people. It keeps our people in ignorance of what is taking place in China. It hampers negotiations for disarmament. It limits the functioning of international organizations. We have a strong hope that the resumption of relationships between the peoples of China and of the United States may make possible also a restoration of relationship between their churches and ours.[15]

When this resolution reached the newspapers, there were repercussions from coast to coast. The resolution was widely interpreted as representing the official view of the Council—which it did not. Spokesmen for the Council pointed out that while the Cleveland conference had NCC sponsorship, it spoke only for itself. Fewer than half of those participating were from the Council; the rest were invited laymen. The purpose of the resolution, they added, was not to put the meeting on record as favoring a fixed point of view but to get the China question out into the open where it could be studied and discussed by the various member churches.

In spite of the disclaimers, however, much damage had already been done insofar as public opinion was concerned. *The*

[15] See *Christian Responsibility on a Changing Planet*, The Report of the Fifth World Order Study Conference, Cleveland, Ohio, November 18–21, 1958 (Cleveland: Fifth World Order Study Conference, 1958), pp. 22–23.

Daily Worker and other left-wing publications had greeted the resolution with delight and distortion. The right had leaped on it as "clear proof" of Communist infiltration of the churches. And the Protestant congregations were themselves involved in diverse reactions.[16] The United Presbyterian Church in the U.S.A. urged study of the message and expressed its "Christian concern that the day may soon come when our government, in concert with other free nations, may enter with honor into normal relations with the government of the Chinese people." The Board of World Peace of the Methodist Church recommended "that the U.S. use every opportunity to seek a settlement of major differences and a better understanding with Communist China." But the American Baptist Convention, while advising Baptists to study the matter objectively, decided to support current policy "until such time as the government of mainland China proves itself worthy of recognition."

An NCC leader said to me later: "We were getting 150 letters a day, many violently opposing our stand. Some church congregations denounced the Cleveland resolution, and the question was raised whether it was the Church's function to be a lightning rod all the time. Some of our people were scared by the uproar. I think it had an inhibiting influence which is still being felt."

The Friends Committee on National Legislation (FCNL), a Quaker group, lobbies energetically and continuously for a revision of American policy toward Communist China. The FCNL sponsors conferences and conducts seminars on international issues and—in its own words—"encourages letters, telegrams and visits to congressmen when they will be most effective." As the Society of Friends, the Quakers have had a long contact with China and during World War II became well known through the operation of their Friends Ambulance Unit, in which more than 150 conscientious objectors participated. The Quakers seek a peaceful settlement of U.S. differences with Communist China, which they view as a key to the solution of most of our other difficulties in the Far East. Early in 1965 they issued a report outlining

---

[16] Catholic organizations have tended, generally, to take a firm position against retreat from our present policy.

their proposals.[17] The FCNL has been unable, however, to counter appreciably the influence of the Committee of One Million on Congress, despite its rather determined efforts to do so.

Nowhere in this country are pressures for a modification of our policies toward China—particularly our trading policies— more pronounced than in the San Francisco region. We have previously noted that among organizations in that area which have taken a position in favor of reappraising our embargo policy are the World Trade Association of the San Francisco Chamber of Commerce, the International Longshoremen's Union and the California Federation of Young Democrats.

Also mentioned was the Committee for a Review of our China Policy, one of whose founders, Ernest T. Nash, issues statements and appeals from his home at Woodland, not far from San Francisco. China-born, Nash is the son of English parents. His mother was the first English child born on the island of Formosa and was named Florence Formosa in honor of the event. An elderly, quiet-mannered, yet persistent person, Nash has devoted much of his effort in recent years to speeches and letter-writing aimed at countering what he describes as "the appalling insensitivity of the vast bulk of American public opinion to the course of events in China since 1959."

The Far Left

The radical Left has exerted little influence on American public opinion toward China in the past decade and a half but has recently shown signs of coming alive again. During its heyday in the 1930s and 1940s it did have a tangible effect on American attitudes through various Communist-front organizations flourishing under pretty slogans of international peace and friendship. That was a period of pink-hued illusions that saw the rise and fall of Communist-infiltrated organizations like the Progressive

[17] *A New China Policy, Some Quaker Proposals, A Report Prepared for the American Friends Service Committee* (Yale University Press: New Haven, 1965).

Party. Leftist liberals got some hard knocks and learned some hard lessons in those fellow-traveling years. They emerged from the experience more hard-headed and wary about communism in general and Chinese communism in particular.

Although the so-called New Left has focused its attentions mainly on civil rights and Viet-Nam, the China problem stands prominently in the background. A few of the left-wing groups —for example, the small but growing Progressive Labor Party (PLP)—make a specialty of their pro-Peking sympathies. Milt Rosen, who heads PLP, was once a member of the American Communist Party but fell out with it when the party showed a preference for the Russian over the Chinese variety of communism. An unabashed admirer of Mao Tse-tung and company, Rosen has described the United States as "the most hated country in the world" and President Johnson's Great Society as a military dictatorship.[18] PLP's Maoist sympathies and its revolutionary fervor seem to have some appeal to Negroes, Puerto Ricans and other underprivileged elements among our people, but its membership, even when combined with that of other like-minded organizations, still represents only a minuscule percentage of the population.

On our college campuses, also, there has been a small but turbulent upwelling of leftist activity, illustrated by the emergence of groups like Students for a Democratic Society, which was largely instrumental in organizing the student march on Washington in the spring of 1965. Such groups can be expected to switch their attention from Viet-Nam and civil rights to questions of China policy, if and when the China problem again becomes a national issue.

On Ideological Labels

Enough has been said in this chapter to point up the fallacy of assuming that all those who are against modifying our China policy are necessarily conservatives or that all those who favor change are liberals or leftists. Political and ideological labels do

[18] See *The National Observer*, May 24, 1965.

frequently provide a clue to a person's views on the China question, but they certainly are not reliable indicators except in the case of the minorities of the Far Right and the Far Left, whose views tend to be frozen into dogmatic molds. The issue is one on which most Americans seem to be guided more by what they see as the national interest than by ideological considerations.

PART THREE

The Lack of Information

CHAPTER EIGHT

Truth vs. Fallacy

The need for a better flow of information from and about China is widely felt by Americans. Time after time, in interviews across the country, people complained about the insufficiency or unreliability of the information they were receiving. Yet, as we shall show, a vast quantity of reliable information on China—some of it highly detailed and specialized—is, in fact, available. The fact that very little of it is reaching the general public is in part the fault of the news media, in part the fault of our educational system, in part a consequence of public apathy. Since American public opinion toward China is determined, to a very large extent, by the amount and kind of information reaching the people, this inadequacy in the flow of information is obviously a serious matter. It lies at the very root of American misunderstanding on China. In exploring this matter, we will examine first the role of the news media and leave for the subsequent chapter a discussion of what our schools and universities are doing—and neglecting to do—in this field.

Before taking a closer look at the problem, we here note a few of the general comments we heard from the Americans we interviewed:

From a businessman: "Press coverage is very poor. It is tied too much to topical events. There is not enough basic interpretive material."

From a professor: "There is too much disposition to handle

the news from the mainland uncritically. The coverage is slovenly."

From a retired Navy captain: "I'd like to know what's going on in China, but I'd like someone to tell me who knows what he is talking about."

From a retired general: "The news coverage from China is wholly inadequate. We don't have sufficient information to put the situation in true perspective—or our policies either."

From a lawyer: "It's a tragedy that we do not know more about the Chinese revolution."

From a trader: "The reports you see are so conflicting that it is very difficult to make judgments. Most of what you hear is highly colored and critical."

Some of these shortcomings are admitted by newspaper editors themselves. This writer sent out a questionnaire to a small sampling of newspaper editors selected at random from across the country. Among the questions asked was this:

"Do you feel that American newspapers and other news media are giving the American people a reasonably objective and well-rounded picture of the situation in China?"

Of the fifty-two who answered this question, twenty-four said No, fourteen said Yes, and the rest gave indeterminate answers. The surprising thing here is not the large number who have doubts about the adequacy of our China coverage but the fact that as many as 26 per cent of the editors queried believe the public is getting a well-balanced picture. The principal complaint of the majority was the lack of direct access to the news— that is, the inability of American correspondents to visit Communist China and report from that country. There was an evident feeling that the news is incomplete, that it is not always to be trusted. Some of the replies reflected a feeling of frustration over the extreme difficulty of pinning down the facts. One editor objected to "too much stress on what obviously is Red China propaganda." Another took the opposite view that the news always makes the Chinese Communists appear in the wrong. "I doubt," he said, "if this is 100 per cent true. We should try to see some good, or at least some 'justification,' even while we oppose their major trends and policies."

American news media, evidently, are falling short of their possibilities and responsibilities with respect to China news coverage. Granted, considerable information is shut off by official secrecy and other insurmountable difficulties. And the task of ferreting out the facts, even when they are to be had, can be time-taking and tedious. Yet unquestionably a great deal more information is available than is being passed on to the American people. Thus there are two leading requisites for obtaining a sharper focus on the situation in China. One is to develop new and more reliable information sources—for example, by getting American correspondents into Communist China. The other, and, for the present, more important need is to make better use of the information obtainable.

To this kind of talk American editors are quick to retort that if they were to give the public only what it *ought* to read instead of what it *wants* to read, they would soon be out of business. This is a problem, indeed, on which generalizations can be misleading. Some American newspapers are, in fact, doing an outstanding job of covering China to the extent that reliable information is available. *The New York Times* is probably pre-eminent in the field. Deserving of equal or greater credit are those certain newspapers in other cities which are going to great effort and expense to provide extensive foreign news coverage to much smaller audiences of internationally minded readers. A few such can rightfully claim to be publishing more news on China and other foreign countries than reader interest would seem to justify. But they are the exceptions.

Obstacles Are Many

No country in the world presents as tough a news problem for Americans as Communist China. Not only is it the most populous and most complex of all countries, it is entirely closed to Americans and large parts of it to other foreigners as well. The Communist regime exercises complete control over the internal-information apparatus—processing, adulterating, delaying or suppressing the news to suit the needs of propaganda and policy.

Statistics are hard to come by and, when obtainable, may be factual or wildly misleading, depending on the purpose they are intended to serve.

In this totalitarian setting, keeping up with developments and appraising their significance takes knowledge, experience, judgment and the deductive powers of a Sherlock Holmes. Hong Kong is by all odds the best listening post for information from Communist China—in some ways better than being stationed in mainland China itself. There correspondents and other China watchers are in a position to keep a close check on Peking broadcasts, scrutinize translations from mainland newspapers, consult China experts and pseudo-experts of many nationalities, interview travelers and refugees from China, maintain contact with diplomats and intelligence agents and occasionally find time for a drink at the Correspondents' Club bar. Much of the information so obtained would be unavailable or inaccessible in Peking. About the only advantage of the Peking correspondent is in matters pertaining to the sights, sounds, smells and "feel" of Communist China. Hong Kong has been disparagingly compared to Riga, a favorite clearinghouse of rumors and reports during the early years of the Bolshevik revolution. But the comparison is not very apt. Hong Kong attracts a vastly greater volume of reliable information and has better facilities for separating fact from fiction.

Blending the diverse bits of information picked up in Hong Kong, an able correspondent can come up with a remarkably accurate analysis of mainland developments. Another reporter, with access to the same facts, might well cable home a wholly misleading interpretation of the same situation. Why? Inexperience, perhaps, or laziness, or excessive haste, or prejudice, or irresponsibility, or headline-hunger—any one of these could account for the wrong twist in a story that will be read by millions of Americans. The desirability of a larger volume of China news is obvious, but only if it is handled by correspondents who know what they are doing.

The Peking broadcasts, monitored in Hong Kong, Tokyo and other centers, provide much of the meat and potatoes of the news from Communist China presently appearing in American newspapers. News and views that the Peking regime wants made known to the world appear in the official government organ, *People's Daily*, and are usually broadcast simultaneously over Peking Radio. The official Hsinhua (New China) News Agency completes the job of world-wide distribution. But for a broader and more clearly defined picture of the situation it is necessary to follow, also, dozens of newspapers and journals serving as mouthpieces for the party, the army, various organs of government and so forth, at both national and regional levels. Digging out the meaningful bits of information, weighing them, checking them, comparing them for hidden meaning, fitting them together into a pattern is a challenging and, for many observers, a highly interesting game. Correspondents who find it an intolerable bore obviously will never be happy covering China under present circumstances and belong elsewhere.

Most important news developments, favorable or unfavorable, are likely to appear, sooner or later, in one form or another, in the mainland press. If the news is unfavorable it may be so heavily camouflaged as to be almost unrecognizable. There are times when a significant happening may be deduced only from its published aftermath. At other times an important story may, for political reasons, be publicized in one part of the country, hushed up in another. News of a crop failure, or a food shortage, or a local disturbance may be withheld for weeks or months until all possibility of unfavorable political repercussions has passed, then suddenly be exploited with big headlines as an object lesson for the party, and the public. And the true significance of a story may not unfold for still more months after it has first broken into print. There are times when the ruling regime speaks out of two sides of its mouth, with one version of a given situation for the general public, another (its real views) for those who have to know the truth. It takes a close watch on obscure publications to find the truth. To overlook one of them could mean missing a vital clue to some significant development.

Covering mainland China from Hong Kong or Tokyo is rather like covering the night sky from an observatory. A star explodes, and it is big news. But it did not happen today.

Translations, Refugees and Travelers

Among the many useful services available to American correspondents and other China watchers is the elaborate press-transla-
tion facility operated by the United States government in con-
junction with its Hong Kong Consulate-General. Here a large
and competent staff translates into English pertinent news items
and articles from dozens of mainland newspapers and periodicals
and distributes the material in mimeographed form to journalists,
China specialists, and others not only in Hong Kong but throughout the world. The output is enormous—about 33,000 words
daily—but researchers plowing or picking through this mass of
Marxist-Leninist verbiage are often rewarded with nuggets of
significant information.

Until a few years ago, mainland newspapers and periodicals
were permitted to flow into Hong Kong without let or hindrance.
After 1958, however, when the humiliating failure of the Great
Leap Forward became painfully apparent, the Communist regime
imposed restrictions on the shipment of provincial papers out
of the country. In view of the heavy demand from consulates,
libraries, research groups and interested organizations, a brisk
bootleg business has developed in hard-to-get publications, with
fantastic prices offered for exceptionally rare specimens. Recently
the situation has eased somewhat, and provincial newspapers have
been coming through in larger quantities, though the ban persists. The demand for Communist publications is not limited to
newspapers and periodicals. Reference works, textbooks, scholarly
studies—indeed any written works that shed new light on conditions and policies on the mainland—are snapped up when they
make their appearance in Hong Kong.

Mainland refugees are second only to mainland newspapers
as an information source. One writer on Chinese affairs told me
that the only information he considers worth using is what he
can obtain or confirm through refugees; but this is an extreme
view. The refugees arrive in Hong Kong and Macao in a continuous trickle, and those who have anything to tell are usually
closely interrogated, first by representatives of official agencies,

later by newspapermen. Most are farmers and fishermen from areas on the south coast whose stories tend to be monotonously parochial and similar. But occasionally a higher echelon Chinese quits the country; and once in a while there are refugees from central China, north China, even distant Manchuria or Sinkiang. Such people are often able to tell much that is interesting. Of course, mainland refugees, like mainland newspapers, have an axe to grind, though of a different kind, and their stories have to be carefully weighed and evaluated.

Through Hong Kong, also, passes a procession of China-bound travelers of diverse nationalities. They go in eager-eyed, and most come out starry-eyed, with their suitcases full of "factual" material and souvenirs from the People's Republic of China. Applicants for visas are carefully screened, and one may be sure that none are admitted who have a known record of hostility to the regime. This does not mean, however, that all persons admitted are necessarily sympathetic. In some cases—for example, in the case of businessmen—practical considerations often weigh more heavily than ideological considerations. But if the visitor is so indiscreet as to take a strongly critical view of the regime after his departure from the country, he can be quite sure that any attempt to obtain permission for a second visit will be a waste of time.

Interviewing these China visitors—or at least the more promising of them—is another of the functions of a Hong Kong correspondent, for there is not one of them, however partisan his views, who cannot add a little something to the mosaic of the "big picture." But here again the information obtained has to be handled with the utmost caution and discrimination if it is to convey an accurate impression to the American reader. Guided tourism on the mainland has been developed into a highly refined technique, full of propagandist pitfalls for unwary visitors. The value of each eyewitness story has to be separately assessed on the basis of the background knowledge, objectivity and reputation of the person telling it. Robert Loh, Richard Walker and other writers on this subject have told of the extraordinarily detailed planning that goes into Chinese arrangements for foreign visitors Nothing is left to chance, not even the possibility that the visitor will demand that he be permitted to see places "off the beaten path." The authorities have an ample supply of such places in reserve. Visitors have come out of China with what they believed to be an exclusive report on some aspects of the Chinese scene, only to discover in some cases that others had been there before them, met the same people and heard pretty much the same speeches.

The average tourist or casual visitor spends about three weeks in the country—entering via Canton, putting in one-third to one-half his time in and around Peking, also visiting Shanghai, Hangchow and, perhaps, one or two other cities. The more serious visitors spend up to two months on the mainland and usually include some of the less accessible areas in their itineraries. Permits may be obtained without too much difficulty for parts of Manchuria and Inner Mongolia and for such towns as Taiyuan, Sian, Wuhan, Leyang and Yenan. The authorities are chary, however, about permitting travelers into the deep interior and particularly the Far West.

On arrival in Peking, the visitor is consulted as to the places and people he would like to see, and arrangements are made for him to pursue those parts of the program which are permissible and practicable. An officially assigned interpreter accompanies him on officially arranged interviews. In his leisure time, which normally is not extensive, he is free to go sightseeing on his own. While traveling or walking the streets, he has occasional opportunities to pick up odd bits of offbeat information, but, in the main, the chances for a free, uninhibited, unsupervised conversation on any politically sensitive subject with any citizen not acting as an agent for the regime are negligible. It is not that the visitor is under constant watch. In a totalitarian system such as China's such measures are quite unnecessary. What is more important, no Chinese in his right mind is going to unload his grievances on a casual visitor, for he well knows the futility and — dangers of doing so. Years of indoctrination have conditioned most Chinese to drab uniformity in their responses, punctuated, of course, with dutiful expressions of extravagant praise for Chairman Mao. Although the observations of casual visitors to China are sometimes of informative value, they are more often a mélange of the same kind of experiences reported by a procession of other before them. Even old China Hands returning to China find the problem of communication a frustrating one. Rarely are they able to make contact with old friends of pre-"liberation" days, and when, on occasion, they do, the meetings are more likely to be mutually embarrassing than helpful.

The controlled flow of foreign visitors into mainland China fell off somewhat during the grim years immediately following the abortive Great Leap Forward but has increased with improving economic conditions in the past year or two. Apparently, a desire to encourage more trade and to earn more foreign exchange was also a factor. There has been an emphasis on tourism since 1964. In that year about 5,000 foreign tourists (as distinguished from other visitors) entered the country. With the inauguration of air service between Karachi, Pakistan and Shanghai, tourist visas have become a little easier to obtain, except, of course, for citizens of the United States, Spain, Nationalist China, Israel, South Korea and South Viet-Nam. In 1965, Communist China offered thirty packaged tours for foreign visitors, most within the Peking-Shanghai-Canton triangle.

An exasperating problem for the visitor to mainland China is the difficulty of keeping informed on current happenings both outside and inside the country. From the moment he steps across the border, he is in a never-never land of controlled news and propaganda where there is no clear dividing line between fact and fiction. It is possible, to be sure, for foreign guests in Chinese hotels to rent short-wave radio receivers, on which they can pick up BBC, the Voice of America, Radio Japan and others. This enables them to keep in touch with the highlights, at least, of international developments. Yet, important events may be in the making under their very noses without their being aware of it. This has sometimes been a cause of embarrassment. Many visitors who were in China, for instance, during the Hundred Flowers uproar and the subsequent student rioting, in 1957, did not learn until after they left China what had been going on. Some of them, indeed, had already sounded off to the Western press about the excellent morale they had found among the youth of the country. Others have gulped down the impressive production statistics handed to them in China, only to discover, in some cases (for example, after the Great Leap Forward), that the figures had been grossly exaggerated. Valentin Chu, China-born writer and author, names Lord Boyd Orr, former head of the United Nations Food and Agriculture Organization and winner of the Nobel Peace Prize, as one of the more distinguished victims of this deception.[1] A more recent example of air-tight control of the news was the convening of a huge Young Communist League rally in Peking (in 1964) without the knowledge of foreign correspondents living there. Foreign reporters in Peking were told of the event only after it was over and had been reported elsewhere.[2]

American newsmen in Hong Kong, interviewing travelers from China and recording their observations, are under a heavy responsibility to their newspapers. It is their duty to report both favorable and unfavorable information, insofar as it is soundly based, and they can afford neither to be too credulous nor too cynical, for to err either way means giving their readers a distorted and misleading picture of conditions in mainland China.

Consider the following quotation:

"Every trip from India to China I get a shock. In India the natives are depressed, dejected, hopelessly poor, ragged, dirty, underfed, skinny, sick, unsmiling, apathetic. In China they have their heads up, they are bright, cheerful, laughing and joking, well fed, relatively clean, independent, going about their business, appear to have an object in life."

One has come to expect observations similar to this from European visitors to Communist China. Such tourists are almost invariably impressed by the smiling, alert faces they see on all sides. The inference is, of course, that the people are happy with Communist rule. Yet the passage quoted above came not from a visitor to Communist China but from a frequent visitor to pre-Communist China, General Joseph W. Stilwell.[3] And it was

---

[1] *Ta Ta Tan Tan* [Fight, Fight, Talk, Talk] (New York: W. W. Norton and Company, 1963), p. 265.

[2] See *Current Scene* (Hong Kong), v. 3, no. 21, June 15, 1965.

[3] Joseph W. Stilwell, *The Stilwell Papers;* ed. by Theodore H. White (New York: William Sloane Associates, 1948), p. 183.

written in January 1943, at a time when the people of Kuomintang China were widely believed to be low in morale, discon-
tented with their government, and near the end of their rope
militarily and economically. What I am saying is that brightness
and cheerfulness were Chinese characteristics long before the
Communists came to power, and that it is dangerous to draw
political inferences from smiling faces without corroborative
evidence of a more substantial nature.

By the same token, editors who treat all unfavorable information from mainland China as news and reject all favorable information as propaganda are being equally dishonest with their
readers. The situation inside Communist China is neither all black
nor all white, despite a widespread disposition to make it seem
so. While this report was in preparation, a hard-hitting but one-
sided book purporting to tell how the American public has been
misinformed about China appeared in bookstores throughout the
country.[4]

Written by a long-time British resident of California, the book
quotes from scores of reports published in the American press
over recent years to demonstrate—sometimes dubiously, often
with damaging effect—how frequently our correspondents, our
scholars, our politicians and our statesmen have distorted and
misconstrued the news from China. Despite his obvious bias,
Greene makes some telling points. Starting from the early years
of the Communist takeover, he cites reports from American newspapers and official American spokesmen about Russian territorial
grabs in China that were largely imaginary. He quotes later press
reports to show how Americans have been misled by colorful and
often fanciful reporting on the Chinese communes. He notes that
American writers have repeatedly had Communist China at the
point of bankruptcy, mass starvation or collapse, only to be
obliged, later, to eat their words or modify them. He deplores
the American tendency to ignore or ridicule eyewitness reports
from mainland China by European and Canadian visitors, some
of them persons of outstanding reputation in their respective
fields.

[4] Felix Greene, *A Curtain of Ignorance* (Garden City, N.Y.: Doubleday
and Company, 1964), p. 282.

For fourteen years a vast number of reports distributed by the great organs of public opinion—the press, radio, TV—and many of our political leaders have stressed the weakness and insecurity of the Chinese government. All predictions so confidently expressed have been proven wrong: the Chinese government has not been 'snuffed out'; the Nationalists have not invaded the mainland; the peasants have not revolted; Shanghai has not been 'choked in mud'; the Chinese have not starved; there is no evidence that the government has at any time been 'out of control'; and the regime of Mao Tse-tung is still with us more secure than ever! [5]

Greene's book would carry a great deal more impact were he not so obviously prone to errors of prejudice, distortion and judgment no less serious than those for which he so acidly indicts his peers. While Greene condemns unsupported statements depicting Communist China in an unfavorable light, he does not hesitate to quote from unsupported statements that happen to agree with his point of view. And his point of view, quite evidently, is that the sun did not rise in China until Mao Tse-tung and company took over. For example, Greene is deeply concerned over the millions who died from shooting, starvation and infanticide in the old China, but wastes not a word of sympathy for the many hundreds of thousands—probably millions—who were brutalized by the Communists in "people's" trials and killed in the name of the revolution.

Yet books like Greene's need to be read, along with those of other viewpoints, if one is to fit in all pieces of the jigsaw puzzle. Greene has made three visits to Communist China and in an earlier book [6] tells much of interest about the country that is unknown to most Americans. Defending the veracity of what he has written, Greene goes on to say that "if only half of the facts that I have presented are true, then it becomes clear that the American people have been seriously misinformed." [7] On this point, I think, any reasonable person must agree.

[5] Same, p. 282.
[6] Felix Greene, *Awakened China* (Garden City, N.Y.: Doubleday and Company, 1961).
[7] Same, p. 389.

Facilities for Direct Coverage

At this writing, the only regular direct coverage of mainland China available to American newspapers comes from British and French news agencies with resident correspondents in Peking and from a roving correspondent for the Toronto (Canada) *Globe and Mail*. A West German news agency is in the process of opening a Peking bureau, and others, no doubt, will follow. Occasional articles are also provided by Western correspondents visiting the mainland for brief periods. The flow of such traveling reporters increased notably in 1964 and included Canadian, French, British, Scandinavian, Dutch, Swiss and West German writers. A number of television teams have also toured the country.

There is a consensus among Americans—and more especially among editors—that the most effective means of improving the news flow from China would be to get American correspondents into the mainland. Many Americans tend to be distrustful of reporting on China from non-American sources. Very few of those interviewed considered such reporting a satisfactory substitute for direct coverage by competent American reporters. However, British and other Western correspondents in Peking suffer from problems which probably would apply equally to Americans, if they are ever admitted. While they have freedom of movement in and around the capital, their travels elsewhere in China are severely restricted. While they can engage in small talk with Chinese encountered in their perambulations, any serious discussion of important issues is virtually impossible except under official auspices. While there is no censorship on outgoing dispatches, there is censorship of news at its source.

Since fraternization between Chinese and foreigners is officially discouraged, the social life of the correspondents is largely limited to contacts with other foreigners—which means members of the diplomatic community, fellow correspondents and foreign visitors. There are, of course, daily contacts with Chinese employees—house-boys, cooks, interpreters and so forth—but these worthies are all presumed to be doing double duty as the eyes and ears of the Chinese secret service. Interviews with high-ranking Chinese officials, which could be a profitable source of news, are seldom granted to resident correspondents, although visitors are sometimes able to arrange a meeting with Chou En-lai or Ch'en Yi, very rarely with Mao Tse-tung. It is hardly surprising that Peking-based correspondents, despite certain attractions of life in the Chinese capital, look forward with relish to their occasional trips to Hong Kong.

Reuters, a British news agency which maintains a correspondent in Peking, has many American subscribers. A check of various papers taking this service showed uneven usage. *The Washington Post* was one of the heavier users, with nine direct-from-China stories in a rather routine month. Of these, two were features, one about Marxist song hits, the other about the "productive labor" program of the People's Liberation Army. Another story told of Premier Chou En-lai's return to Peking from a three-month Afro-Asian tour, the welcome he received from Mao Tse-tung, and something about Mao's current state of health. Then there were a piece about the mysterious postponement of a pro-Arab, anti-American rally in Peking and a Shanghai story quoting the vice-mayor on the progress of suburban construction in that city. The remaining dispatches were based on material appearing in the Chinese Communist press and probably could have been picked up as well in Hong Kong.

Even if we presume that *The Washington Post* used only a part of Reuters' China file, the limitations on direct coverage are rather painfully evident from this sampling. Could American correspondents, if admitted to mainland China, do a better job than their British, Canadian or French colleagues? The rather obvious answers are (1) that there would probably be more of them and (2) that they would be looking at China through American rather than British or French spectacles. From the viewpoint of American editors this would be all to the good.

A large number of American publications have indicated their desire to send correspondents to China if and when the barriers are let down—most for a quick look, a few to establish bureaus there. The wire services, of course, would set up Peking offices. Initially, at least, Communist China would receive greatly increased attention in the American press. Public interest in that critically important area would undoubtedly be stimulated. After a time, the novelty would wear off, and the news flow out of China would become routine. But the output would certainly be bigger than now and, because of the multiplication of effort and the intensified competition, probably better. However, without some dramatic change in Peking's policies of news management, the improvement would probably fall short of expectations. And chances are that Hong Kong would remain, as now, the main center of mainland China news.

There is yet another catch in the problem of direct news coverage from China. That is, that any reporter or writer hoping to visit Communist China more than once suffers from a built-in handicap. He is obliged to think twice before writing anything that might cost him a visa the next time he applies. Herbert Passim takes note of this inhibiting factor in a monograph on *China's Cultural Diplomacy:*

> The journalist who wishes to return to China will be very cautious in what he writes; he will often suppress unfavorable material, confining himself to the favorable things he can honestly say or, in some cases even bending the truth. In either event, his reportage will lack balance. The same problem arises for scholars who hope to get into China or, having been there, to return.[8]

Undoubtedly this factor helps account for the insipid tone of much of the news that is sent out of Peking by foreign agencies. Its effects are apparent, too, in some of the books that are written by China visitors. Authors-who-want-to-go-back are likely to avoid criticism on particularly sensitive points, and such criticism as they indulge in may be so qualified and tortuously stated that it loses much of its impact.

It would be unfair to suggest that all writers and reporters visiting China fall into this category. There are surely those who do not, as is evidenced by some of the reporting of Canadian newspapermen which has appeared in the American press. A correspondent who has worked in Peking said:

> This is important to clear up, because if people think that we are always holding back for fear of being thrown out, they will not take

[8] *China's Cultural Diplomacy* (London: *China Quarterly*, 1962), p. 124.

our work seriously. There may be others, but I know of only two resident correspondents who have been expelled or not had their credentials renewed. What we are told is this: The Chinese authorities expect us to "report the facts as you see them." We are explicitly told that the authorities do not expect us to agree with everything we see. They say to us that they don't mind political and economic criticism. What they object to is any distortion, and any speculation on the health or personal relations or current status of the leaders (which doesn't stop us from indulging in such speculation, since it is an important part of the job).

For the present, the problem of getting American correspondents into mainland China is purely academic. No exchange of correspondents is in sight at this writing. The Chinese Communists made it known immediately after their takeover, in 1949, that American reporters would be excluded from the mainland pending diplomatic recognition of their regime. In 1956, however, during a phase of "peoples' diplomacy" and "peaceful coexistence," they extended invitations to a group of fifteen American newsmen to visit China. The State Department withheld permission but later weakened under public pressure. Thirty-two American reporters obtained passport validations in Washington, and some hurried hopefully to Hong Kong in order to be first into China when the gates opened. But Peking had cooled. The United States was informed that the Americans would be admitted only if an equal number of Chinese newspapermen were admitted into the United States under reciprocal conditions. The State Department hedged, and said that under American law it could not agree in advance to the admittance of an equal number of Chinese without knowing their identities. To this the Chinese Communists said "No," and they have been saying "No" ever since. As matters stand today, the State Department remains favorable to an exchange, but Peking has closed the door, except on the basis of an over-all political settlement including withdrawal of U.S. military and naval support from Taiwan.

Only two American reporters have visited China since 1957. They were John Strom, who went in 1958, and Edgar Snow, in 1960 and again in 1964. Both had State Department validations, but in each case the Chinese Communists carefully avoided designating them as newspaper correspondents. Strom was received as an "agricultural expert," Snow as a "writer."

Sampling Shows Defects in Handling of China News

The truth is, of course, that the ban on direct access to the news is only one of several reasons for the inadequacy of American reporting on mainland China and that even the lifting of it would not wholly solve the problem. For the present more can be accomplished by improving the quality and the quantity of the news obtainable under the existing limitations. To get a rough picture of current China coverage in the American press, a check was made of a dozen newspapers over a period of one month.[9] The papers analyzed included two of our most internationally minded journals—*The New York Times* and *The Washington Post*—and a daily in each of the following cities: Cincinnati, Ohio; Denver, Colorado; Sacramento, California; Spokane, Washington; Tucson, Arizona; Des Moines, Iowa; Peru, Indiana; Shreveport, Louisiana; Wilkes-Barre, Pennsylvania; and Natchez, Mississippi.

It was probably a near-average month for China news. The stories that got most attention were the continuing Sino-Soviet quarrel, Chou En-lai's trip through Asia and Africa, Peking's flirtation with de Gaulle, Chinese involvement in Southeast Asia, and a report that the United States was making reconnaissance flights over the China mainland. Not surprisingly, *The New York Times* led all papers in the amount of space given, with a total of 660 column inches of news about or relating to Communist China during the month—in other words, more than a column a day. This was about half the space given to Soviet Russia in the same period, but three times the amount given to Japan.

The Washington Post ran the *Times* a fairly close second during the month, but all other newspapers were far behind—ranging from eleven columns of China-related news in the Cincinnati paper down to less than two columns in Natchez. In all newspapers studied, Soviet Russia fared better than China in space received, and Japan fared worse. An ironic touch was that Taiwan

[9] March 1964.

—the "China" we recognize—was largely ignored by most of the newspapers checked. Even the *Times* gave Taiwan only one-tenth of the amount of space devoted to mainland China, and most of this was taken up by a comprehensive article in the Sunday magazine. In five of the newspapers studied, diligent search failed to turn up any news at all of Taiwan origin. To be sure, it was a dull month in Taiwan, with no headline-making flare-ups on Matsu or Quemoy, but the lack of interest was nevertheless painfully apparent.

The newspaper analysis revealed other significant inconsistencies in the treatment of China news by the American press. One was the evident imbalance between the space given to China-international news and China-domestic news. In all newspapers examined except *The New York Times*, *The Washington Post* and the Spokane paper (*The Spokesman-Review*) Peking's international relations almost wholly dominated the space given to Communist China. None of the nine printed more than one or two articles dealing with internal developments in a country embracing one-fourth the population of the globe. Among the subjects: "Red China Isn't Folding"; "Red China's One Tooth Dragon"; "Sinkiang Pits Soviet, Chinese in Deadly Game"; "The 'Old Comrades' of China"; "New Oil Fields in China"; "English Replacing Russian in Chinese Schools."

This preoccupation with Peking's international adventurism is to some extent understandable. Certainly the Sino-Soviet quarrel and Peking's intrigues in Southeast Asia, Africa and Latin America are matters of the utmost concern to the United States and the whole free world. But the neglect of the news from China's home front, where social and political experiments of massive scope are being put to test, is regrettable and could, indeed, prove very costly. It has created an appalling gap in American comprehension of the Asian scene and is probably a primary cause of much of the confusion, uncertainty and contradiction so evident in American attitudes toward Communist China.

Editors give many reasons for not using more news on developments inside Communist China, and we will examine some of them. Perhaps the most common complaint is that reliable information is practically unobtainable. This is not entirely true. I asked a State Department analyst who has devoted a great deal of time to the study of Pekingology whether the United States government is doing better than the newspapers in obtaining an accurate picture of mainland conditions from information available. He replied:

We have pretty good information on the general picture—the general agricultural situation, the general industrial situation. But we do not have a very good breakdown in detail. For example, we have been able to make very accurate estimates of grain production, calculated on a basis of what refugees tell us about weather conditions, food supplies, and so forth. We have an accurate picture of the situation in the coastal areas—Kwangtung, Fukien, Chekiang, Shantung, Hopei. Down the main line, as it were. We know what life is like in those areas. Also, by analyzing the Communist press, we can tell what the regime is thinking and what it is likely to do. We have a fairly good picture of political conditions and economic conditions—enough on which to base policy.

The areas on which we are in the dark are in far western China, where travelers don't go and from which few refugees come. For instance we did not realize the gravity of the border dispute in Sinkiang until the revelations were published in the Communist press. Information is scanty from the fringe areas—Tibet and Mongolia. The whole area of the minorities in China is pretty much a blank spot. Yet if there is trouble, that is where it is likely to be.

Also, we would like to know more about the differences of view among top leaders of the Communist regime. What are the strains? Outwardly, there is a remarkable monolithic unity. We hear about Mao Tse-tung and Liu Shao-chi and Chou En-lai but very little about the others among the seventy-five men who run the country. There are things we sense but cannot confirm. But even if we had diplomatic representation in Peking we would not know.

Thirdly, there is the question of the mood of the people, very difficult to determine with any exactness.

My State Department informant insisted that virtually all the information on which this assessment is based is available to any American correspondent stationed in Hong Kong. True, not many of these reporters have sufficient staff, or time or patience to do the painstaking research needed to get the most out of the China story, and with their editors crying for dramatic and spot news there is not much incentive for them to do so. It is so much easier and—from the headline-making standpoint—so much more profitable to concentrate on the story of the day, be it some new development in the Sino-Soviet quarrel, some fresh outburst against the United States, or some new bid for influence in Southeast Asia or Africa. Stories like this can be skimmed like cream off the daily outpouring of wordage from Peking Radio or the Hsinhua News Agency. And they stand a better chance of making American front pages than the longer and heavier pieces which are the products of careful research.

Yet it is the latter material which tells the story behind the story in mainland China. As we have said, it requires a close watch on the mainland press supplemented by information from refugees, travelers, diplomats and intelligence agents. It requires an ability to separate truth from propaganda and to interpret the information obtained in a way that will be interesting and meaningful to the American newspaper reader. A tough assignment, yes; but there are short cuts. Responsible newspaper correspondents in Hong Kong have access to much carefully researched information on China prepared for official agencies of the United States government and other friendly governments. Academic experts on mainland China are also fairly plentiful in Hong Kong and often are generous in sharing the results of their research with repo;ters they trust.

Wire Services Have Key Role

Our one-month analysis of twelve American newspapers showed that nine of them relied primarily on the Associated Press or the United Press International for their mainland China coverage, while the other three gave major play to their own and syndicated correspondents and used the wire services only for back-stopping purposes.

The role and responsibility of the press associations in informing, or misinforming, the public about China is enormous. Separately or together they serve virtually all American daily newspapers. Most newspapers are wholly dependent on them for their routine China coverage, although many subscribe also to one or more syndicated feature services which provide them with occasional background articles on China. Even well-heeled newspapers like *The New York Times* which have their own bureaus in Hong Kong often use wire-service material. Both wire services maintain news bureaus around the fringes of Communist China, both religiously monitor Peking broadcasts, both do a certain amount of background research and both interview anybody they think might have a headline-making story. Out of these efforts comes a file of miscellaneous information studded with isolated incidents but deficient in the background, perspective and continuity so necessary to give the news real meaning to the average reader.

Nobody can question the basic integrity of the two major press associations. Their reporters are in the main capable newspapermen, under standing instructions to get the facts. Yet they would be less than human if they did not try to provide their client newspapers with what they think they want. A former wire service correspondent in the Far East put it this way:

The climate in New York and on editorial desks discourages a truly liberal interpretation of the news from China. Editors seem to want black and white treatment of the China news. They don't like unpleasant truths about confused situations that have no apparent remedy. If you come up with a new idea that doesn't conform to the ancient clichés, it is almost sure to end up in the waste basket. I see no way to improve coverage in China as long as this attitude exists. The problem is not one of the quantity of the news, but of the quality.

His parting comment was that "people are a hell of a lot more interested in China than editors give them credit for."

What this news agency veteran was saying is that the press associations are giving the editors what they want, that the editors are giving their readers what they think they want, and that the readers are dissatisfied with what they are getting.

For some years after the Communist takeover of mainland China both the major wire services (AP and UPI) maintained their main monitoring facilities in Hong Kong. It became necessary, however, to move the facilities to Tokyo where transmission was faster and more reliable. Since the move, Hong Kong has been less intensively exploited as a listening post, though both agencies retain bureaus there. It seems that thoroughness has been sacrificed for speed. As any Asia correspondent knows, Tokyo simply does not compare with Hong Kong as a source of detailed information on developments inside mainland China. But a wire-service executive in New York noted that his organization has recently (in 1965) distributed to its clients a large number of informative first-hand reports on China written by non-American observers. He said that the use made of them has been spotty, with many newspapers not using them at all.

A count of AP and UPI stories used in the twelve newspapers checked showed that fewer than two per cent of the items relating to Communist China originated in Hong Kong. Approximately 25 per cent of them carried a Tokyo dateline, and the remainder, mostly concerned with China's international relations, came from cities around the globe. The weakness of this situation is shown by the fact that only a small fraction of the wire-service material published in these newspapers during the month dealt with conditions inside Communist China. Hong Kong is by all odds the best source of information of that kind.

What's Wrong with Our China Coverage? Some Answers

While a majority of editors, as was noted earlier, feel that the American press is not giving the public a well-rounded picture of the China situation, they are inclined to blame Peking's closed-door policies rather than the news-gathering organizations. A majority of editors queried felt the news services were doing an adequate (some said good or excellent) job, in view of the difficulties they have to buck. Many editors seem unaware of the possibilities for improvement, or just don't care. Here is a cross section of editorial reaction to the news coverage they are receiving on China:

"Good, with the obvious reservation that no country can be covered adequately from outside its borders."

"Sufficient."

"Satisfactory as far as it goes."

"Lacks depth and true insight of China."

"I suppose it's the best they can do under the circumstances, but it is inadequate."

"Thorough and objective."

"They do not seem to be writing about real people. We are unable to get information on how the Chinese live and work and think."

Lay members of the public were less charitable in their views. The testimony was overwhelming that we are, in general, being given a disjointed picture of happenings in China and that the American press has neglected its opportunities for improving the coverage. Both mainland news coverage and Taiwan news coverage were criticized, but it was the former that caused the most concern. It may be useful, at this point, to examine the main points of criticism.

Distortion of the news. This takes many forms, some of them common to all foreign-news coverage. Editors cannot resist giving major prominence to dramatic and offbeat stories, often at the expense of material that is more important but less exciting. There is a disposition to play up isolated incidents without giving them the setting and perspective that would make them meaningful to the average reader. Newspapers are printing more than enough of the stuff that is broadcast over Peking Radio, not enough of the news behind the news that has to be dug out at the cost of considerable effort. There is a tendency to play up adverse news—for instance, stories of natural disasters, crop failures, food shortages and so forth are usually sure of headlines—while the more favorable developments are less likely to be given prominence.

Distortion can be the result of inexperience, or neglect, or lack of judgment, or even prejudice on the part of a reporter. Every official pronouncement, every editorial, most news items in the Chinese Communist press carry some political significance. Faulty interpretation can lead to a serious warping of the information reaching the American public. There is probably no field of foreign news writing in which background and experience are so important. Even information obtained from official American sources can sometimes be misleading, and it takes a knowledgeable correspondent to know how to check it and make best use of it. I have no doubt that most of the American correspondents covering China are motivated by completely honest intentions; a few of them rank among the ablest foreign correspondents anywhere. But the China issue is so emotionally charged that objectivity is often difficult. For the occasional irresponsible reporter the temptation to interpret the news to fit his own views or the views of his clients is irresistible. And who is there to prove him wrong?

A number of persons interviewed charged American correspondents with bias in their handling of China news. The editor of a well-known Eastern newspaper said: "American correspondents suffer from a built-in difficulty in reporting on Communist China from distant sources. They are bound to show that communism is a terrible enemy and that it has a fatal flaw because it is communism. Reporters are pushed by these two motives into writing distortions of the facts." There were others who expressed similar views, but less bluntly. A few felt the bias, if any, was in the other direction.

Conflicting versions of mainland developments. Many persons said they did not trust the news out of Communist China, chiefly because it is so full of contradictions. Some wondered how different experts could reach opposite conclusions from the same set of facts. As this is written, some authorities find Communist China in a rather desperate state economically, others find her making a strong economic recovery. "I get impatient with the newspapers," said a Californian. "One day China is collapsing, the next day it is a threat to our security. What can you believe?" This is a problem closely related to the problem of distortion, and it stems from much the same causes—poor judgment, bias, oversimplification, too much guesswork. Valentin Chu refers scornfully to those China watchers who are addicted to instant punditry, and he continues:

Some of the Western dragonologists are excellent. But some are blundering amateurs or cynical quacks whose writing consists either of timid, non-informative intellectual acrobatics, or unguided emotional missiles that hit everything except the bulls-eye. As a result the overall picture of the China situation is incoherent. The experts disagree and the public is confused.[10]

Mishandling of China news by American editors. Responsibility for the uneven coverage of China by American news media lies not alone with the reporters in the field but with the editors at home. Few American editors have sufficient background knowledge of China to be able to judge the accuracy, bias or propaganda content of a China story, much less to draw well-reasoned editorial conclusions from it. This may mean giving prominence to a story of only superficial significance, while burying or wastebasketing an article of utmost importance. Many editors are, by tradition and training, more Europe-minded than Asia-minded and assume—perhaps correctly—that the majority of their readers are the same. In many newspapers it takes a big story from China to get the same play as a lesser story from Europe.

Even when the facts emerge unscathed from the wire service mills, they run the hazard of mutilation or misinterpretation when they reach the telegraph desks of individual newspapers. A news-agency executive complained that some editors are so anti-Communist they will not publish or, in any case, will not give fair display to dispatches reflecting favorably on any Communist government. Others adopt a free-wheeling, flippant attitude in their handling of news about mainland China and other Communist countries which they do not show in their handling of similar news from friendly countries. Inevitably these editorial attitudes influence reader attitudes in the long run.

Only a few of the very largest American newspapers can afford the luxury of a full-time foreign editor. On most other newspapers the foreign file is handled by the telegraph editor, whose judgment is often decisive on the evaluation and play to be given a foreign news story. Traditionally, the telegraph editor has been little more than a glorified dot-and-dash man, with little prestige and scant incentive for self-improvement in international problems. It was only rarely that a knowledge of foreign affairs

[10] Chu, cited, p. 264.

was considered a necessary qualification for the job. This is changing. In recent years, with the help of continued prodding from the wire services, many newspapers have upgraded the status of their telegraph editors and, in some instances, encouraged them to become local experts in international affairs. Some of them have been sent off to seminars for telegraph editors sponsored by the American Press Institute. A few have been given new titles—for example, World Affairs Editor—and find themselves in demand for talks in local schools and civic organizations. These practices are not yet general, but they are catching on. They should lead to a more intelligent handling of foreign news in the country's press and, consequently, more depth in the treatment of news from China.

The editorial orientation of a newspaper—whether it is Democratic or Republican, liberal or conservative, internationalist or isolationist—is also a factor of importance in determining its handling of China news. Indeed it can be argued that the generally conservative attitude of the American public on China is more attributable to this influence than to any other. Newspapers of conservative outlook—and they are predominant in the smaller cities and towns—tend to give prominence to news and background stories that favor their point of view. They also tend to use columnists of a predominantly conservative viewpoint. The total impression of China conveyed week after week to the readers of such a newspaper is likely to be different from that conveyed by a militantly liberal or independent newspaper.

Since newspapers remain the principal source of information on China for the general public, the failure of many publications to give their readers a balanced picture is a cause for concern. Fortunate is the city that is served by two or more newspapers of differing outlook or by a single newspaper that believes in giving all sides a hearing.

Public Only Mildly Interested in China, Editors Say

One of the questions put to our sampling of newspaper editors was concerned with the extent of public interest in news and features from China. Twenty-nine replied that their readers were only mildly interested in China news, ten said they were interested only in sensational developments. A scant eight believed their readers were much interested. One who said his readers belonged in the "mildly interested" category added that "some of this may be our fault." Another felt that "intelligent readers" would like to know more about Communist China than newspapers are telling them. And yet another said readers were interested "only in developments affecting the United States and its international posture."

We followed that question with this: "Would you and could you print more news on Formosa and/or Communist China if you could get it?" Twenty-nine of those who responded said "Yes," and fifteen gave a qualified "Yes." Only eleven answered with a flat or qualified negative. Asked what kind of news they wanted, one replied: "Interpretive and humanistic. Who are these people? How do they live? What do they want? But please, no quaint features." Another said: "More emphasis on the people of China, less on the leaders and politicians." Another: "What the common people are doing and thinking. The truth about agriculture, food shortages, population explosion and what, if anything, China is trying to do about it."

The editors volunteered dozens of other suggestions, of which the following are a representative selection.

"More effort to weigh their point of view against ours."

"More objectivity. Less 'experting' by reporters and more interviews with partisans of both sides."

"Less emphasis on propaganda announcements and more periodic roundups that look at the over-all situation and put it into perspective."

"If we could adequately staff even Peiping with enough reporters, this should help. But it would not be the answer as long as reporters and editors insist on evaluating such news only in terms of the cold war."

"Perhaps the reader would be more interested if we had reliable articles coming out of Red China. Certainly much of the Peiping Radio propaganda relayed to our press services via Tokyo is so much pure bunk that the reader couldn't care less."

"We need more what-people-are-doing stories, particularly on Red China."

"We need more personality stories; more interpretive pieces, not written for headlines but for better understanding of the problem involved."

"More news of actual living conditions and attitudes of the people of Red China."

As is evident from the foregoing, many editors felt that the news from Communist China is too much concerned with situations and not enough with people. To Americans, the Chinese seem more like automatons or "blue ants" than people. Several, in interviews, referred to the "faceless mass" of China. Yet this is hardly a problem that can be satisfactorily solved as long as we are barred from direct contact with the Chinese people. The admission of American reporters to mainland China would help but is not a final answer.

And what of Taiwan? There, there is no problem of travel restrictions. Correspondents can go where and when they please. Officials are approachable and, in the main, friendly. Yet it is apparent from the reactions I have received that the news from Nationalist China is viewed with only slightly less distrust than that originating on the Communist-ruled mainland. Editors are mainly impressed by the superficiality of the coverage, the over-emphasis on official pronouncements and the lack of hard reporting on the true state of affairs between the mainlanders and the native Taiwanese. Some could not understand why a greater effort was not being made. Others provided what they believed to be the reason: lack of public interest. An editor said: "I believe that the average U.S. citizen is not especially interested in Formosa." Several agreed.

A pronounced note of skepticism and an antipathy for Chiang Kai-shek ran through some of the comments. For instance:

"I suspect that the Chiang government colors the news flow."

"The hand of Chiang appears too often."

"The true picture probably never has been given."

"Sometimes there seems to be a propaganda tinge (in the news from Formosa) as if the line of Chiang's government is being echoed without further checking."

Editors who were interested in more news from Taiwan complained about the absence of stories in depth. One said: "Apparently the Chinese on Formosa are bitterly resented by the Formosans, who may or may not be burdened by their presence. There is little written about this, if indeed it is true. I don't know, and I doubt that many editors do."

The China Story on Television and Radio

United States television and radio coverage of China is no better —and in some ways inferior—to that of the daily press. Many stations rely on the two major wire services for routine information, others on the network news services. Since American TV and radio reporters in the field suffer from the same handicap as their newspaper colleagues in being unable to enter Communist China, they are obliged to glean their information from the same second-hand sources. TV-radio coverage of day-to-day developments in mainland China differs from newspaper coverage only in that it is more fragmentary.

Most television networks have tie-ins with European and Canadian sources of film that can sometimes be used on news programs. The National Broadcasting Company, for one, has access to a limited flow of official Chinese film, through an international (British-Canadian-Australian) distribution company. Only part of it is usable. Not many Americans are interested, for example, in watching Premier Chou En-lai bear-hug an arriving dignitary from Albania at the Peking airport.

Perhaps the only important advantage of television over the newspapers in its coverage of China is in being able to offer occasional filmed documentaries and live panel programs. NBC's *White Paper on China* (1962) and a CBS program *China and the World* (1964) are examples. *White Paper* had an estimated audience of 19 million. Yet such programs are few and far between and not always successful. A troublesome problem is the scarcity of usable film footage from Communist China. A producer trying to put together an hour-long show on mainland China for a major network complained to this writer:

I have looked at film from four different sources. The stuff is so much alike and so obviously shot under official supervision that it has very little value. Apparently each photographer was taken to the same clubs, the same truck and bicycle factories, the same fertilizer plant. There was complete conformity.

Now and then, a European or Canadian photographic team comes out of China with unique and exciting material. But the big networks have set such stiff standards on film of this kind and are so shy of being "used" for propaganda purposes that much technically excellent and interesting film is rejected on grounds of being "loaded." Moreover, even when such film is usable, the producer often finds it necessary to insert a disclaimer mentioning the restricted conditions under which the pictures were taken and to introduce enough material from the "other side" to give balance to the production, with the result that the hapless viewer comes through it all feeling more confused about China than ever.

Some of the smaller networks, notably National Educational Television and Westinghouse Television, suffer from fewer inhibitions on China than their big brothers and have given the subject relatively more attention in greater depth. They reach, of course, a somewhat more sophisticated audience and are more inclined to welcome controversy than avoid it. With China very much in the news, TV panel discussions have become increasingly popular within the past year or two, especially in the larger cities. But when the writer wrote to a representative list of TV and radio executives across the country asking whether it was possible to conduct an uninhibited and rational public debate on China without provoking a flood of hostile mail, eleven of the nineteen who responded said "No," and only eight said "Yes." Some of the specific comments from specific areas are illuminating:

From Louisiana: "I am not aware of any cooling whatsoever of public emotions on the China question."

From New York: "I think the situation will improve if media begin a debate."

From Massachusetts: "I think you could do an objective program here and only expect hostile reaction from the usual small minority."

From Alabama: "Apathy is the problem here."

Recently, National Educational Television produced a 90-minute show on modern China, much of it consisting of film taken on the Communist-ruled mainland. Ben C. Markland, director of the University of Arizona's Station KUAT, which used the program, wrote me as follows:

"We had four or five rather irate telephone calls while the program was on the air and immediately afterward. The tenor of most of them was that KUAT was a mouthpiece of Red China, that the university staff is communistic, and that this was a propaganda effort to gain public support for the admission of Red China to the United Nations. There was also a letter to the editor of the *Tucson Daily Citizen* expressing some of the same attitudes. Within three days after the broadcast, we had at least ten complimentary comments on the program and no additional derogatory comments. Both the local Tucson papers, including the rather conservative *Citizen*, commented on the broadcast in a favorable way."

Books about China

Do Americans read books about China? In these days, not many and not much. Many good books on China, both fiction and non-fiction, were written in the years between the two world wars, and a few continue to sell. Pearl Buck's classic, *The Good Earth*, has sold over 2,500,000 copies in the United States and is still going strong in four editions. Its foreign sales (it has been translated into more than thirty languages) are uncountable. But *The Good Earth* is a sensational exception to the rule.

An important nonfiction work of the same period was *Red Star Over China*, by Edgar Snow, the first detailed, definitive account by a Western writer of the Long March and of conditions in Chinese Communist territory. First published in 1937, the book sold about 125,000 copies in England but only about 15,000 in the initial Random House edition in this country. Total sales in the United States have added up to about 65,000. It has been translated into many languages, with sales in Japan alone (paperbacks) of around 30,000.[11]

Since the Communist takeover in China, there has been a great falling off in the output of books of general interest on China written by Americans. This is attributable in part to the fact that Americans are excluded from China, in part to simple lack of interest. However, books written for the academic and library market—textbooks, analytical studies of various aspects of the China scene, reference works—have been coming off the presses in increasing numbers. This is a good sign. It is evidence of intensified research on China and of increased attention to China in our schools and universities. But academic works of this kind are of little interest to the public at large.

The writer discussed this matter with several New York publishers and book editors. One said: "It is impossible to reach the general public unless you have an unusually good book by somebody who has been there. Credibility is a necessary ingredient." But the real need of the moment, this publisher continued, is not for eyewitness books but for simple, central, straightforward, basic books that tell us about contemporary China and the nature of Chinese communism in terms that any intelligent American can understand. These "core" books, as he called them, would be "read by that very limited but very influential sector of the population that is starved for understanding of China but finds the scholarly literature on the subject too specialized and too dull."

---

[11] Some of the better selling books on China in recent years have been the following: A. Doak Barnett, *Communist China and Asia* (New York: Harper and Brothers for the Council on Foreign Relations, 1960), sales 33,345; Edgar Snow, *The Other Side of the River* (New York: Random House, 1962), sales 21,281; Felix Greene, *Awakened China* (Garden City, N.Y.: Doubleday and Company, 1961), sales 12,000; Alice Hsieh, *Communist China's Strategy in the Nuclear Era* (Englewood Cliffs, N.J.: Prentice-Hall for the RAND Corporation, 1962), sales 12,000; Robert Loh, *Escape from Red China* (New York: Coward-McCann, 1962), sales 8,569; Valentine Chu, *Ta Ta Tan Tan* (New York: W. W. Norton and Company, 1963), sales 8,000; Felix Greene, *A Curtain of Ignorance* (New York: Doubleday and Company, 1964) sales 6,300. The list is by no means complete or comprehensive and does not include books intended primarily for textbook use. Circulation figures were supplied by the publishers named, early in March 1965.

A leading book editor agreed. "What we want," he said, "is the translation of true scholarship into a style that people will read."

What about the many books written on China in recent years by foreign writers, some of whom have visited and traveled in that country?

"No," was the reply. "No matter how good the book, it will make no real dent on Americans unless it is filtered through an American consciousness."

"What has happened," mused an editor, "to the great American public which devoured books on China in the 1920s and 1930s? I wish I knew. Maybe they all grew older and died, leaving a younger generation with no links to China." He admitted, however, that good manuscripts are hard to find; his company has not published a book on China for fifteen years. He wondered if there was any connection between this situation and "the absurd ostrich policy" of the United States and Chinese governments. "I certainly could not prove any," he went on, "but China is the only major region of the world on which we have this record over the past fifteen years."

China and the Magazines

The influence of leading national magazines on American thinking about China is difficult to assess, but is certainly not inconsiderable. Viewpoints differ widely. The traditionally conservative *Saturday Evening Post*, for example, startled its readers one summer issue in 1964 with an editorial entitled "Let's Open the Door to China." [12] The mass circulation *Reader's Digest*, on the other hand, has featured articles by former Congressman Walter H. Judd warning against any softening of policy toward Communist China.[13] *Look, Life* and *United States News and World Report* have also taken an interest in China, from varying viewpoints. Of special importance in terms of influence are the news

[12] *Saturday Evening Post*, July 25/August 1, 1964.
[13] See, for example "Keep Red China Out," *Reader's Digest*, November 1964.

magazines *Time* and *Newsweek*, primarily because so many busy Americans rely on their capsulated reporting as a primary source of information and guidance on international affairs. What they say about China week in and week out undoubtedly carries a considerable impact, for better or worse, on a highly influential segment of the population.

CHAPTER NINE

China in Our Schools
and Universities

Millions of Americans have grown to adulthood without even elementary instruction in the geography, the history, the politics or the culture of China. In this educational neglect, surely, lies one of the root causes for the apathy and ignorance on China so commonplace in the United States. We have watched the upsurge and felt the impact of great changes and powerful new forces without clearly understanding what lay behind them. We have lacked the background knowledge on which to base sound judgments. Small wonder that our emotions have so often taken mastery over our insufficient comprehension.

This is a kind of problem, of course, that is not related solely to China. In recent years, all of Asia, Africa and Latin America seem suddenly to have sprung to life. We were not prepared for this. For generations our schooling in foreign affairs had been geared to the history and culture of Europe, as if that were all that really mattered, as if all else were peripheral. A more balanced presentation of history would have taught us that from the very beginning of the United States as a nation our fortunes and destiny have been closely linked also to the Far East. Dr. Chitoshi Yanaga, a Yale scholar, notes:

Had it not been for the tea brought from China by the British and sold to the American colonists, there might not have been any Boston Tea Party and the chain reactions which followed. Had it not been for the incredibly lucrative trade with China that began with the end of the War of Independence and was carried on by the New England clipper ships, the struggling new nation could not have possibly lifted itself out of virtual bankruptcy and gotten on its economic feet; the great seaports of the Atlantic Seaboard would not have prospered; New England fortunes would not have been created. Nor could the Northwest Pacific fur trade of John Jacob Astor have flourished to make him one of America's earliest millionaires.[1]

Dr. Yanaga goes on to point out that the lure of the China trade was a major factor in hastening the building of our transcontinental railroads and that Horace Greeley's admonition to young men to go West was indirectly tied to the quest for the riches of Asia. He points also to the role of Chinese labor in the building of the Union Pacific and Western Pacific railroads and the effects of Chinese and Japanese immigration on the political and economic development of California and, for that matter, on the foreign policy of the United States.

These are a few of the early instances of Asian impact on the United States which have not always received the attention and emphasis they deserve. But there are, of course, many other and even more obvious reasons why we can ill afford to remain in ignorance of the history, culture and characteristics of a dynamic people who make up more than one-fifth of mankind. The uniqueness of Chinese civilization, the fact that it developed largely in isolation from our own and has influenced at least as many people, the many original contributions it has made in the fields of science, human relations, government organization, art, literature and philosophy—all of these make some knowledge of China an indispensable part of the equipment of an educated American. We have much to learn *about* and *from* China, enough, indeed, to add a whole new dimension to our thinking. For a people steeped, as we are, in the "Confucius say" concept of Chinese philosophy, the world of Chinese thought offers an exciting field for study and exploration—as increasing numbers of serious-minded young Americans are discovering. Professor H. G. Creel, an authority on ancient China at the University of Chicago, commented a few years ago: "I have been told by more students than

[1] Chitoshi Yanaga, "Needed: Emphasis on Asian Studies," *The Independent School Bulletin* (Milton, Massachusetts), November 1959, pp. 1–2.

I could estimate that their contact with Chinese thought was the *most stimulating single intellectual event of their lives.*" [2]

Although his specialty is ancient China, Dr. Creel is no less concerned with China today. He said that of all countries lying entirely outside the orbit of Western culture, China poses the most urgent problems for the present and the foreseeable future. He continued that "for Americans to continue in ignorance of China is not only benighted but perilous. To say that any institution of higher education worthy of the name cannot afford one faculty member who devotes his time wholly to China is indefensible."

The necessity for a broadened outlook on world affairs and for a sharper focus on non-Western cultures in our schools and universities is now widely recognized in American educational circles. Significant headway has been made toward filling this gap in recent years, yet it would be presumptuous to suggest that what has been accomplished is more than a good beginning.

The High Cost of Ignorance

Public ignorance of China has been of two principal kinds: (1) ignorance of its history and culture; (2) ignorance of the nature of Chinese communism. The two shortcomings are, to be sure, interrelated, for Chinese communism can be understood only in the historical context. And both deficiencies have cost us dearly—the first because it has left us easy prey to propaganda, dangerous myths and false assumptions, the second because our failure to understand Chinese communism (or Maoism) led us into miscalculations and dubious decisions. But for our deficiency of information and knowledge, the sudden collapse of traditional China and its takeover by the Chinese Communists might not have taken us so by surprise.

Formal education is, to be sure, no guarantor of correct conclusions and decisions on a problem as complex and involving so many questions of national interest as our China policy. China

[2] H. G. Creel, "Chinese Culture and Liberal Education," *Journal of General Education*, v. 12, no. 1, January 1959, p. 34.

studies and academic debate have often trailed behind the fast-changing China situation. Yet the desirability of a wider dissemination of basic knowledge on this and other "neglected" areas of the non-Western world is self-evident. For well over a century, Americans had direct contact with China through missionaries, businessmen, diplomats and scholars, and the store of expert knowledge built up by them over the years is truly impressive. What is unfortunate is that so little of this vast fund of available information has reached the general public through educational channels.

Asian studies in the popular sense are quite new in the United States, and the number of educated Americans who possess sufficient knowledge of China and the inner nature of Chinese communism to appraise current happenings in China with reasonable accuracy is disturbingly small. Until recently, China was a field mainly for specialists. Only a few of the leading universities had sufficient resources, qualified personnel, or, indeed, interest to undertake Asian study programs. It was quite common—even usual—for an American youth to run the full gamut of primary school, high school and university without ever being exposed to any knowledge of the world's "other half" except in the most superficial terms.

World War II forced a change in this casual attitude toward Asian studies—first by revealing our insufficient knowledge of an area in which we were fighting a major war, second by creating a sudden need for interpreters, translators and persons knowledgeable in Asian matters. The acute shortage of Asian experts made it necessary for the military services to launch crash language training and military government programs, which gave many institutions of higher learning an interest and incentive in Asian studies that they had not had before. Large numbers of young people got their first exposure to Asia in these quickie courses, and most took to them enthusiastically. Later, with the benefit of direct experience in the field, some returned to the universities and colleges for further study and became specialists and teachers in their own right.

Thus, postwar progress in the field of China studies got off to a good start, only to be slowed down, in the early fifties, by the drying up of the G.I. influx and the damaging consequences of the Communist takeover in China and McCarthyism at home. Americans were excluded from the China mainland; and in the United States the academic community was attacked from without and shaken from within on the China issue. The anti-Communist hysteria of that period, of which Senator McCarthy was a symbol, left deep wounds. Scholars of outstanding reputation in the China field were held up to ridicule as "Reds," "revisionists," even traitors, because of their antipathy to Chiang Kai-shek or their disposition to favor recognition of Communist China. The McCarran Committee's hearings on the Institute of Pacific Relations[3] were particularly disruptive. Exposure of undue leftist influence in the IPR was both an embarrassment and a blow to Asian specialists in this country. Moreover, with experts testifying against experts, the McCarran hearings laid bare a schism between so-called liberals and conservatives within the scholarly establishment.

It is difficult for anyone outside the academic community to comprehend the disquieting repercussions of the McCarran hearings among Asian scholars. For two decades, from 1925 to 1945, the IPR had been the leading American organization promoting the serious study of Asia. Besides publishing the periodicals *Pacific Affairs* and *Far Eastern Survey*, it had organized international conferences, teacher-training programs and research projects. It had published scores of serious books on the Far East. The final and fatal blow to the organization came after the hearings, when the U.S. Treasury Department withdrew the IPR's status as an institution qualified to receive tax-exempt contributions. This, of course, closed off all foundation and corporate gifts, on which the organization had been heavily dependent. The IPR won back its tax-deductible status several years later after a bitter court battle in which prominent lawyers, scholars and businessmen rallied to the support of what they considered an important civil-rights principle. But the damage had been done, and the publica-

[3] *Institute of Pacific Relations,* Hearings before the Subcommittee to Investigate the Administration of the Internal Security Act and Other Internal Security Laws of the Committee on the Judiciary, U.S. Senate, 82nd Cong., 1st sess. (Washington, D.C.: GPO, 1951–52).

tion *Pacific Affairs* (now edited and printed in Canada) is all
that survives of a once vigorous and influential organization.

The Reluctance to Speak Boldly

In my interviews with academic people across the country, I
found that while inhibitions stemming from the McCarthy period
have greatly faded, many scholars of liberal inclinations are still
timid about taking a strong stand publicly on China issues.

"When you have been burned once, why ask for it again?"
said one who was singed rather badly in the early fifties. Others
explain their silence with the observation that in the absence of
a national debate nothing they say is going to make any difference. So what is the use, they ask, in stirring up a hornet's nest?
There are some who admit that their thinking has moderated
with the years. A China scholar whose name was much in the
headlines during the McCarthy era remarked in an interview:

My attitude has undergone some changes. Until the end of 1957, I
tended to feel that the Chinese Communists were being fairly clever
in their handling of the economic situation. But the attempted Great
Leap Forward was so inexpert that it became apparent these people
were capable of great blunders. It had been thought, also, that they
would be fairly expert in the international field. But recent actions
against the Soviet Union and efforts to seize control of the revolution
look rather like stupidity. They are not as clever as we thought. Yet
I have not changed my views on U.S. policy. My feeling has been
from the beginning that in Communist China you have a great country
that is going to be a big force. In such circumstances things like embargo, isolation and so forth just don't make sense. We should put
Communist China in the same category as the Soviet Union and Albania, re-establish contacts even if we don't like the shape of the government. Our present policy leaves us isolated in east Asia. We have
no international support on Quemoy or Formosa. Some day, Chiang
is going to die, and the roof will fall in on us in Formosa. If the
situation shifts, you want to be in a position to take advantage of
the shift.

In a Midwestern university situation in a conservatively
minded community, I met a young professor of Asian studies
who not only favored prompt normalization of our relations with

Communist China—in return for reciprocal concessions—but did not care who knew it. More than that, he felt it his duty to spell out his views from the lecture platform whenever the opportunity offered. Things have not been too easy for him.

For the past 10 or 15 years, the situation has been such that a man talking about China has to start each speech almost with a loyalty oath. I am called upon to clear myself several times a year. Fortunately, this is a private institution, so we are not subject to the State legislature. Who is responsible for this absurd situation? It is easy to blame right-wing organizations, but my feeling is that the primary responsibility rests with my colleagues of the academic profession. If they would speak out frankly on China, I think we would see a change of public opinion, at least in the urban areas. But we are living in an era of academic luxury. Professors are no longer marginal people. We are making good salaries. We are very comfortable. We do not want to stir up trouble.

Time has softened the animosity between the conflicting China camps in intellectual ranks, and there has been some modification of views on both sides. But memories of past feuding and harassment still rankle. Those who are called conservative because they tend to go along with the *status quo* in our China policy complain that they have sometimes had cavalier treatment, amounting to intellectual ostracism, from the liberal majority. Here are some recollections and impressions from a well-known authority on Asian affairs:

The division among the China specialists began to develop during the war. For example, there was the issue of what to do with the Japanese emperor. Those who advocated keeping him were regarded as reactionaries. We wound up the war with our friendship unbroken, but with latent differences. Emotionally, the attitude of the liberals was based on a dislike for Chiang Kai-shek. This prepared them to accept the Communist line. Ill feeling grew, and the academic world went through a bad time in 1947–48 and during the McCarthy period. The liberals held the majority and the power and presented their case as if they were the injured parties. Nobody is as gifted in character assassination as the liberals. At that time, anybody not in favor of recognizing Red China was regarded automatically as a fascist. Many of the liberals, though strongly anti-Communist, are unwilling to do homework that might give them a true understanding of the nature of communism. This is their big weakness.

The professor who spoke these views has himself gone through some change of thinking on China. Although opposed to recognition and admission to the United Nations at this stage, he does favor more communication through an exchange of newspapermen and scholars. And he would like trade, under the right conditions. "I formerly favored a complete boycott," he said. "But we have not been able to develop one. I formerly felt we should make the Russians pay for the Chinese. Now that's impossible. So I see no reason why we shouldn't trade with them, if we use trade as a means of obtaining political concessions from them."

In general, the academic community prefers not to wash its linen in public, and most of the attacks on academic liberalism on China have come from outside sources. One such is contained in a book entitled *The Red China Lobby*, jointly authored by Forrest Davis and Robert A. Hunter. This violently partisan volume denounces as "revisionist" those liberals who want a change in U.S. policy toward China and refers acidly to the attitudes of the academic community in general:

The university professors who steadfastly enjoin us to indulge Red China constitute a fraction of the faculties throughout the country. Yet the professors who defend the China policy are but a fraction of that fraction. The refusal of the academic punditry to appraise the Great Confrontation according to the interest of our society and Western culture is a symptom of the deep malaise that afflicts the Western intelligentsia.[4]

In light of the bitter wrangling that followed the collapse of Kuomintang China and the closure of mainland China to Americans, it is hardly surprising that interest in China studies fell off appreciably in the early 1950s. There were some gains in the academic field, but there were also setbacks. A west coast professor lamented: "It was almost a lost generation; it was as if we had washed our hands of the world's most populous country." Not until the middle fifties did this psychosis begin to wear off. Interest in China studies picked up as they regained some of their old respectability.

[4] Forrest Davis and Robert A. Hunter, *The Red China Lobby* (New York: Fleet Publishing Corporation, 1963), p. 167.

Recent Expansion in China Studies

A series of developments in the late 1950s gave great impetus to research on China and to Asian studies generally. A small company of scholars had led the way for this upsurge through the careful groundwork they laid in the prewar years. Also deserving of recognition is a much larger band—trained mostly at Harvard, Columbia or California before the war—who, after the war, came into leadership in those graduate centers that have provided the basis for the great expansion of the late 1950s and early 1960s.

The remarkable transformation of the last few years can be attributed to three principal developments: (1) an increased outpouring of funds for China studies from the big foundations—notably Ford, Rockefeller and Carnegie; (2) the enactment, in 1958, of the National Defense Education Act (NDEA), which authorized the establishment of language and area centers throughout the country and provided funds for the teaching of "uncommon" languages, including Chinese; (3) the creation, by China scholars, of a joint Committee on Contemporary China to stimulate research on modern China.

The role of the Joint Committee on Contemporary China has been particularly significant, though little publicized. The Committee was born at a meeting of China specialists called together at Gould House, Westchester, in 1959, on the joint initiative of three well-known China scholars. Present were about twenty experts, who represented conflicting points of view in the China controversy. All were agreed on the urgent need for a special committee to encourage and activate more research on present-day China, but old animosities made it difficult to agree on the proper sponsorship. However, a proposal for putting the proposed committee under the neutral joint auspices of the Social Science Research Council and the American Council of Learned Societies proved acceptable to all factions. Thus, formation of the Joint Committee had the happy result of bringing together into one team a wide variety of points of view on China and China policy.

The Joint Committee has been instrumental in opening up

many new avenues of exploration in the long-neglected China field. With strong financial support from private foundations, individual scholars have completed or got underway dozens of detailed studies on various facets of the contemporary Chinese scene. A picture long blurred, even to the experts, is coming into focus, at least in its larger aspects. A founding member of the Committee told me:

We felt our first big job was to encourage specialists to increase their grasp on China. Since 1959, there has been a marked increase in the amount of money and the number of people involved in this effort. A number of universities have strengthened their staffs in China studies. Graduate students are emerging in increasing numbers. Formerly most of our centers of Far Eastern studies were concentrating on history and linguistics, with very little attention to the social sciences, political sciences, anthropology and other fields so important to an understanding of modern China. These fields are now getting more attention. Intensified research is producing more and more books of an informative nature on an expanding range of subjects.

John M. H. Lindbeck of the East Asian Research Center at Harvard has noted that perhaps the most significant single development causing American scholars to take account of China is "the tremendous shift of the social science disciplines into new fields." The social sciences are the academic sectors which tend to focus on contemporary events, and up until recently they had taken little account of Communist China. Now they are showing a lively, if delayed, interest in the country, including even its legal system, which they are subjecting to scholarly analysis.

Yet despite augmented research, there is still no early prospect of "catching up." Trying to keep pace with developments on the Chinese mainland in the face of Peking's secrecy, censorship and truculence has strained the ingenuity of political scientists, historians and other students of the Chinese scene. Unable to enter Communist China, these researchers are heavily dependent on newspapers, periodicals, books and documents shipped or smuggled out of the mainland. There is hot competition for rare items. Some American universities have managed to establish direct arrangements with the Peking National Library, the

Academia Sinica and other institutions on the Chinese mainland for an exchange of scholarly publications on various subjects. This requires a permit from the United States government, which is not difficult to obtain. Enough material has come through to impress American specialists with the quality of the research that is going on in Communist China in such fields as history, linguistics, archaeology and art criticism. But while the supply of material is more than adequate on some subjects, it is woefully deficient in others. I heard many complaints on this score, including this one from a professor in a southern California university:

My specialty is education, and my problem is to study the techniques used by the Chinese Communists in influencing the minds of the people. This is a matter of great importance. What is happening to the minds of the Chinese is surely more significant than what is happening to their stomachs. Yet we know a great deal about the food situation in mainland China, very little about the educational techniques. I have had extreme difficulty, for instance, in obtaining textbooks used by the Chinese Communists, especially grade school and college textbooks.

Another China specialist remarked: "Some important aspects of the China picture have been barely touched. For example, I know of only one manpower study dealing with Communist China, only one paper on the role of the sciences, very little on the social transformation that is going on inside the country. I have not seen a single good book on the military structure. Only a bare beginning has been made in the study of decision-making in Red China. The field for research is still enormous." [5]

In some areas the difficulty is plainly and simply lack of information; in others it is lack of qualified scholars to deal with the overwhelming quantities of information available. The attack on these problems is, of course, growing in intensity as our universities step up their output of China specialists. And it must be said that despite innumerable difficulties, including lack of access to Communist China, the United States has probably made

[5] In light of these comments, I should call attention to the other books to be published as part of the Council on Foreign Relations' series on The United States and China in World Affairs. These will cover most of the areas mentioned.

greater progress in the field of higher Chinese studies than other non-Communist countries, with the possible exception of Japan. The advance has been accelerated by improved facilities for collecting, cataloguing and translating available materials and making them more readily accessible to scholars who need them. The cooperation of the State Department and other government agencies has been invaluable.

Any American needing reassurance with respect to the standing of American scholarship on China needs only to examine almost any issue of the *China Quarterly*, the leading outlet for scholarly writings on that subject. Although the *China Quarterly* is edited and published in England, issue after issue shows a heavy preponderance of American contributors. This in spite of the fact that American scholars are denied the advantage enjoyed by most other nationalities of visiting the mainland.

Until the middle 1950s, China hardly figured in the curricula of our universities and colleges except as a subject for specialists, and usually at the graduate level. The past decade, however, has seen a notable growth in emphasis on non-Western studies as a desirable, even necessary, part of any liberal education. This quiet revolution has brought Asia (and particularly China) into the sphere of undergraduate education in a far bigger way than was imaginable a decade ago. Major universities like Harvard, Columbia, California, Chicago and Michigan—each with well-established Asian study centers—led the way in this development, but many others have taken it up, either with Asia "programs" or simply by the addition of one or more courses to their undergraduate offerings.

The benefits of exposing young Americans to some knowledge of the larger world of which we are now so unavoidably and inextricably a part have been touched upon in previous pages. Comparative study of the Chinese and other great civilizations not only gives us valuable insights into our own culture but serves also as an antidote for patronizing and superior attitudes which, all too often, are the by-products of our ignorance. Thus, by improving our understanding of Asian peoples, we improve, in a sense, their understanding of us. Another of the more important consequences of introducing China to college undergraduates lies in the interest it may stir in some young minds in the possibility of making Asian studies a specialty and a career. Students who might not have had any contact with this fascinating field until late in their college career—or even after graduation—now encounter it at a stage when there is still time to make a choice.

It will be some years, at best, before Asian (or non-Western) study programs are generally adopted in liberal-arts colleges across the land. Difficulties abound—including lack of qualified instructors, lack of financial resources, competition of other fields of study and, at times, lack of interest. But striking changes are in progress and, no doubt, will continue.

In some cases where individual colleges have lacked the resources to start programs of their own, they have pooled their resources with other nearby colleges and offered instruction in Asian and other non-Western subjects on a cooperative basis. Earlham and Antioch colleges provide an example of just such an arrangement. Amherst, Smith and Mount Holyoke Colleges and the University of Massachusetts are also taking a cooperative approach. Bryn Mawr, Haverford and Swarthmore Colleges have a joint program on Asia. In Indiana, where there are more than thirty institutions of higher education, the problem of stimulating non-Western studies in the field of general education has been tackled by setting up a state-wide cooperative project, in which about half the colleges have been participating. Known as the Non-Western Project (and, by the facetious, as the "Un-American" Project) it provides counsel and other assistance in such matters as arranging faculty fellowships, faculty seminars, regional institutes, special consultants and televised lectures. This frankly experimental project aims at exposing student and faculty at all levels to some useful knowledge of the non-Western world. China, of course, figures prominently in the studies.

The new ferment is being felt, though to a lesser extent, even in our high schools, where there is increasing pressure for a rewriting of textbooks and revision of the social science curriculum to give pupils a more balanced perspective on the world in general and Asia in particular. Nationally, a good deal of the impetus for this reform has come from the National Council for the

Social Studies of the National Education Association. The Council's director, Merrill Hartshorne, has been pushing Asian studies, in the face of considerable apathy, for more than a decade.

No doubt some of the clichés, stereotypes and misconceptions on China which are so widely prevalent in this country can be traced to impressions gleaned from badly written textbooks on world history and from teachers devoid of any special knowledge on Asian matters. It is in the world history course, at about the tenth grade, that most American youngsters get their first schooling on China and Asia; and a very sketchy schooling it is. Too often, high school textbooks treat Asia as if it were some kind of three-ring circus in which many strange and entertaining things are happening but where, somehow, nothing seems very important compared to the triumphal march of Western civilization. Another difficulty is that very few of the teachers themselves have had much instruction, in college or afterward, in Asian subjects. A survey made in Kansas in 1956–57 showed that while 79 per cent of all world history teachers in Kansas high schools had completed courses in world history and 85 per cent in American history, only 9 per cent had taken any credit in Eastern and Asiatic history. Things were no better in New York, where Ward Morehouse, consultant in foreign area studies to the state of New York, reported in 1962 [6] that the average secondary school student probably spends less than 2 per cent of his time studying "about those regions of the world which contain a majority of its people and by all odds have experienced the greatest amount of human history."

Thanks in part to Mr. Morehouse's efforts, New York State has taken the lead in the broadening of public school education to include more study of non-Western peoples and cultures. This is not as simple as it sounds. It involves a thoroughgoing re-examination of the social studies curriculum in elementary and secondary schools, expanded facilities for teacher training, improved teaching material, and more and better textbooks. Teacher education, according to Mr. Morehouse, is crucial. Teachers

[6] *The International Dimensions of Education in New York State: A Summary View* (Albany: State Education Department, The University of the State of New York, 1962).

willing to attend summer institutes or regular university courses in Asian or other non-Western subjects are eligible to receive tuition grants from the state. Other states are active or interested in similar programs. Help in the field of teacher education has come from organizations like the Asia Society and the China Institute. The Asia Society, a nonprofit, nonpolitical organization based in New York, has a mailing list of 4,000 teachers and educators throughout the country to whom it supplies up-to-the-minute reference material on Asian subjects. It also assists in teacher-training programs at both the college and high school levels.

Help from the Foundations

Asian studies in our schools and universities would be in a less robust state today were it not for the financial encouragement provided by our leading foundations. The Rockefeller Foundation was the first to recognize the need, with a program of assistance that began in the early 1930s. It was a modest program but paid off handsomely during the war years when the specialists it helped train were to prove indispensable to the war effort. The Carnegie Corporation entered the field in 1947 and, like Rockefeller, helped leading universities to develop non-Western studies at a time when funds for such purposes were hard to find.

Since 1952, the Ford Foundation has been the principal private contributor to non-Western area and language studies. Its grants in this field have totaled approximately $70 million, while in the same space of time the Rockefeller Foundation has spent $5 million and the Carnegie Corporation $4 million for similar purposes. East Asian and China studies have been, of course, among the principal beneficiaries of these windfalls. The foundation grants have not only given great stimulus to graduate training and research, they have helped also, through fellowship awards, to train large numbers of teaching personnel for colleges and universities wanting to add Asia-related courses to their curricula. Government agencies have also recruited many of the specialists trained under these grants.

Substantial sums of foundation money have also gone into the field of China research and thus enlarged our store of basic knowledge on China and other non-Western areas. Among many outstanding grants in this field have been the following: $420,000 to Columbia University, for research on the political evolution of modern China; $277,000 to Harvard University, for research on the economy of China in modern times; $910,000 to the Social Science Research Council, for research on the economy of Communist China.

Washington Gives a Hand

It was not until World War II created a sudden and insatiable demand for specialists on China and other Asian countries that the United States government recognized the necessity for giving direct support to Asian language and area studies in this country. The crash program inaugurated in 1942 gave a big push to such studies, but the flow of federal money soon dried up after the war's end. Later, our increased international involvements created a new demand for experts and linguists and it became apparent that our schools and universities would require federal help if they were to cope with the situation. The National Defense Education Act of 1958 was, in part, a response to this need.

The effects of the NDEA have been felt, in varying degree, throughout the whole spectrum of China studies in the United States, from the graduate schools in our universities, down to our secondary schools. The Act understandably gave emphasis to language training. But another of its objectives was to encourage the "center concept" in higher education—that is, to promote establishment of programs of centers in which study of a particular non-Western civilization, such as China's, would be closely integrated with study of the language of that civilization. By 1964, fifty-five such language and area centers were receiving some federal support, of which eleven were concerned solely with East Asia. Centers of this kind are usually an expensive luxury for the university operating them. Hence the assurance of federal help quite often spells the difference between existence and nonexistence. This helps explain the fact that at least two-thirds of the language and area centers receiving NDEA support were established after the Act was passed in 1958. In those teaching Chinese, enrollments in Chinese language courses have more than quadrupled during this period.

Teaching Chinese in Our High Schools

Even our high schools are feeling the influence of this upsurge of interest in the study of China and the Chinese language. While the wheels grind slowly in the revision of world history textbooks, China has been brought dramatically into many high school classrooms through the introduction of Chinese language study. Abraham Lincoln High School in San Francisco was probably the first public school on the U.S. mainland to offer a course in Chinese. That was in 1952. But it is only within the past five years that the innovation has really taken hold. By 1965, the teaching of Chinese had spread to about one hundred secondary schools in cities ranging from Fairbanks, Alaska, to Boston, Massachusetts.

The spectacle of American youngsters scrawling complex Chinese ideographs on schoolroom blackboards is enough to convince wide-eyed parents that at last they have seen everything. Yet in the context of world affairs and our educational needs, the development is a perfectly logical one. Dr. Frederick H. Jackson of New York University, who has been closely associated with this development almost from the beginning, feels it is high time we gave more attention to a tongue that is spoken by one in five of the world's population.

"More people speak Chinese than any other language in the world," Dr. Jackson noted. "It is also the basis of the written language of 90 million Japanese and 30 million Koreans. Finally, Chinese is the linguistic key to one of the half-dozen greatest civilizations the world has produced, one much older than European civilization." [7]

To which we might add that an understanding of China is

[7] "Instruction in Chinese and Japanese in Secondary Schools," *The Annals of the American Academy of Political and Social Sciences*, v. 356, November 1964, p. 114.

vital to our national existence, and a knowledge of the language greatly improves the prospects for such understanding. Chinese has been one of the neglected languages in our universities and secondary schools. A knowledge of it is essential to advanced research in some branches of Asian study. Exposing younger students to it serves a two-fold purpose: it whets their curiosity about China, and it filters out those who are seriously interested in later specialization in Chinese studies and gives them a head start in preparation for it.

Teachers report that students often enroll in the Chinese language course more for novelty than for knowledge but later become fascinated by the language itself. A part of the learning process that students particularly enjoy is using a brush and inkpot to practice in Chinese calligraphy. Students' reactions to the Chinese language course are sometimes refreshingly unexpected, like this one, from a Thayer Academy student: "I feel extremely at home in the Asian wing of a museum, and this feeling is accompanied with a happiness of partially understanding another's culture. This is something I wasn't sure I'd find, but it is one of the unexpected rewards and one of the most delighting."

The financial push behind the high school language program has come mainly from the U.S. government (through NDEA), the Carnegie Corporation and the Ford Foundation, each giving support to a separate aspect of the program. Primary wants are adequately trained tearchers and properly prepared teaching materials. From the beginning, the movement has had strong support from the larger universities with a special interest in Asian studies. A pioneer in the language program was Thayer Academy in Boston, which, in collaboration with Harvard and Yale Universities, was instrumental in introducing Chinese language study to high school students in the Boston area. The students have shown surprising proficiency, and many have gone on to advanced study in universities and language institutes. Several who entered Harvard as freshmen were able to step immediately into the third-level Chinese course.

Institutes for training secondary school teachers in Chinese have been set up, with federal support, at San Francisco State Teachers College and at Seton Hall University, New Jersey. Other training programs are afoot elsewhere, and we now find Chinese being taught to high school students in such widely scattered centers as Chicago, St. Louis, New York, Los Angeles, Minneapolis, Pittsburgh, San Francisco, Fairbanks and Honolulu. And this is by no means a complete list.

Short Cuts to Language Learning

What is important in all this is that learning Chinese is no longer the formidable problem it once was. In the past (before World War II) the Chinese language could be studied in only a few American universities and never before the junior year. Learning it properly invariably involved time-consuming postgraduate study. Many a prospective specialist in China studies turned to something else rather than face the grueling business of mastering the language. The picture has changed enormously. Today, a student can begin learning Chinese in high school. Later, if he wishes to pursue the subject, he can enroll in one of more than fifty institutions of higher learning that offer instruction in the language. There are also many summer institutes to choose from; and for advanced training, there is Taiwan.

Even those who have not the benefit of high school language study can find short cuts. Dr. William Theodore de Bary of Columbia University, a leader in the promotion of Asian studies in American schools and universities, points out [8] that it is now possible for an incoming graduate student to telescope the equivalent of four ordinary "years" of Chinese or Japanese into fifteen months. This is made feasible through the use of intensive learning methods and summer study. It means that the student specializing in China can anticipate spending much less time in language study during his postgraduate years and much more time in interdisciplinary study of his chosen area of specialization. De Bary gives credit both to the foundations and the federal government for making these improvements possible.

[8] William Theodore de Bary, "East Asian Studies: A Comprehensive Program," in same, p. 65.

Teaching about Communism

We venture here into a highly contentious area, yet one which cannot be avoided if we are to do full justice to the role of education in shaping American attitudes toward China. It goes without saying that no true understanding of modern China is possible without some knowledge of the theory and practice of communism, particularly Chinese communism. Lack of such basic knowledge certainly has been a factor in our errors of calculation and decision in East Asia since World War II—for example, our tendency, during the Chinese civil war, to underestimate the Chinese Communists, our failure to foresee Chinese intervention in the Korean War. Mistakes of this kind might have been circumvented or minimized through a more serious study of communism *à la* Mao Tse-tung. Mao accommodated us by laying down in advance his strategy for revolution in China and "wars of liberation" abroad. While his forecasts have often been wrong and his tactics have fluctuated, his basic pattern has been followed. If knowing your enemy is a sound precept, Mao's writings should be "must" reading for any public official or private citizen who presumes to speak with authority on the China problem. Too often we have erred in dismissing as propaganda what to millions of indoctrinated Chinese is scripture.

For some years after the war, Americans were inclined to regard communism as a subject too distasteful or too "touchy" for close examination. We clung to the wishful notion that in China, anyway, communism would fail if we snubbed it. And anyone who ventured to examine and discuss communism objectively was regarded at best as peculiar and at worst as contaminated.

Examples are plentiful of the then-prevailing attitudes. A California professor who teaches a course in Chinese government and politics in which the nature of Chinese communism is explored asked his students, several years ago, whether they had had any unfavorable external relationships because of their study of communism. Half of the students raised their hands. One reported that his fraternity brothers were apprehensive that he would be checked by the FBI. Another said her father was concerned about the course. A girl reported that a bus driver had been insulting to her because she was carrying a copy of a book entitled *Communist China Today*.

These incidents and others like them represented, no doubt, a hangover from the McCarthy era, when carrying a book on communism could be construed as guilt by association. In those days it was "smart" to be ignorant insofar as communism was concerned, and the price we paid for that ignorance was underlined during the Korean War by the inability of some American boys taken prisoner by the Chinese to cope with Communist brainwashing techniques. The brainwashing revelation, though perhaps exaggerated in its implications, did a lot to impress on the American public the need to provide our youth with a broader education in competing ideologies, including Chinese communism.

"There has been a tremendous change in atmosphere on this matter since 1953–54," a professor of political science in a west coast university remarked. "In the early fifties I began teaching a course in Comparative Marxism. Some students said they would like to audit it but didn't want it on their records that they were studying communism. But by 1959 even the ROTC was asking me to teach it."

Today, in most parts of the country, it is no longer considered queer to attend classes in Communist theory and practice. Teaching about communism is in fashion in colleges and is "catching on" in public schools. As Dr. Rodger Swearingen of the University of Southern California has pointed out,[9] sex and communism are two things every student is going to hear about and wonder about sooner or later, and in both cases he is better off with the facts than with gossip and rumors. Dr. Swearingen believes that teaching about communism should begin in high school, preferably not as a special course but as part of a more general

[9] The references to Dr. Swearingen are taken in part from "Students Getting More Facts on Communism," *Los Angeles Times*, September 15, 1963, and in part from an interview.

course dealing with "problems of Democracy," or "World Governments," or the like. Since this is a subject that leaves no room for amateurism or irresponsibility, Swearingen considers teacher-training as all-important.

Up to this point most educators would go along with Dr. Swearingen. But from here on, in such questions as program content, teaching methods and choice of textbooks, we encounter profound differences of opinion among educational authorities. Teaching about communism is still a new and rather experimental development, especially in high schools. And the subject is so sensitive politically and so full of booby traps that the selection of teachers, textbooks and methods of approach is often a cause for much agonizing and acrimony among school authorities and the public. The basic problem is how and where to draw a line between serious study of the subject and resort to propaganda.

A number of state legislatures have passed laws or resolutions requiring teaching about communism, but this mixing of politics with what is essentially an objective educational need has not often had satisfactory results. The General Assembly of Georgia in 1962 adopted a wordy resolution requiring short courses of instruction in all high schools, colleges and universities in the state on the subject of Americanism vs. Communism. The resolution stipulated that students must be shown by comparison of the two systems "why Communism and Socialism are evil and vicious, why they destroy the freedom, well-being, dignity and happiness of the individual, and why they are our implacable enemy, to the end that students will understand the propaganda and dishonesty of Soviet Russia, Red China and other apparatus and affiliates of organized communism and national socialism." [10]

Educational authorities in most states would prefer to devise methods of teaching about communism on their own, without "benefit" of legislative supervision. What is required, of course, is an approach that has general acceptance. Otherwise the temptation to yield to local pressures and to treat the subject in black-and-white terms will prove irresistible in some localities.

Speaking at the annual meeting of the Council of Chief State

[10] Senate Resolution 105, as passed in the Senate and House, 1962.

School Officers in 1962,[11] Dr. Richard I. Miller of the National Education Association said that complete objectivity on a subject as sensitive as communism is a myth and the goal should be intellectual honesty. In the same speech, he advanced a number of suggestions for improving the teaching about communism in this country. He pointed out that a stronger and more deeply rooted faith in the American way of life almost inevitably flows from a systematic, rational study of conflicting ways of life, including communism. But he was opposed to the black-and-white approach, which, in his words, amounts to "benevolent brainwashing" and "has no place in education for democratic citizenship where free inquiry and reasoned judgment are vital."

Dr. Miller felt that inadequately prepared teachers constitute the greatest obstacle to effective school programs about conflicting ways of life. He remarked that while the number of summer courses or seminars for teachers on the subject of communism is increasing year by year (there were about two dozen in 1962 in widely scattered states), the number is still "woefully inadequate."

Among influential national organizations which have taken an active interest in this problem are the American Legion and the American Bar Association, both with strong feelings on the need for a sharpened public awareness of the Communist danger. The American Legion collaborated with the National Education Association in 1962 in preparing a booklet containing guidelines for high school teachers on teaching about communism. This material has been widely distributed and rather extensively utilized. But some educational authorities have misgivings about its usefulness.

Even with guidelines, there remain such problems as finding properly qualified and suitably thick-skinned teachers and providing them with teaching materials and textbooks that will not be criticized either as dishonest or subversive. The textbook problem is particularly delicate, and I have heard complaints that some textbooks currently in use are "loaded." Nervous teachers

[11] *Teaching about Communism in the Public Schools*, an address to the annual meeting of the Council of Chief State School Officers, November 21, 1962, Miami Beach, Florida, mimeographed.

are likely to turn to books like J. Edgar Hoover's *A Study of Communism*,[12] as being at least "safe."

At the university level, teaching about communism is less subject to outside pressures than in the high schools. But even there, it has been difficult to develop a sophisticated approach. For most students, a catch-all political science course in world ideologies or comparative governments is about the extent of the exposure to the study of communism in its various manifestations. But some are stimulated to go on into deeper study of individual countries—for example, Communist China. China specialists tend to be skeptical of the value of courses devoted solely to the study of communism. They point out that a full understanding of Chinese communism can be acquired only by studying it in the perspective of Chinese history. As a leading China scholar remarked to the writer: "Mao owes as much to Confucius as he does to Lenin, and both consequently have to be taken into account when studying Mao." The problem of how best to blend the old and the new in Chinese history and in what quantities is a problem our graduate schools are still struggling with. An authority on Asian studies in an Eastern university put it this way:

The difficulty is that there is an extraordinarily seductive quality about Chinese history and civilization. Once the young student is exposed to this history, he often does become very excited by it and is led into a whole new field of knowledge which can increasingly take him away from matters that are relevant to an understanding of contemporary China. Time after time, we have had young people come to graduate school with the intention of studying Communist China, but once they got into Chinese history, they seemed to drift away from the modern periods and went into the earlier periods because of the inherent interest and novelty of it all. This of course has meant not only a decline in the study of contemporary China but also a strengthening of the tendency to romanticize traditional China and China in general.

[12] *A Study of Communism* (New York: Holt, Rinehart and Winston, 1962).

The Summing-up

To recapitulate. There is a new awareness of China in our schools and universities, a new emphasis on Asian and non-Western studies, generally, at all educational levels. There is also a growing realization of the necessity of promoting more teaching about communism as an essential to understanding countries like Communist China and the Soviet Union.

Concerning China, the main concentration of effort up to now has been in the field of graduate study and research. This is as it should be, for there are big gaps in our basic information on modern China which only the specialists can fill. As the corps of experts grows, as the stockpile of information increases and as teacher-training programs expand, knowledge of China will spill over, increasingly, into the other levels of our educational system.

The process is well started. Taking the academic establishment as a whole, one finds that China studies are still an unusual feature of undergraduate education—but rapidly less so. The ever-widening interest is being felt also, to some extent, in the high schools. In the field of Chinese language study, particularly, the advance has been striking.

We are still in the first mile, however, of an arduous educational journey. There are still not enough China specialists to deal even with the information on China that is available, though many are in the making. The preparation of textbook and teaching materials on modern China is lagging, and teachers well qualified in Asian subjects are far from plentiful. Teacher-training is vital to the expansion program and is being encouraged in many ways.

What about our young people? To what extent are they interested in China, and what are their attitudes? I put such questions to faculty members in universities and colleges and got a variety of answers. As might be expected, the degree of interest varies from institution to institution, depending on the amount of exposure to the subject, but the usual condition is apathy. This is hardly surprising. Most students, after all, enter college devoid of any knowledge of China beyond what little they have picked up from the headlines of their hometown newspapers. Such feeling as some of them may have is more likely to be motivated by cold war considerations than by any particular interest in the country and its people.

A professor on the west coast told me that he finds students less knowledgeable but more open-minded on the subject of China than the college generation of a decade ago. Students of ten years ago could hardly have avoided knowing something about the Communist takeover of China, the Korean War and the activities of Senator McCarthy and many of them, no doubt, would have had some emotional involvement in the matter. Today, our universities are receiving students who have no recollection of the Chinese civil war or the Korean War and who were untouched by the emotional upheaval that followed. Such young people tend to have a detached attitude on China.

Several professors commented on this state of mind. A California instructor said: "They don't have fixed ideas on whether we should recognize Red China or not." Another, at a nearby university, remarked that students often ask why we don't go ahead and recognize Peking—that is, until they go into the question. And an Oregon professor made this observation: "Students don't seem to have strong opinions but tend to think it foolish not to recognize China." At a university situated in a strongly conservative community in Texas, however, it was apparent that student viewpoints had been influenced to some extent by parental feelings. A professor of political science in that institution told me that he found student attitudes "generally hostile" to the Chinese Communists—"but curious." Strong student attitudes for or against American policy toward China are most likely to be found on campuses where conservative youth groups or groups of the so-called New Left are unusually active.

Interest in China is easily aroused if students are given opportunities for contact with the subject. As yet, however, few liberal-arts colleges or universities provide such opportunities on a significant scale. A professor in a Midwestern university who teaches a postgraduate course on politics and government in Communist China complained that he has to spend half the term giving his students a basic preparation on traditional China. This wouldn't be necessary if suitable background courses were provided in the undergraduate curriculum.

A further reason for student indifference to China is the impression that with mainland China closed to Americans, Chinese studies offer little promise of leading to a satisfying or gainful career. Certainly the prospects are mixed, but it is possible to be over-pessimistic, as is probably the case with a professor in a large Midwest university, who said to this writer:

I tell my students that China is the burial ground of many a fine career and will continue to be. Why? Well, for one thing, the effects of the McCarthy period are still being felt, and anybody working in the field is liable to be criticized if he is not careful. Secondly, I can see no detente in Sino-American relations that will open up China for us. I warn my students of these dangers, but I tell them that at least they will find China a fascinating subject.

Fascinating, yes. But extremely complex. Complex enough to scare off many an interested college student if, as is often the case, he does not come in contact with the subject until late in his career. Career possibilities, though limited, are more numerous and rewarding than is generally supposed, notably in such fields as research, teaching, government service and business.

PART FOUR

Public Attitudes and U.S. Policy

CHAPTER TEN

Congress, the Administration and the State Department

United States policy toward China is a product of the interplay between the administration, the Congress, public opinion and various pressure groups. It has remained unchanged, except in superficial details, since the termination of the Korean War. Yet the mood of the public has not been entirely static. Soundings of public opinion taken in connection with this study and spelled out in earlier chapters indicate that while the American people are still basically committed to a firm policy toward Communist China, there is more elasticity in their outlook than commonly supposed.

Why has there been no serious effort to translate this beginning of change in the public mood into the actuality of a more realistic official approach to the China problem? Why no more serious attempt at restudy or re-evaluation of the present official line? There are many reasons, but several stand out: first, a kind of congressional paralysis, based on the assumption that any suggestion of change would provoke a hostile public reaction; second, the reluctance of the administration and of influential private groups to take the initiative in encouraging a new look at the China situation; third, the quite evident conviction of a large sector of Congress that our present policy is right and offers the only acceptable choice under existing circumstances.

China policy did not become a contentious political issue in this country until near the close of World War II. Until then

Republicans and Democrats had found little to quarrel about, and the approach had been largely bi-partisan. But beginning in 1943, interparty acrimony set in and built up steadily through controversy after controversy until, by 1949, bi-partisanship on the China issue had largely disappeared. It does not take a long memory to recall the emotion-charged climate of the period. The Stilwell recall, the visit to China of Henry Wallace and his strangely assorted entourage in 1944, the ill-fated Marshall mission, the Wedemeyer report, the dispute over economic and military aid to the faltering Nationalists—these and other politically loaded developments whipped up party antagonisms.

It was a time of frustration, bitterness and ugliness, of mud-slinging, skeleton-rattling and name-calling. Who was responsible for the "loss" of China? This was the question of the day. The Republicans made every effort to pin the blame on the Truman administration. They charged the Democrats with selling out Manchuria to the Soviet Union, betraying the Chiang government to the Chinese Communists, and withholding from the Nationalists critically needed military aid previously authorized by Congress. The wrangling grew in intensity until after the outbreak of the Korean conflict; it reached a high-water mark of bitterness during the presidential election campaign of 1952.

Meanwhile, the Nationalist collapse, the insulting hostility of the Peking regime, McCarthy's disquieting though enormously exaggerated "revelations" of Communist infiltration at home and, above all, the blood-letting in Korea helped to stir a nationwide feeling of revulsion and bitterness toward the Chinese Communists and of distrust and antagonism toward those in this country who sympathized with them. It was, understandably, a period of deep national anger in which persons with moderate and conciliatory views on China kept their silence because they knew that to speak up would mean being labeled "pinkos" or appeasers.

Congress also was in accord with this mood; and the policy fashioned by John Foster Dulles was a natural outgrowth of it. Both major parties gave their support to the Dulles policy. No one arose to challenge it, and few have challenged it since. Meanwhile, though the Asian and world situations have changed considerably, our China policy has changed hardly at all.

As a nation and as individuals we are only now emerging from the trauma produced by the China upheaval of the late forties and the Korean conflict that followed. Clearly the climate for public discussion of the China problem has been improving; it is possible to debate controversial aspects of the problem with more candor than was the case only a few years ago. Yet it is equally apparent that many of the inhibitions generated in the years between the middle forties and the late fifties are still with us. The nagging fear of the "pro-Communist" smear mutes many voices. In talking about China with opinion leaders around the country one cannot but observe that very often there is a marked difference in emphasis between a man's public and private views on this subject.

What is being said here is in no sense an attempt to argue for or against present United States policy toward China. We seek only to underline the fact that in the many years since that policy was formulated it has not been put to the test of a thoroughgoing public re-examination. The responsibility for this immobility on what is perhaps the gravest foreign policy problem of our time is attributable in large part to the inaction of Congress and the administration. It must be shared, however, to a significant extent, by influential citizen groups and the press, which have shown equal timidity in facing up to the issues. There are those, to be sure, who are so completely satisfied with the *status quo* that they would resist even a discussion of the pros and cons of our policy as it stands for fear of "rocking the boat." There are others who have misgivings yet see no alternatives in the light of the unremitting hostility and intransigence of the Chinese Communists. But, as our surveys indicate, there are millions of Americans who have only a vague comprehension, or no comprehension at all, of the issues at stake. Plainly, both the American public and government would benefit from a full-scale review of a policy which has, with the passage of time, become a little shopworn, to say the least.

China and China Policy

It is natural for Americans to look to Congress to take the lead in debating and evaluating problems of transcendent national importance. Discussion of China, however, has tended to be more emotional than informative; and members of Congress are obviously chary about coming to grips with an issue so loaded with political dynamite. Yet there is probably no problem of international relations in which the American public is in more need of enlightenment. This need is made the greater by the extreme complexity of the China situation, which seriously limits public understanding of it.

The change from violent interparty discord on China policy in the late forties to the relative uniformity of view today is well illustrated by the tone of the rival party platforms since 1952. In that year, the China planks were in jarring disagreement.[1] The Republicans charged that the leaders of the Democratic administration

. . . required the National Government of China to surrender Manchuria with its strategic ports and railroads to the control of Communist Russia. They urged that Communists be taken into the Chinese Government and its military forces. And finally they denied the military aid that had been authorized by Congress and which was crucially needed if China were to be saved. Thus they substituted on our Pacific flank a murderous enemy for an ally and friend.

The Republicans then went on to promise to "end neglect of the Far East which Stalin has long identified as the road to victory over the West. We shall make it clear that we have no intention to sacrifice the East to gain time for the West." Moreover, they vowed to

. . . again make liberty into a beacon light of hope that will penetrate the dark places. That program will give the Voice of America a real function. It will mark the end of the negative, futile and immoral policy of 'containment' which abandons countless human beings to

[1] The 1952 Republican and Democratic platforms may be found in *The New York Times*, July 11 and 24, 1952.

a despotism and Godless terrorism which in turn enables the rulers to force the captives into a weapon for our destruction.

The Democrats, in contrast, maintained:

We are convinced that peace and security can be safeguarded if America does not deviate from the practical and successful policies developed under Democratic leadership since the close of World War II. We will resolutely move ahead with the constructive task of promoting peace.

They added, however, that "our military and economic assistance to the Nationalist Government of China on Formosa has strengthened that vital outpost of the free world, and will be continued." In 1956, the platforms were sweetly similar—indeed so much so as to be virtually interchangeable. Both parties declared themselves against recognition of Communist China and its admission to the United Nations. Even in 1960, when that liberal internationalist, Chester Bowles, had a big hand in drafting the Democratic platform, Democrats and Republicans both again supported a hard line toward China. In 1964 the China planks of the two parties were as follows:

(a) The Republican party

We are opposed to the recognition of Red China. We oppose its admission into the United Nations. We steadfastly support Free China.

Republicans reaffirm their long-standing commitment to a course leading to eventual liberation of the Communist-dominated nations of Eastern Europe, Asia and Latin America including the peoples of Hungary, Poland, East Germany, Czechoslovakia, Rumania, Albania, Bulgaria, Latvia, Lithuania, Estonia, Armenia, Ukraine, Yugoslavia, and its Serbian, Croatian and Slovene people, Cuba, mainland China, and many others.[2]

(b) The Democratic party

. . . We continue to oppose the admission of Red China to the United Nations.

We pledge unflagging devotion to our commitments to freedom from Berlin to South Vietnam. We will:

[2] *The New York Times*, July 13, 1964.

Encourage by all peaceful means the growing independence of the captive peoples living under Communism and hasten the day that Albania, Bulgaria, Czechoslovakia, East Germany, Estonia, Hungary, Latvia, Lithuania, Poland, Rumania and the other captive nations will achieve full freedom and self-determination.[3]

The renewal of bipartisanship on China reached its full flower in January 1955 with the adoption, by both houses of Congress, of the so-called Taiwan Resolution. This remarkable document authorized the President to utilize the armed forces of the United States in such manner as he might deem necessary to safeguard the security of Taiwan. It was adopted by nearly unanimous majorities in both houses of Congress—409 to 3 in the House and 85 to 3 in the Senate. What Congress was doing, in effect, was writing a blank check for the President on Taiwan. Not only did Congress thus abdicate some of its remaining control over China policy, but it also helped institutionalize that policy to such an extent that much of Congress' flexibility in dealing with the China problem was lost. And our commitments to Taiwan are still on the books.

Thus on the three major issues—recognition, admission to the United Nations and defense of Taiwan—Republicans and Democrats in Congress now find themselves standing on more or less common ground. In fact, however, there is considerably less harmony than meets the eye. In conversations with members of Congress one soon discovers that a fair number of them have private reservations regarding our present policy but feel that political expediency demands conformity with the majority view. Several have told me of their feeling that Congress is neglecting its duty in failing to re-examine and re-evaluate our China policy in the light of changing conditions in the Far East and the world. But politically (and inelegantly) speaking, most of them regard the China question as a can of worms which they would rather walk around than pry into. A number of the honorable members pointed out that there is almost no public demand for a change of policy at this time. So why stir up a messy public controversy? The first principle of a politician is to be elected or re-elected, and on this basis the less said about China the better.

[3] *The New York Times*, August 24, 1964.

As one said: "There is no political mileage in making an issue of the China question." Another remarked: "No congressman or senator was ever elected because of a stand he took on foreign policy—and particularly on China policy."

Even though the China issue has been, so to speak, swept under the congressional rug, it has remained politically sensitive; and every so often new developments in the international situation have smoked out frank expressions of congressional feeling. In 1957, for example, some senators became vocally indignant over the British government's decision to lower its restrictions on trade with Communist China. They urged the administration to re-examine American policy on this matter. Again, in 1958, China became a subject of congressional debate (and, in 1960, of political debate) when the Quemoy crisis provoked some sharp exchanges over the strategic importance of the offshore islands and the ambiguity of the American attitude regarding them.

In more recent years there have been scattered signs in Congress of increasing impatience over the inflexibility of our China policy and even isolated demands for its re-examination. These stirrings have been apparent in both Senate and House. For example, there was a noteworthy attempt to break the ice in 1959. In May of that year the freshman Senator from California, the late Clair Engle, made a bold speech from the Senate floor urging a revision of policy based on a calculated and realistic look into the future rather than on a reaction to the past. His recommendations did not go as far as recognition but urged (1) a serious effort to arrange an exchange of newsmen, (2) a relaxation of the trade embargo, (3) continued support of the Taiwan regime, but with the clear understanding that we would support no military adventures against the Chinese mainland, (4) àn international solution for the question of Taiwan's future status, and (5) high level talks with the Peking government on issues of substance. All talks, said Engle, should be on a *quid pro quo* basis and should be accompanied by continued military and economic vigilance against Communist expansion in the Far East.[4]

The speech drew laudatory comments from several of Senator

[4] Speech in the U.S. Senate, May 21, 1959. For the full text, see the *Congressional Record*, v. 105, pt. 7, pp. 8760–8762.

Engle's liberal-minded colleagues. Press reaction was mixed. A British periodical, *The Economist*, noted with some astonishment that Engle's careful plea for gradual revision went unmentioned in *The New York Times* and was relegated to page 7 of the internationally minded *San Francisco Chronicle*. But *The Economist* took the hopeful view that the speech might "mark the beginning of the end for that masterpiece of diplomatic immobility, the policy of the United States toward Communist China." [5] For once *The Economist*'s crystal ball was cloudy. The speech failed to spark the extended public debate that Senator Engle had hoped for. Two weeks later, a southern Democrat, Senator Robert Byrd, rose to defend current policy. And that was about the end of it, though the Engle speech was not without impact.

Later in 1959 the Senate Foreign Relations Committee let pass a new opportunity for public airing of the China policy question. The opportunity arose with publication of the so-called Conlon Report, an independent study of American policy in Asia, prepared for the Committee by a private research firm in San Francisco. [6] The China section of the report, written by Professor Robert A. Scalapino, of the University of California, reviewed the pros and cons of our current China policy and suggested alternatives. It recommended a step by step program of change, beginning with exploratory moves to test Communist China's willingness to coexist with us and following this up, if practicable, with a more dynamic, flexible and positive approach within the limits of our present commitments to the Taiwan regime and other friendly governments. Among the specific objectives sought would be an exchange of newspaper correspondents, withdrawals of Kuomintang forces from the offshore islands and international consultations on such questions as Communist China's admission to the United Nations, recognition of Taiwan as the "Republic of Taiwan," the seating of this Republic in the Assembly, and the enlargement of the Security Council to include

5 *The Economist*, v. 192, July 25, 1959, p. 221.

6 *Report on Asia*, Prepared at Request of the Committee on Foreign Relations, U.S. Senate, by Conlon Associates, Ltd. (Washington, D.C.: GPO, 1959).

India and Japan as permanent members, as well as China. "If feasible," the report added, "the United States would negotiate a treaty of commerce with Communist China, and if successful, this would be followed by *de facto* recognition." The authors of the report recognized the difficulty of obtaining acceptance for such a program but insisted that it formed "the only basis for any possible agreement among major elements within the free world."

The China section of the Conlon Report received a friendly reception from many academic people and others interested in a review of our China policy, but much of the press reaction was lukewarm or hostile. The Committee of One Million took after it hammer and tongs. Nevertheless, the report went through a number of printings. It had been expected that its release might be followed by public hearings in which controversial aspects of our China policy would be ventilated. The Foreign Relations Committee, itself, favored such hearings but was reluctant to hold them without at least the tacit approval of the Department of State. In the end it was decided not to proceed with hearings when it became apparent that the Executive Branch of the government was not willing to offer testimony on a voluntary basis. Thus the Conlon Report, like the Engle speech, passed into history as an interesting but somewhat futile intellectual exercise.

Congressional inertia on China continued until, on March 25, 1964, Senator J. W. Fulbright, chairman of the Senate Foreign Relations Committee, made a speech that gave fresh significance to the subject.[7] Senator Fulbright's speech was not devoted exclusively, or even primarily, to China, but it did touch on two of the more vulnerable aspects of our China policy: (1) its inflexibility and, (2) the shaky foundation of myths and misconceptions on which parts of it are based. He referred to the "elaborate vocabulary of make-believe" that had become compulsory in both official and public discussion of China. His remarks were in effect an appeal for a re-evaluation of policy and a more flexible approach. The big obstacle to a rethinking of policy, he said, is "the fear of many government officials, *undoubtedly well-founded*, that

[7] See the *Congressional Record*, v. 110, no. 56, pp. 6028–6034.

even the suggestion of new policies toward China and Viet-Nam would provoke a vehement public outcry."

The italics are our own. The words they emphasize deserve attention, for they contradict the view of some observers that congressional timidity on China is based largely on groundless fears of hostile public reaction. Senator Fulbright feels they are not groundless, and none of our national legislators is better qualified to speak with authority on this matter.

In his speech Senator Fulbright also said he did not believe the United States could or should recognize Communist China or acquiesce in its admission to the United Nations as long as the Peking regime maintained its attitude of implacable hostility toward this country. He added:

I do not believe, however, that this state of affairs is necessarily permanent. As we have seen in our relations with Germany and Japan, hostility can give way in an astonishingly short time to close friendship; and as we have seen in our relations with China the reverse can occur with equal speed. It is not impossible that in time our relations with China will change again, if not to friendship then perhaps to competitive coexistence.

It would therefore be an extremely useful thing if we could introduce an element of flexibility or, more precisely, of the capacity to be flexible, into our relations with Communist China.

To do this, said the Senator, would mean casting off the myths which clutter up our thinking. It would mean facing realities. It might even mean thinking "unthinkable" thoughts. And it is the responsibility of our national leaders both in the Executive Branch and in Congress to acknowledge and act upon these realities, even at the cost of saying things which will not win immediate widespread enthusiasm, he continued.

Senator Fulbright received more than 12,000 letters in response to his speech, a spokesman for his office told this writer. More than two-thirds of them were favorable.

The New York Times hailed the Fulbright speech as the opening of a great debate on foreign policy, and there was indeed a nationwide flurry of comment, both favorable and unfavorable, on this senatorial effort to open new ground. But the "great debate" soon fizzled out. Plainly, in the case of China anyway, neither the majority in Congress nor the general public shared Senator Fulbright's feeling of immediacy over our policy problem. Moreover, while Senator Fulbright has had much to say about the need for fewer myths and more flexibility in our thinking on China, he has not himself come forward with any notable recommendations for policy changes. It may well be that the Senator from Arkansas feels genuinely unable, at this juncture, to propose any satisfactory alternative to our present China policy. Or is it that Senator Fulbright, being a politician and being human, shares to some extent the caution of his congressional colleagues on this prickly subject?

Probably the most informative congressional hearings touching on China in recent years were those conducted in March 1965 by a subcommittee headed by Clement J. Zablocki (D., Wisconsin), in the lower house. The subject was the Sino-Soviet conflict.[8] The committee took testimony from a score of expert witnesses, including, besides Secretary of State Dean Rusk, many of the leading authorities on China and the Soviet Union in the United States. Among its findings was a recommendation that "at an appropriate time" consideration be given to the initiation of limited but direct contact with Communist China through cultural exchange activities, with emphasis on scholars and journalists. The committee took a negative attitude toward trade with mainland China but urged recognition of Outer Mongolia. Notwithstanding the very real significance of the committee's proceedings and findings, most newspapers gave the hearings only cursory attention; and congressional reactions were scanty.

We have been told that no representative or senator was ever elected because of a stand he took on China policy. It would be interesting to know whether any candidate was ever defeated because of such a stand. There have been two or three recent cases in which candidates with a particular interest, pro or con, in China policy have been beaten at the polls, but whether their interest in China played any significant part in the voting for or

[8] See *Sino-Soviet Conflict: Report on Sino-Soviet Conflict and Its Implications* by the Subcommittee on the Far East and the Pacific of the Committee on Foreign Affairs, House of Representatives, together with Hearings Held by the Subcommittee on the Far East and the Pacific, March 10, 11, 15, 16, 17, 18, 23, and 31, 1965 (Washington, D.C.: GPO, May 14, 1965).

against them is debatable. One such was the defeat of Dr. Walter Judd, long a missionary in China, in his bid for re-election to Congress from Minnesota in 1962. During his long and distinguished service in Congress, Dr. Judd was a consistently militant critic of the Chinese Communists and a staunch supporter of the Nationalist government. He was one of the organizers of the Committee of One Million. But he seems to have been much more the victim of gerrymandering and domestic issues than of his stand on China.

Charles O. Porter, a former congressman from Oregon, who was defeated in a bid for re-election in 1960 and again in 1964, was China-minded in quite a different way. He was highly critical of Chiang Kai-shek and openly advocated increased communication and trade with Communist China. His opponents said, "Porter wants to shake hands with Chou En-lai." Porter lost on both occasions. Certainly his views on China and Cuba were no help to him, but there were other issues that probably had more effect on the outcome of his campaigns.

Nor can we overlook the colorful case of Byron Johnson, who was elected to Congress from Colorado in 1958 but was defeated in his campaign for re-election in 1960. Discussing his experience with this writer, Johnson described himself as "the guy who thinks you ought to put the word 'candid' back into 'candidate.'" Johnson has a distaste for hypocrisy in politics. To use his words: "It is terribly important that people have the truth. Otherwise, there is no way to act honestly. If we act on the basis of a lie, we will live with the consequences of our act, whether we like it or not."

Johnson believes that many politicians are living a lie insofar as China is concerned. He thinks they have one view for the State Department and another for their constituents. When he was up for re-election, Johnson met the China question head-on: "I asked my audiences, 'Wouldn't it be better to negotiate?' I pointed out that we had a whole packet of issues that were negotiable. We should do something while we still had some trump cards. It was just possible that it would be better to have the Chinese in the UN than out of it."

Johnson's outspokenness on China worried even his friends.

"They would come up to me," he said, "and they would say, 'Byron, it isn't that you are wrong, but you shouldn't be saying this,' or 'Byron, you're ahead of your times.'"

When it was all over, Johnson, a Democrat, was well ahead of John F. Kennedy in his district, was one of the leading Democratic vote-getters, but had lost to his opponent by 35,000 votes. Some Democratic leaders in Colorado believe that Johnson's candor on China was a significant factor in his defeat. Johnson doubts it but admits that "it did have a lot to do with my public image."

Another political figure who found that taking a stand on China was in the end more of a liability than an asset was William F. Knowland, prominent publisher and former senator from California. When Knowland ran for governor of California in 1958 against Pat Brown, his opponents did a private "popularity" poll on him. They found that Knowland was being hurt politically by the label, "Senator from Formosa," which had been tied to him. Knowland lost the election, and this may have been one of the factors in his defeat.

The least that can be said is that taking a stand on China did not get any of these candidates elected. One can also cite instances in which a candidate has been elected in spite of a supposedly unpopular position on China. Quite a number of members of Congress who have refused to sign the petition of the Committee of One Million opposing admission of Communist China to the United Nations are consistently re-elected, despite the pressures to which they have been subjected. One such is Congressman John V. Lindsay of New York. In declining to put his name to the petition, he said he preferred to remain independent, did not want to be trapped in a fixed position. There was a move among Young Republicans to censure him. Yet he has won his elections by tidy majorities.

The truth is that a candidate's position on China is, more likely than not, but one of dozens of issues on which he or she is judged. And the weight given to it in an election is certain to vary greatly from area to area, depending on the political, educational, religious, even racial, composition of the population.

Experienced members of Congress recognize that the way

to win elections is to give first priority to the needs of the home folks. This "tend to the folks" psychology means that all too often senators and congressmen have neither the time nor the inclination to keep abreast of international or even national developments. Ignorance of China is a common phenomenon in both houses of Congress. "We hardly ever get down to a discussion of the China situation," said a congressman. "We talk around it. We seem proud of what we don't know." When we asked newspaper editors around the country whether they thought congressmen and senators could do more to improve public understanding of the China question, most said yes, but many doubted whether their elected representatives were sufficiently well informed to be of much help. One said: "The debates in Congress rarely indicate much knowledge, let alone reflection, on this subject. It's much easier to give 'em hell. More popular, too." Another complained that "our congressmen don't know much more (about China) than the rest of us, if as much." Several editors remarked that the best service the lawmakers could do for their constituents on China was to learn more about it themselves.

Fortunately, there are individuals in both houses who have made a speciality of foreign affairs, including several who are outstanding experts on China and the Far East. One such is Senator Mike Mansfield (D., Mont.) whose reports on conditions as he has found them in East Asia are shining examples of reportorial competence.

Many of our legislators have discovered that a pleasant and painless way of improving their comprehension of international affairs is to travel. Each year dozens of them take off on taxpayer-financed trips to the four corners of the earth. Most are Europe-oriented, but increasing numbers are heading for teeming Asia. The nearest approach of our legislative tourists to Communist China is invariably at Hong Kong, where, if they wish, they can drive to the border and see live Communists patrolling the customs barrier. There is also much they can learn in Hong Kong about developments on the other side of the bamboo curtain. But the counter-attractions of Hong Kong, with its fascinating streets, its exotic shops and its low prices, are hard to resist, and it is indeed a conscientious legislator who can hold fast to the dull business of fact-finding while there. Whether diligent fact-finders or not, the majority of these congressional travelers come home with an augmented understanding of international problems.

Talking to individual members of Congress one finds little disposition to criticize our China policy in public, regardless of the doubts some members may entertain privately. Most are convinced, on the basis of correspondence received, editorial opinion in their hometown newspapers and their own public opinion soundings that their constituents generally are opposed to any modification of our present tough policy toward the Peking regime. There are other reasons for congressional caution; one is the pressures involving China policy to which they are subjected. These pressures come in part from the Committee of One Million and its allies and in part from organizations of the extreme right with a special penchant for letter-writing. As one author observes: "A large part of the history of American foreign policy since World War I might be interpreted as a series of successful intimidations by pressure groups." [9] The applicability of this statement to the China situation is self-evident.

The fact is that most members of Congress have been maneuvered into a position where they are heavily committed on the China question through their affirmative votes on repeated resolutions opposing the admission of Communist China to the United Nations.[10] In the House, particularly, the introduction of such resolutions has been an almost annual occurrence. Frequently, also, similar declarations opposing admission have been attached as riders to important appropriations bills, particularly those relating to the State Department and the Mutual Security Act.

It can hardly be doubted that the primary purpose behind these resolutions has been to keep the members of Congress lined up in opposition to any drastic change in our China policy. The

[9] Robert Dahl, *Congress and Foreign Policy* (New York: Harcourt, Brace and Co., 1950), p. 54.

[10] See *Expressions by the House of Representatives, the Senate, and the Committee on Foreign Affairs That the Chinese Communists Are Not Entitled to and Should Not Be Recognized to Represent China in the United Nations*, a Publication of the Committee on Foreign Affairs, House of Representatives, 36th Cong., 1st sess. (Washington, D.C.: GPO, 1959).

success of the strategy is shown by the fact that, in the House at least, the resolutions are nearly always approved unanimously, or without recorded dissent. Such unanimity on political questions is common in totalitarian countries; it is rare in the United States. While there is no doubt that congressional sentiment overwhelmingly and sincerely opposes admission of Communist China to the United Nations, it stretches credulity to believe that the sentiment is as uniform as the votes have indicated. Political expediency is undoubtedly a factor—political expediency cleverly exploited by pressure groups.

A member of the House who declined to vote on the anti-admission resolution the last time around said: "The thing I resent about these resolutions is that we never have a real confrontation with the issue. It is your patriotism that is questioned. To prove your patriotism you are expected to vote 'Yes.' "

This view is challenged by a former congressman with a deep interest in China who contends that there has been more discussion on China in the House than is generally realized, although the press has largely ignored it. Such discussion, he said, has always wound up on the same note: that there is no alternative to present policy until Communist China changes its behavior.

A well-known political scientist, interviewed by the author, put the matter in this perspective:

Congress is frozen between the pressures of the right, on one side, and the failures of our China policy on the other. The situation now is in kind of a stalemate, where senators and congressmen are afraid to move because they take it for granted that any attempt to do so would bring adverse reactions from their constituents. Members of Congress are easily terrorized by a state of public opinion which is more or less fixed. There is no incentive for them to take the initiative in an unpopular direction. The administration is in much the same position.

Boxed in by pressures and commitments and, more particularly by Peking's intransigence, members of Congress are indeed in a poor position to modify their attitude toward China policy, even if so disposed. The few willing to criticize that policy make up a lonely company. Unquestionably there are those among the majority who have private doubts about some aspects of our policy and would like to see it at least reappraised. But they will continue to support existing policy and keep their doubts to themselves as long as they are convinced that neither the American public nor, for that matter, the Chinese Communists are interested in change.

The Question of Presidential Initiative

Clearly there is more flexibility on China in the Senate than in the House. Yet even in the upper chamber, the margin of "give" is relatively small. In these circumstances, with Congress entangled in its own web and inclined to follow rather than to lead, it is rather futile to expect effective initiative from Congress in respect to China policy. Time after time, I was told by persons inside and outside Congress that the initiative for a reappraisal of policy, when the time arrives for it, must come from outside, preferably from the President. This indeed would be in line with tradition. In the past nearly all significant policy moves relating to China have come from the Executive Branch. Here are some views on the subject:

A senator from a Western state: "There is no way for Congress to get out in front on the China issue. New initiatives have to come from the Presidency."

A writer and lecturer on political affairs: "When the time comes for policy to be modified, the lead will have to come from the President, in consultation with certain members of Congress. Without such leadership, Congress will not change its line."

A nationally syndicated columnist: "The general feeling is that this is a problem for the President. The question of China policy is too complex for the average person—too God-damned complicated."

A west coast exporter: "Congress today is nothing but a rubber stamp. Any change of policy has to come from the President. I think the public would go along with him."

A California professor: "The President should take the initiative in influencing public opinion. If the administration decided that improved communications with China were desirable, Congress would find a way."

Of those who had an opinion on this matter, there were few who dissented appreciably from the views expressed above, except that some felt critics of Congress were too harsh in their judgment of that body. One who knows Congress well said:

It is unreasonable to expect congressmen with a narrow political basis to take a lead in calling for a reassessment of China policy. Senators Engle and Fulbright exhibited far more guts, in my opinion, going as far as they did, than has been evident in the administration during this entire period.

Another knowledgeable Congress-watcher commented: "Congress follows, not leads, in foreign policy and has essentially a critical, even kibitzing, role."

But an academic specialist on China, in an Eastern university, took exception to this interpretation of the congressional role.

"It is my assumption," he said, "that the Executive is waiting for *Congress* to take the initiative for any change in the China policy. Does not the Congress in theory represent the popular sentiment? And how can an Executive that was trounced for its China policy by the Congress in 1950–54 be expected to take off on a new line not even sanctioned by its own party in Congress in 1964—especially given the treaty with Formosa? Congress in the past has often enough taken the initiative to the extent of passing resolutions categorically opposing any change in the China policy; it passed the January 1955 joint resolution (the Formosa Resolution) with remarkable alacrity. Why must it now wait for the Executive Branch, lacking all visible means of support, to strike out alone along a new path?"

This much is evident: neither the present administration nor previous ones have shown enthusiasm for taking the lead in any move for a thorough public airing of the pros and cons of our China policy. Even President Kennedy, who had indicated during his campaign for election that he would like to do something about China, failed to do anything about it during his tragically curtailed term of office. In a memorandum released early in 1960, before his election, Kennedy had said:

This is not a proper time for the recognition of Red China. In view of the Peking government's failure to free American prisoners, its aggressive designs and actions against Tibet and South Asia and its unwillingness to guarantee the integrity of Formosa, there is strong reason to withhold recognition. I feel there is merit in the view that China should not be allowed to 'shoot its way' into the U.N. and thence to recognition by the U.S. I do not see it as a moral issue primarily, but I do think we have every right to expect reciprocal benefits from such recognition. On the positive side, I believe it would be well if there were more open windows between the peoples of China and the peoples of the western nations. Some promising approaches to this end could be made by allowing the press and other private individuals greater latitude in visiting and reporting on China.[11]

Kennedy deeply felt the importance of China as one of the major international problems with which the United States would have to cope in the years immediately ahead. Prior to his election, during the Quemoy-Matsu flare-up, he displayed an interest in the "two-China" idea. There were indications that he hoped, after election, to make some move toward a re-evaluation of our China policy. But the President, too, functions in a political context. When, on assuming office, Kennedy came to realize the impressive strength of congressional and public support behind our present policy, his interest in reform cooled. China was not then an urgent issue, and the President needed all the help he could get from Congress on matters of higher priority. China could wait; and it did. Earlier in this chapter, we have noted how the Executive discouraged the Senate Foreign Relations Committee from holding public hearings on China policy at the time of the Conlon Report. There is little doubt that Kennedy always had China in the back of his mind as something that should be attended to when the right time came along. And this was certainly a view that was shared by his more liberal advisers. Yet there were times when he seemed to exaggerate the threat from China, almost as if to justify doing nothing about China policy.

With President Kennedy's passing, the prospects for any display of presidential initiative on China policy became problem-

[11] Quoted in Joseph G. Whelan, "The U.S. and Diplomatic Recognition; The Contrasting Cases of Russia and Communist China," *The China Quarterly*, no. 5, January/March 1964, p. 72.

atical. President Johnson seems less "China-minded" than was his predecessor, but his proved disposition to act boldly in international matters when he feels the national interest is at stake could yet produce some Executive surprises in the field of China policy.

China and the State Department

In Washington, most of the "heavy thinking" on China is done in the Department of State. Among its functions is keeping Congress and the Executive informed of significant developments relating to China; another is to recommend pertinent legislation or policy changes. A vague barrier of mutual suspicion, occasionally flaring into open acrimony, stands between Congress and the State Department. Congress has the capacity to block or sabotage foreign policy moves dear to the heart of the administration and over the years has often used that power. Hence State Department planners are likely to regard congressmen as people who are forever getting in the way of an intelligent foreign policy. Congress, for its part, tends to see the State Department as being constantly pushed by assorted "eggheads" in a more liberal and internationalist direction.

The State Department took a heavy beating from Congress during the McCarthy era, and today China remains a particularly sensitive issue between the two. For the present, however, there are no conspicuous differences between Congress and State on this subject, chiefly because the administration is not pressing for any alterations in our China policy.

Yet there have been stirrings. The much-scarred State Department, though still understandably gun-shy on the China issue, has made a strong recovery from the grievous hurts of the postwar years—so much so that it has even dared to put the old China policy under hard scrutiny and, without materially changing its substance, presented it to the public in a more modish garb. The occasion was the speech delivered by Roger Hilsman, then Assistant Secretary of State for Far Eastern Affairs, before the Commonwealth Club of San Francisco on December 13,

1963.[12] Great care went into preparation of Hilsman's address, which was the first significant public exposition of China policy in nearly a decade. Many of the China specialists in the State Department had a hand in it, and Dean Rusk, Secretary of State, gave it his blessing. The basic difference between the old Dulles approach on China and the new look, as delineated by Hilsman, was this: Dulles had said that communism on the Chinese mainland was a passing phase; Hilsman, reflecting the "new" thinking in the State Department, indicated that Communist China was probably here to stay. Forensically, this was a rather important distinction. It meant that the State Department had dropped its pose of waiting for a miracle in China and was prepared to open the door to improved relations with Peking on the basis of existing realities—provided, that is, that the Communist regime were to adopt a more reasonable attitude.

After the Hilsman address, China specialists in the State Department waited anxiously for the roof to fall in. Instead, the speech received favorable reactions from an overwhelming majority of the newspapers commenting on it. From China, predictably, came only ridicule and insults. Some in the State Department had hoped that in the wake of a favorable public response the administration might find an opening for a concrete gesture or two—to propose, for example, a lifting on both sides of restrictions on travel in the two countries. President Kennedy, had he lived, might have responded to the occasion, although the worsening situation in Southeast Asia made it problematical. In any case, his death put an end to these hopes for the time being.

Congress is inclined to be more conservative on China than the people in the State Department. In the words of a congressman: "The State Department is less concerned with what it thinks ought to be done about China than with what it thinks it can get Congress to approve." This, of course, is no more than a proper carrying out of its constitutional functions. Congress, to be sure, expects the administration to take the lead in policy matters, but in a way that will make its proposals palatable to

[12] For the full text, see *Department of State Bulletin*, v. 50, January 6, 1964, pp. 11–17.

the voting public. Sometimes, as we have shown, our legislators have an exaggerated notion of how strongly the public feels on such issues as China policy. A bigger problem is their own lack of perception on the subject.

Some congressmen complained, during interviews, that the State Department does not keep them adequately informed on China developments. But one said the fault lies not with the State Department but with congressional apathy. Present channels of communication between the State Department and Congress include frequent contact between Department officials and the Foreign Affairs Committees of the two houses. State Department people also testify before other congressional committees on pending legislation, proposed appropriations and investigative matters. Weekly briefings (with two written notices in advance to every congressman) are provided for the House by the top echelon of the State Department. Major international developments, often including developments in China and the Far East, are discussed. Yet rarely are the briefings attended by more than 35 or 40 congressmen out of 435. Two briefings on China for all members of the House in early 1964 drew an audience of only 20 congressmen—surely a sad commentary on congressional indifference. The speaker was an outstanding authority on the Far East.

There are still other contacts between Congress and State, not the least of which occur on the Washington cocktail circuit. Moreover, congressional parties leaving for the Far East receive State Department briefings before departure and are usually provided with additional information by American diplomats in the field. Yet some congressmen feel "left out" and resentful. One problem, of course, is congressional distrust of the State Department. A congressman with a particular interest in international affairs told this writer briefings would be better attended if they included experts of diverse views from outside as well as inside the State Department. This would obviate the complaint that briefings are just a device for disseminating the State Department "line." This same lawmaker felt that the administration and the newspapers could do a lot to jolt congressmen into taking a more serious view of the need for restudying China policy.

The State Department and the Public

In respect to China, the State Department's image still suffers
somewhat from damage incurred during the McCarthy era. Traveling about the country, asking questions about China, I found
distrust particularly apparent in parts of the country where the
radical right is strong and the memory of Joe McCarthy is
cherished. A former China service officer (later an ambassador
to an Asian country) related to the writer an experience that
illustrates this attitude. While on a trip to the American South-
west, he decided to seek out relatives and friends he had not seen
for years. He looked forward to an amiable exchange of reminis-
cences and pleasantries but instead found himself defending the
Department against a bombardment of half-baked charges and insinuations. The parting shot—the one that really shook him—came
from one of the women present. "You are just what I expected of
the State Department," she said, "only worse."

Such incidents, fortunately, are not typical, and it is recognized, even in the Department itself, that more direct contact
between foreign service officers and the public is desirable.
Traveling about the country, I often heard the complaint that
the United States government is not doing an adequate job of
keeping the public informed on China. Although the State Department is a favorite target for such criticism, the White House
and the Pentagon also come in for their full share of it. Obviously federal agencies cannot be expected to tell all they know.
However, there is a serious question whether they are providing
as much information as they should on a situation in which reliable
information and accurate perspectives are badly needed.

Most Americans seem quite unaware of the rather extensive
facilities in the State Department for disseminating information
to the public on foreign affairs. The bulk of this information, to
be sure, reaches the people through the news media and the mails,
but there is also considerable face-to-face communication at
national and regional foreign policy conferences and through
local appearances by State Department speakers. The Department also maintains a Public Opinion Studies staff for keeping in

touch with the ebb and flow of American opinion on foreign countries, including China. This office regularly examines and analyzes a formidable influx of incoming materials including editorials from seventy-one American newspapers, the writings of forty-four syndicated columnists, articles on foreign affairs from twenty-one magazines, statements and speeches relating to foreign policy from a dozen leading national private organizations, the results of all public opinion polls, congressional statements and debates on foreign policy, news stories, letters to the editor and so forth, relating to foreign affairs. Out of this mass of printed matter are distilled periodic reports on shifting public attitudes and their significance, for the guidance of policy makers.

There is at least one public relations job concerning China on which the State Department got a well-deserved pat on the back from most observers. That was in the way it helped prepare the American public for the announcement of China's first nuclear detonation. The job was well done—perhaps too well done. The Chinese blast, when it came, occasioned no shocked surprise, no panicky reaction. On the contrary, there was a rather disquieting element of complacency in the public's response—a tendency perhaps to underestimate the eventual consequences of this development.

CHAPTER ELEVEN

Conclusions

On the question of China, Americans are caught in a web of circumstance which makes it extremely difficult for them to view the issue with cool objectivity. Not only are we heirs to a mythology dating back to our earliest contacts with China; we are also closely involved in a cold war which inevitably influences our thoughts and attitudes with respect to the second most powerful Communist state. Nor is our factual information as full or as clear as it should be.

The record as outlined in these pages shows that a host of factors has contributed to the shaping of present American attitudes. Throughout a century and a half, but especially in the past thirty years, the history of Chinese-American relations has been punctuated by an extraordinary sequence of dramatic developments, many of which have left lasting marks. Among them were the war with Japan, the wartime visit of General and Madame Chiang Kai-shek to the United States, the Stilwell recall, the unsuccessful outcome of the Marshall mission, the McCarthy charges, the Korean War with its heavy loss of American lives, the Sino-Soviet split, the Viet-Nam hostilities, Communist China's attainment of nuclear status.

Experts disagree on the relative impact of these and other events on American attitudes. But I found some of their views surprising. A distinguished American with long experience in Washington was convinced, for instance, that the wartime visit

229

of Chiang and his wife left a deeper imprint on our thinking about China than most Americans, looking back on that almost-forgotten episode, now realize. "Personally," he said, "I think the public and congressional attitudes toward China were pre-emptively crystallized by the visits of Chiang and Madame Chiang to the White House during the Roosevelt administration and that everything after that merely reinforced the situation."

In more recent years, we have witnessed a steady buildup of public antagonism toward the Chinese Communists. There are few who will dispute that the Korean War profoundly affected the American outlook. It was that tragic conflict which first fixed firmly in American minds the concept of Communist China as an aggressive nation and alerted us to China's basic strength. Many of our present views—one might even say, stereotypes—on Communist China date from this period.

In view of these influences and our dearth of direct contact with mainland China for the past fifteen years (one writer predicts Americans may be seeing the other side of the moon before they see Communist China), it is hardly surprising that the public has great difficulty in reaching objective, analytical judgments about that country. There are those who argue that if the United States and Communist China are on a collision course, it is because they so utterly misread and misunderstand each other. One needs but to examine a single day's output of Radio Peking and the Hsinhua (New China) News Agency to realize that the people of mainland China are receiving, through their controlled information apparatus, a wildly misshapen image of the United States. And it must be admitted that despite our vaunted press freedom, the picture we are getting of mainland China is blurred, full of gaps and streaked with black and white. Even our government has fallen short of fulfilling its responsibility to provide the public with a clear perspective of the situation.

We are, in fact, in a situation in which we are disposed to believe the worst of Communist China and they the worst of us. It is a situation which tends to encourage exaggerated fears, illusions, false reasoning and self-serving arguments on both sides. To make matters worse, it is being continuously aggravated by Communist China's posture of arrogance, contempt and hostility for the United States. This posture has, in American eyes, contributed heavily to the building up of China as an implacably hostile country, more fanatical, more ruthless and potentially more dangerous than the Soviet Union.

This ominous—if exaggerated—image began to develop in the closing stages of the Communist takeover of the Chinese mainland, at a time when the American public had to all intents and purposes written off the defeated Nationalists and was psychologically resigned not only to Communist victory on the mainland but also in Taiwan. Even diplomatic recognition seemed to many Americans, at that time, only a short time off. Yet with deliberate recklessness, encouraged, no doubt, by the apparent indecisiveness of our mood and policy, the Communists ignored this opportunity to gain just about everything they were after, at no cost. They chose, instead, to harass American nationals in China and to attack us in Korea, at a time when a little understanding would have gone a long way.

We now know that the North Korean attack on South Korea (presumably with the concurrence of Moscow and Peking) represented a colossal miscalculation of our mood. Overnight, the American attitude toward the Chinese Communists was transformed from frustrated indifference to outraged determination, and Taiwan, the sitting duck, became suddenly an unassailable fortress. Although the Chinese campaign of cold hatred and hostility for the United States had started months before the Korean outbreak, it is nevertheless arguable that United States relations with Communist China might be on a friendlier basis today but for the Korean War.

After Korea it was *our* turn to be handed an opportunity and *our* turn to throw it away. In the late 1950s, the U.S. State Department dillied and dallied on the Chinese offer to admit to China an invited group of American newspaper correspondents—until the Chinese attitude hardened, and it was too late. Since then, Communist China has done nothing to improve our view of her.

Our survey makes it quite evident that China's posture of truculence constitutes a serious obstacle to friendlier American attitudes toward the Peking regime. On the other hand, our interviews also indicate that the American public would respond readily to evidence on the Chinese side of a real interest in discussing U.S.-Peking differences in a spirit of mutual effort to improving relations. It was only a few years ago, as Samuel Lubell has pointed out, that Americans viewed Soviet Russia with the same extreme antagonism and concern as they regard Communist China today. In substituting China for Russia as the main villain and in attributing to the Chinese extravagantly fearsome qualities, Americans demonstrate once again their penchant for going overboard emotionally where China is concerned.

It is human nature, of course, to exaggerate a danger which is only imperfectly seen. What we know about China is disturbing enough. What we do not know worries us as much, or more. We know China as a big country, teeming with industrious people, subjected to continuous anti-American indoctrination and dominated by a fanatical, hostile regime capable of hurting us (as in Korea) and intent on stirring up the entire non-Western world against us. On such foundations, and in the absence of the full facts, it does not take much imagination to build up a specter of truly alarming proportions.

The Cold War Psychology and Its Influence on American Attitudes toward China

The cold war continues deeply to influence our attitudes and to color our information about Communist China. As Americans, most of us are anti-Communist both by upbringing and conviction—which makes it difficult for us to view the news from China in other than cold-war terms. Except for the far left, few Americans would advocate compromise with the Communist Chinese at the expense of key positions and principles. There is in this country a "built-in" consensus strongly opposed to any expansion of Communist influence beyond its present limits. This does not deter many Americans from advocating varying degrees of flexibility to cope with the danger. Suggestions range from "endless flexibility" to no flexibility at all.

In the course of our interviews for this survey we encountered a hard core of Americans so convinced of the utter incompatibility of the American and Communist systems that it accepts with fatalistic resignation the possibility, even probability, of an eventual military showdown. As this school sees it, we are already engaged in World War III; we are at war with a system dedicated to Communist revolution on a worldwide scale and the eventual destruction of our way of life, and unless and until the Chinese Communists provide convincing proof of a change of heart, they argue, we would be simpletons and dupes to let down our guard or give ground anywhere. Allied with these militants are others who hold similar convictions but with isolationist overtones. They see the United States as overextended in the world struggle and would reduce our military involvement overseas to concentrate on the defense of Fortress America and its environs.

We have noted that those in this country who are prepared to risk war with the Communist world rather than compromise on any significant issue represent a relatively small percentage of the total population, yet are numbered in millions. They include some high-ranking officers in the armed services, active and retired, and a considerable number of businessmen and industrialists of conservative outlook. They include those organizations of the Far Right which have become so numerous and stridently vocal in recent years. They include many others of less rigid views, as well. And in a crisis, their number would probably swell. The concept of coexistence, as these Americans see it, is nothing more than a delusion and a trap. They insist that the United States continue firmly to press its policy of isolation and containment and seize every opportunity for advantage to frustrate the expansion of Communist power and influence.

There are not many Americans who would challenge the basic premise of the fundamentalists that the Chinese Communists and their allies are out to get us. Yet, despite the fact that Peking has shown not the slightest interest in discussing compromise on other than "impossible" terms, our survey indicates that most Americans refuse to take a hopeless view of the future. The desire for East-West harmony lies very close to the surface in most American minds. This is shown by the consistently favorable response in public opinion polls to any suggestion of negotiation with the Chinese Communists for the alleviation of existing tensions. It is not a mood of appeasement, but rather an underlying desire for peace, if attainable on honorable terms. It reflects the persistent hope that in the end the Chinese Communists, like the Russians, will "mellow" and become "more reasonable."

So runs American thinking. The cold war persists, however, with the result that initiatives are inhibited. Even the news about China in our newspapers is couched in cold war terms. A story which makes Mao Tse-tung look foolish is assured a better "play" than one which makes him look good; and the temptation to cater to this mood is not an easy one for reporters and editors to resist. Many of us no longer view the Chinese people as individuals but as faceless pawns in a gigantic chess game. In view of the cold-war milieu in which we live, these are understandable reactions. But they do complicate our problem of understanding contemporary China.

We have noted that the consistently hostile attitude of the Peking government combined with the basic anticommunism of the American people keeps public apprehension at a high level and serves as a continuous deterrent to friendlier attitudes. This does not mean, however, that the public is happy with the *status quo*. We have seen that while there is little public pressure for a change in our China policy, there are a great many people who would condone and even welcome modest changes. On no single point did we find more general public support than on the need for increased contact and communication with the Chinese mainland. Undoubtedly, a lifting of all restrictions on travel from the United States to Communist China would be widely applauded in this country, even if the Chinese reduced it to a mere gesture by refusing to cooperate. It is true that public opinion in this matter is based, in part at least, on the dubious assumption that through direct contact we would be able to establish lines of communication and channels of information far more satisfactory than those which are presently open to us. These expectations are doubtless highly exaggerated. There is no reason to suppose that Americans visiting China would be able to see more or, for that matter, do more than nationals of other countries. Their reports might carry more credibility in the United States, however, and might be more widely read than the information we are receiving today.

Furthermore, although our opinion samplings revealed a split down the middle on the question of trade, it is apparent that many of those who said they opposed trade with Communist China did so out of deference to current U.S. policy rather than from conviction. It is this writer's opinion, based on interviews across the country, that a majority of the nation's business community and probably of the general public would welcome a U.S. government decision to modify the total embargo on trade with Communist China and to put that trade on the same basis as our commerce with the Soviet Union. We must note, however, that the hard core opponents of trade with Communist China hold their views with greater intensity than those who favor it and would certainly contest vigorously any letting down of the barriers, be it ever so slight.

There is of course a serious question as to whether any easing of our policies at this stage would be reciprocated. It is a commentary on the lack of public awareness that many Americans still view such matters as trade and recognition as bargaining counters for which the Chinese Communists might be willing to pay a high price. In truth, the Chinese Communists have shown a complete disinterest in trade, recognition or even people-to-people exchanges, except on the condition that the United States withdraw its military and naval support from the Taiwan area. Even so widely publicized a matter as the ban on American reporters visiting mainland China is widely misunderstood in this country. Many Americans are under the totally mistaken impression that the present prohibition is of Washington's making, rather than Peking's. The fact is that any responsible American newspaperman can obtain a passport validated by the State Department for travel in Communist China, but he will find the gates of China closed to him. As of this writing, about forty-five validations have been issued. On the other hand, except for newspapermen and relatives of Americans held captive in China, such validations do not come easily. Appeals to the State Department to lift *all* restrictions on travel to China have not been favorably acted upon. Obviously such action would have little more than propaganda value under present circumstances.

In interviews and polls we have observed a wide range of flexibility in American attitudes toward China. There is a continuous shifting in public viewpoints, and even the "limits" of our flexibility are far from constant. What is unthinkable today may be considered a necessity tomorrow. As an example, a majority of the American public is evidently opposed today to the diplomatic recognition of the People's Republic of China and the admission of that regime to the United Nations. Yet many consider both developments inevitable in the long run.

Some Suggestions for Improvement

There are no pat solutions for the dilemmas described in these pages, no dramatic denouements. However, there are two important aspects of the problem which deserve spotlighting. The first is the matter of improving the quantity and quality of information on China reaching the American public. The second is the need for rational public discussion and reappraisal of our China policy.

On the information problems, it will suffice at this point merely to underline certain specific needs. The difficulties here are fundamental, serious, and susceptible of improvement. Long-range solutions lie with our educational systems, short-range answers with our news media.[1] The common supposition that the problem stems from our lack of contact with mainland China is only half-true. Contact certainly would be a help, especially in arousing greater public interest in the China question, but whether it would add materially to the knowledge available to us is problematical. The fact is that an immense and expanding store of knowledge on Communist China has already been accumulated in this country through the combined efforts of our scholars, journalists and official agencies. Yet only a trickle of this material has filtered down to the general public. One of the major tasks, then, is to make more of this basic information available, with-

[1] For a fuller discussion, see chapters 8 and 9.

out distortion or bias, to the public at large. A still bigger task, perhaps, is to persuade the public to read it.

Not long ago, an important newspaper chain decided to assign one of its top reporters to the job of digging out some of this hitherto unpublished background material on China. The reporter did a thorough and competent job. He talked with dozens of China specialists in universities, foundations and government. He examined scores of informative documents. His reports were published in thirteen newspapers and were favorably commented on. But evidently news in depth about China does not sell papers. An editor of the newspaper chain described the China series as a valuable public service but a "lonely" effort.

Nevertheless, the responsibility of the newspapers and the wire services in shaping public attitudes and in influencing official behavior on China policy is enormous. The influence of the press, nationally, in this matter is to be judged less by the big internationally minded newspapers like *The New York Times*, the *Washington Post*, the *St. Louis Post Dispatch* and the *Los Angeles Times* than by the hundreds of smaller regional papers which tend, in the main, to be conservative in outlook but which are becoming less and less so. Legislators in Washington may read *The New York Times* for information on China, but when they want to check the pulse of public opinion on the subject they are much more likely to turn to the hometown newspaper.

On our second point—the need for a national, rational, uninhibited re-examination of China policy—the urgency grows greater month by month as our differences with Communist China multiply. True, the worsening situation has provoked an appreciable increase in public concern and discussion on the problem, but the popular tendency to play it safe and dodge controversial facts and facets of the issue greatly reduces the value of the dialogue. Meanwhile, Communist China and the United States drift willy-nilly toward a situation of extreme crisis without the people of either country knowing for sure whether the trip is necessary.

The desirability of an exhaustive debate on China policy, on a national scale, has become increasingly self-evident since the Korean War choked off argument on the question a decade and a half ago. Our survey demonstrated that while the public takes a more elastic view of China policy than either the administration or Congress, it is on the whole very poorly informed. Clichés, illusions and taboos are still widely prevalent. Public discussion is shallow and limited to a very narrow framework. The American people seem unable or unwilling to come to grips effectively with the problem. This situation is hardly surprising. Our China policy has been in cold storage so long that most Americans have lost familiarity with it and tend to take it for granted. They can hardly be expected to grapple with issues of which they are only dimly aware.

This is not to say that no progress has been made. There has been, in fact, a perceptible buildup of public concern over the China problem and some intensification of public discussion of it. Although, in general, congressional timidity on the subject continues, isolated efforts to start a debate have not been lacking. In an earlier chapter we told how the late Senator Claire Engle of California tried, without success, to trigger a debate on China in Congress as far back as 1959. And more recently, there was Senator Fulbright's widely noted speech of March 25, 1964, in which he called for the casting off of old myths in the face of new realities, "even at the cost of saying things that will not win immediate widespread enthusiasm." Since then, several of Senator Fulbright's colleagues have spoken up, from widely different points of view, for a new look at our handling of Asian affairs.

We have also mentioned—and do so again, with emphasis—the highly informative but under-publicized hearings and findings of the Zablocki Committee on the Sino-Soviet conflict. The report of this committee sheds much new light on policy problems of the utmost importance to this country's national interest.

But generally speaking, members of Congress see little point in making an issue of China policy. They assume, probably correctly, that a more flexible attitude toward Communist China is not going to win them new votes. They deem it more likely to cost them some. Congress evidently lacks the stomach, the incentive or, perhaps, even the influence, to take the lead in a national debate on our China policy. Moreover, some remember unhappily the bitter political storm over China in the early 1950s and are fearful that China policy might again become a hot and exasperating domestic political issue. Why stir up latent political animosities, they ask?

It is perhaps worth noting that if a new free-for-all debate over China were to develop, it would be with a revised line-up of contestants. Not many of the gladiators of a decade and a half ago are still around; some are no longer interested. The *Washington Post* recently noted how death and retirement have taken their toll of these stalwarts:

Of the people most prominently identified with the "China Lobby," Senators McCarran and McCarthy, as well as Senator Styles Bridges (R.-N.H.) are dead. Senators William F. Knowland (R.-Calif.) and William E. Jenner (R.-Ind.) are obscurely out of office. Of the military members, General Claire Chennault and Patrick R. Hurley are dead; General Albert C. Wedemeyer and Admiral Arthur W. Radford are retired. Of the civilian officials, Ambassador William C. Bullitt, Pennsylvania Governor George A. Earle and Walter Robertson, Secretary of State for Far Eastern Affairs, are long retired. Of the private citizens, Alfred Kohlberg, the importer of Chinese lace handkerchiefs who headed the American China Policy Association, is dead; Henry R. Luce, Publisher of *Time*, Inc., now takes a less active role in his organization; his wife, Clare Boothe Luce, recently did a public turnabout on United States-China policy; William Loeb, publisher of the Manchester (N.H.) *Union-Leader*, has lost voice in his own state, and author Freda Utley, the frequent congressional witness, is now introducing herself at Washington cocktail parties.

The one member of the "China Lobby" still active, former Representative Walter H. Judd (R.-Minn.), a one-time missionary doctor in China, now speaks for the "Committee of One Million," a group which one American official guardedly called "a term rather than a reality."[2]

While congressional immobility on the China question continues, the problem grows in complexity and gravity. Commenting on the state of mind in the nation's capital, Max Frankel of *The New York Times* wrote recently: "Haunting most of the men who guide U.S. foreign policy is the feeling that on one question or another opportunities are slipping by because their own perception and the mood of the country are years behind

[2] *Washington Post*, November 29, 1964.

the times." [3] This concern over passing opportunities, real or imagined, is shared also by a widening sector of the general public. The deepening crisis in Viet-Nam, the Sino-Soviet breach, Peking's intrigues in Africa and Latin America, the Chinese nuclear explosions—these and other developments have forced China increasingly and, for the most part, unpleasantly on the consciousness of the American people. The spectacle of our allies talking and trading with the Chinese Communists has raised the question in many minds: Are they out of step, or are we?

The Developing Dialogue

There has been, since mid-1964, a modest upsurge of public interest in and discussion of our China policy in the United States. Evidence of it is to be found in the leading newspapers, in mass-circulation magazines and in the broadcasting media. A recent spate of conferences, seminars and local debates on the China question also demonstrates the rising concern. To nobody's surprise, the liveliest reactions have come from the San Francisco Bay area, where, for example, early in December 1964 a committee of the World Trade Association of the San Francisco Chamber of Commerce issued a report [4] recommending that the United States "should reopen communications with the government and the people of the 'People's Republic of China'" and urging that newspapermen, businessmen, scientists, economists, political scientists, cultural leaders and others should be enabled to engage in free intercourse between the two countries." The report concluded:

Whether the Chinese will react in a like spirit should we seek to make contact and to trade with them is, of course, beyond our knowledge. However, we will never know this until we cease our current negative attitude and begin in accenting the positive.

[3] *The New York Times*, March 26, 1964.
[4] *Report of the Committee to Explore Trade Possibilities with the People's Republic of China, Prepared for the San Francisco Area World Trade Association of the Greater San Francisco Chamber of Commerce* (San Francisco: San Francisco Area World Trade Association of the Greater San Francisco Chamber of Commerce, December 3, 1964).

In the same month, at Berkeley, across the Bay, a panel of experts and a large audience of students and interested citizens engaged in a spirited discussion on "China Today." [5] It was the kind of meeting that might be duplicated with great benefit to public understanding on a much wider scale. The panelists spoke from diverse points of view, and there were the inevitable clashes of opinion and flareups of emotion that accompany any "gloves-off" discussion of this sensitive subject. But there was no one who attended the meeting, including the panelists, who did not leave it with a deeper knowledge of the subject. During 1965, there were other symposiums, seminars and institutes on China, including the annual "Great Decisions" program of the Foreign Policy Association, with "Red China: Menace or Paper Tiger?" as one of eight foreign affairs topics studied and discussed in meetings across the country. Television and radio stations, newspapers and magazines, have contributed to the growing cacophony. Panel shows on China, for example, have become more numerous.

Prominent individuals have also been declaring themselves with increasing outspokenness on the subject of China policy. One of them is Thomas S. Gates, a former Secretary of Defense (in the Eisenhower administration), who suggested in a speech before an audience of business executives in January 1965 that once the United States establishes a position of strength in Southeast Asia it should open negotiations with Communist China. "From a position of strength and clear policy," Mr. Gates said, "there is no reason not to talk and to compromise on a whole package of problems." [6] The slowly developing dialogue on China has been in some ways stimulated, in some ways dampened by the controversy over Viet-Nam. In any case, Americans seem gradually to be coming to the realization that China is the real focus of our Asian problems if not of our global difficulties.

Possibly the most significant recent indicator of the shifting

[5] An institute on "China Today" at Wheeler Auditorium, Berkeley, under the auspices of the Department of Political Science and the Committee for Arts and Lectures, University of California, in cooperation with the World Affairs Council of Northern California and the American Friends Service Committee, December 12, 1964.

[6] *The New York Times*, February 10, 1965.

emphasis in public opinion is the emergence of the intellectual community—or an important part of it—as an organized influence in the foreign policy debate. Undoubtedly, the academic establishment can provide, under fully democratic conditions, an unexcelled forum for thoughtful dialogue on questions like Viet-Nam and China when such dialogue is unemotional and objective and combines the special knowledge and experience of faculty members with the fresh, uninhibited outlook of the students. Most of the expert knowledge on China in this country reposes, on the one hand, in the government and, on the other, in the academic community. Each has its own points of view, and public discussion and re-examination of our China policy would be meaningless without the participation of both. Prior to the McCarthy era, the professors were an articulate, if poorly organized and not always realistic, influence on American attitudes toward China. But thereafter, and until quite recently, not much was heard from them on China policy. Now they are again beginning to speak up, although, in the main, cautiously. And with the setting up of an inter-university committee on foreign policy they are no longer lacking in organization.

This is not to say that intellectual opinion on foreign policy is homogeneous or that it necessarily reflects public opinion. In the case of Viet-Nam, for example, public opinion polls showed the people generally favorable toward United States policy in that country, while various "teach-ins" across the country showed the intellectuals generally critical of it. It is only a small step from teach-ins on Viet-Nam to teach-ins on China. These could make a useful contribution to the national debate on China policy if fairly and judiciously conducted. As a counter-weight to the official line, the intellectuals play an important role. New perspectives on our China policy, based on expert knowledge, are badly needed if the public is to have a basis for comparing official policy with the alternatives available. While the public may not always agree with the professors, it can learn much from them. But teach-ins lose much of their value when, as has happened in a number of recent instances, they are exploited by pressure groups inside the academic establishment as an outlet for emotional outbursts and attempts to drown out dissenting voices.

There has been, indeed, an appreciable increase in public discussion of China, although we are still far from anything resembling a national debate. Intensive discussion on a comprehensive scale is hardly likely to catch on unless pegged to specific issues sufficiently important and controversial to stir widespread public interest. What could spark it? Perhaps a new and urgent crisis situation in Asia. Perhaps an Executive decision or a proposed piece of national legislation touching on our China policy. Perhaps an important statement by the President of the United States on some aspect of that policy. A broadening of sober public discussion, however modest, on a matter as little understood yet as important as this one would be a gain.

There are difficulties: To be realistic it must be noted that restraints on critical discussion of our China policy still prevail in parts of our country. People in cities like New York, Washington and San Francisco, where free-for-all debate is a matter of course, find it hard to believe that McCarthyism is still a living influence in large areas of the United States. They prefer to think that people who hesitate to speak up on China are suffering from groundless fears of a bogey that no longer exists. Not so. While it is true that the climate for debate has improved greatly throughout most of the country, there are many cities and towns —strongholds of the Far Right—where the inhibitions are well-founded. In such places, any suggestion of a revision of our China policy invariably provokes an abusive reaction from organizations or individuals who regard that policy as sacrosanct in its present form. Thus the fear of being labeled soft on communism continues to be a barrier to uninhibited public discussion of the China problem.

Complete Candor Essential

Public discussion of our China policy will have maximum value only if it involves a thorough, serious and candid consideration of all relevant questions. This means moving on from the threadbare and decreasingly significant issues of recognition of Communist China and its admission to the United Nations and coming to grips with the more central problem: Can we or can we not find a safe and mutually acceptable formula for living at peace with Communist China? Or, to put the matter a little differently, is coexistence with Communist China feasible and desirable, or is it, as some contend, the path to national suicide? Few Americans have sufficient knowledge of the China problem to venture a confident reply to these questions. Most want peace, but not at any price. Most have hopes—usually for a "middle" way—but lack convictions. Most realize, in any case, that they do not possess enough facts on which to base a sound opinion.

Whether a fuller knowledge of the facts would tend to modify our views or simply stiffen our determination is, of course, a moot point. But plainly there are a large number of neglected questions on China which will require public ventilation if our attitudes toward that country are to be soundly based. To debate them, to be sure, will necessitate, on many occasions, giving vent to those "unthinkable" thoughts which Senator Fulbright has rightly said are unavoidable if we are to know what we are doing in matters of foreign policy. Here are some of the principal matters requiring careful public consideration:

1. Of first importance is the need to bring Communist China into reasonably accurate focus and perspective. We can hardly expect to understand China and the exasperating attitudes of her present-day rulers unless we view them against the backdrop of 5,000 years of Chinese history and recognize that we are dealing here not only with a small clique of power-hungry zealots but also with more than a half-billion people deeply conscious of their greatness, their rich culture, their traditional role in Asia and their present potentialities. Whatever the feelings of the Chinese people about communism—and no doubt they are very mixed—we can safely assume that they all share an ambition to see China restored to a place of prominence in the world, if not as the "Middle Kingdom," at least as an equal among the great powers. Only against this historical background can we see and study Mao and his associates for what they are, the latest principals in a drama which has been going on for a very long time, on a very big stage, with frequent changes of cast and stage business.

2. One of the reasonable assumptions to be drawn from this

survey is that American public opinion would, on the whole, welcome a public reappraisal, in Congress and among the people, of our China policy. We cannot afford to treat any aspect of that policy as too sacrosanct for public discussion. All alternatives need to be exhaustively examined. Our policy is based, as we know, on the principles of isolation and containment of Communist China. These principles, though usually treated together, are not irrevocably joined. The isolation principle has come in for considerable criticism from specialists, while containment has been more often applauded, though neither has been publicly talked out. Who is isolating whom? Are we in fact isolating the Chinese Communists to a greater extent than they are isolating us? Have we put ourselves in a box from which it is becoming increasingly difficult to advance or retreat without risking world disaster? Are we missing chances to exploit the day-to-day situation because of our rigidity? Would efforts at accommodation be interpreted as weakness by the Chinese Communists and make them more truculent? Or should we perhaps be considering questions like the following, which was raised by a nationally known educator in an interview: "Why, in the light of Chinese hostility to the United States and its rejection of all overtures, doesn't someone suggest that United States intransigence is playing into Chinese hands—that the *status quo* is just what Peking wants?"

3. The techniques of Chinese expansionism and how best to cope with them also require a thorough public airing. Americans generally tend to regard Communist China as a recklessly aggressive power out to conquer the world, or much of it, by military and political means. But as our survey shows, many of our people have wildly conflicting opinions on Communist China's strength and capabilities. Our stereotyped views on Chinese aggression stem from the attacks in Korea, Tibet and India. For a better understanding of Chinese expansionism, we will need to draw a distinction between Peking's territorial and political goals and analyze them carefully. We will need to understand the true extent of China's power and the limitations on it, also whether the threat is primarily regional or global, military or political. Only then will we be able to satisfy ourselves that the policy we are following is right or wrong. In this connection there are many other com-

monly held assumptions that need closer public examination than they have had up to now. The so-called "domino theory" is one of them.

4. High up on our list of "unthinkable" thoughts should be the subject of Taiwan and its future. We have declared firmly that we will not abandon Taiwan, and on this matter the public stands almost solidly behind our government. The Chinese Communists, however, have said that no agreement with them is possible unless we withdraw our military and naval support from Chiang Kai-shek's island domain. Here lies the crux of our present differences with Peking. There is no obvious solution, yet various alternatives have been suggested; and sooner or later an acceptable one has to be found. We should not be deterred from subjecting the issue to the anvil of free public discussion.

5. There is also the matter of Communist China's emergence as the self-appointed champion of the non-white peoples of the world against their white "exploiters." In interviews some Americans evoked the nightmarish possibility of eventual racial conflict on a global scale. Fantasy, perhaps, but with a hard core of reality that calls for careful consideration and discussion. The racial aspect of the Chinese Communist problem touches Americans at a vulnerable point, yet few seem to have given it more than superficial attention. Unquestionably there is much in Mao Tse-tung's widely published preachings on liberation through violence that appeals to American Negroes, though most have shown a preference, fortunately, for the nonviolent doctrine of Mohandas K. Gandhi. This could change if the world situation were to shift in communism's favor. Meanwhile, Mao's few disciples among American Negroes keep abreast of developments on the revolutionary front by listening to "Free Dixie" broadcasts from Havana and reading English-language propaganda from Peking. Writing about this problem,[7] a Negro reporter, William Worthy, quoted the following passage from a statement addressed to non-white peoples by Mao Tse-tung: "We are in the majority and they are in the minority. I am firmly convinced that with the support of more than 90 per cent of the people of the world, the American Negroes will

[7] "The Red Chinese American Negro," *Esquire*, October 1964, pp. 132 and 173–179.

be victorious in their just struggle." The Los Angeles riots of August 1965 provided the Chinese Communists with more fuel for their propaganda offensive among non-white peoples. Peking termed the riots a "veritable revolutionary movement." [8]

6. Another "unthinkable" question—perhaps the most difficult of them all for Americans to consider without emotion: Are we giving sufficient consideration to the Chinese point of view? To answer this one honestly means trying to see ourselves as the Chinese see us and, more difficult still, trying to appraise our policy in the light of China's legitimate national interests. Foreign critics of our policy are fond of taunting us with such comments as: "How would you feel if you had a Communist army camped on the Mexican side of the Rio Grande or a Communist fleet patrolling the Catalina Straits?" We know, of course, that the problem is vastly more complicated than that, even though such considerations undoubtedly do account in part for Peking's hostility toward us. The fact remains that few Americans have bothered to analyze the Chinese point of view or to weigh carefully the arguments for and against. Unless we do so, the prospects for understanding are not only remote, they are nonexistent.

Finally, we must ask ourselves what results we would hope to achieve from a public discussion and reappraisal of the kind described. There is no sure reason to assume that a wider discussion of China problems would lead to any fundamental change in the view that our present policy, in its essence, represents the only choice tolerable to us. Nevertheless, such debate would serve to clarify the issues posed and perhaps provide a clearer answer in the public mind to the basic question of whether the conflict between the Chinese Communists and the United States is, by its nature, irreconcilable or not. True, complicated foreign policy questions are not usually resolved by public debate. But debate does, on occasion, produce fresh thinking and new perspectives, both of which should be helpful to our policy-makers in the search for feasible alternatives in what seems, at present, to be a hopeless impasse.

There is another important benefit to be derived from a public reappraisal of our China policy: it could provide the basis for

[8] *People's Daily*, August 16, 1965.

a more confident national posture with respect to the China problem. While our policy toward Peking is firm, our public posture is not. We are sadly in need of a posture based on realities and unfettered discussion rather than on the uncertainties which presently support it. Our public stance is at present weakened not only by our refusal to face facts but also by wishful thinking. The foundation of a confident posture is a sure knowledge and synthesis of the facts and a firm recognition of our capabilities, combined, of course, with a conviction of the rightness of our policy. Moreover, we would be playing falsely with our humanitarian traditions if we did not make a distinction in China between the rulers and the ruled. Americans have more and more fallen into the habit of condemning all Chinese for the iniquities of a few. There is a need to clarify our thinking on this—to make it plain that whatever our attitude at any given time toward the Communist regime, our attitude toward the Chinese people is one of unwavering compassion and goodwill.

On Presidential Initiatives

The desirability of a frank and searching public discussion of our China policy and a re-examination of this policy both inside and outside Congress is implicit in the findings of this study. It does not matter whether such discussion does nothing more than confirm our present policy as the best available under the circumstances or, on the other hand, points the way to new and better approaches. If such discussion succeeds in clarifying public thinking on a matter of grave concern to our national interests, it will have served a useful purpose.

It is not enough, however, to advocate a public discussion in general terms. A haphazard, meandering discussion would lead too far afield to produce satisfactory results. Of equal or greater importance is the *how* of such a discussion. If the debate is to be confined to crucial issues, if it is to accomplish anything, it must have effective leadership. It was clearly the predominant view of opinion leaders interviewed during this survey that prospects for a sound national debate and re-evaluation would be minimal *unless* the President himself were to take the initiative. Most Americans, including the members of Congress, are inclined to lean heavily on the Executive Branch for essential facts, guidance and policy decisions in matters concerning China. Many are apprehensive of becoming involved in a public discussion of so sensitive an issue without a cue from higher up. Only the President, it was felt, could command sufficient prestige to trigger an uninhibited reappraisal of China policy with any prospect of fruitful results.

But, as the late John F. Kennedy discovered, the President himself suffers limitations in this field. Like Congress, he is subject to the demands of practical politics and can hardly be expected to recommend a re-examination, much less a modification, of our China policy except under reasonably favorable circumstances. His hand could be forced, of course, by a crisis situation in Asia, as has happened in the past. Otherwise, he is likely to wait for clear signs of strong public interest, and support, as expressed by prominent opinion leaders, influential private organizations, the press and, of course, leading figures in Congress.

Here we run into a serious practical difficulty. If, as our survey indicates, a majority of Americans would welcome a new look at our China policy, not many of our national leaders seem to be getting the message. This is in part because pressure groups favorable to the *status quo* are better organized and speak with a louder voice than those advocating reappraisal or change. It is in part because groups favoring a searching look at our policy seem to be more timid, to lack organization and to be hampered by public inertia. A remark attributed to a congressman by a lobbyist seeking support for such a reappraisal is relevant here as well as perhaps typical of the congressional dilemma. "Give me something to stand on," the legislator said. "I have to be able to show that the people want change. Otherwise the papers at home will put the skids under me."

Re-examination of our China policy is of course inhibited also by the Peking regime's chronic truculence. "Why," asked one of the Americans interviewed, "should I take a more understanding attitude toward a fellow who keeps kicking me in the face and telling me how much he hates me?"

The President will have little incentive to take the initiative in this matter unless and until he is convinced that there is enough public interest to justify it. There are overt signs of increasing interest. For example, as I have already noted, the United States Chamber of Commerce, in April 1965, called for "opening channels of communication" with the people of mainland China. Roger Hilsman, former Assistant Secretary of State for Far Eastern Affairs and now a professor of government at Columbia University, in a speech at San Francisco, November 18, 1964, urged the following measures: arrange to have the Chinese Communists invited to the arms-control talks in Geneva; lift U.S. travel restrictions; re-examine our trade policies toward Communist China; and proceed to the recognition of Outer Mongolia.[9] Another straw in the wind was the so-called Zablocki Report, issued May 14, 1965, by a subcommittee of the Committee on Foreign Affairs in the House of Representatives. This report, previously cited, suggested initiation of cultural exchanges with Communist China and also recommended that recognition of Outer Mongolia be considered. Most of the really influential private groups and business associations which might be inclined to favor a reappraisal and public airing of our China policy have tended, however, to be very reluctant to commit themselves publicly on the subject.

To sum up: if there is to be a re-examination of our China policy, those Americans who want it will have to make themselves heard in stronger, clearer and more insistent tones. Only in such circumstances is the President likely to consider taking the initiative in the matter. The late President Kennedy once said that he favored opening windows toward China. He was never able to do much about it because of the need to keep Congress in line on higher priority issues. President Johnson, with a much larger popular mandate and a stronger hold on Congress, has enough political elbow room in which to initiate a public discussion and thoroughgoing restudy of our China policy—if he would.

9 Not to be confused with Hilsman's speech of December 13, 1963. See remarks by Roger Hilsman before the World Affairs Council of Northern California and Columbia University and Barnard College Alumni, San Francisco, November 18, 1964.

The American Public's View of U.S. Policy toward China

A Report prepared for
the COUNCIL ON FOREIGN RELATIONS
by the Survey Research Center
UNIVERSITY OF MICHIGAN

MARTIN PATCHEN
Project Director

Contents

The American Public's View
of U.S. Policy Toward China

SUMMARY

This report presents results of a national survey of American opinion on the subject of Communist China and Viet Nam. The survey was conducted in May and June 1964.

· More than one-fourth of the public is not even aware that mainland China is now ruled by a Communist government. But of those who know there is a Communist China, a large majority think there is reason for the United States to be concerned about it. Reasons given for such concern reveal a widespread fear among Americans that Communist China may attack the United States or may try to rule the whole world.

Most Americans who know what kind of government mainland China has also recognize that the United States has recently had more dealings with Russia than with Communist China. Asked about their understanding of the reasons why we have had little to do with Communist China, Americans most often mention either aggression or unfriendliness by the Chinese.

A sizable proportion of those interviewed were not able to think of any Chinese government other than the Communist one. These data indicate that the presence of the Nationalists as an alternative Chinese government is not a salient reality for most Americans.

Those who are aware of both Chinese governments were asked whether they feel we should deal only with the Nationalist government or deal with both governments. A majority of those expressing a direct opinion favor dealing with the Communists as well as with the Nationalists, but a large minority favor dealing only with the Nationalists. Of those who favor dealing with the Communists, most justify such a policy as fitting the reality that the Communists actually rule most of China. Those who oppose dealing with the Communist government give such reasons as our commitment to the Nationalists and aggressive actions by the Communists. Support for a policy of dealing with the Communists as the government of most of China is strongest among those with more education, among younger people, among women, and among those who are Independent or moderately Democratic in their politics.

An overwhelming majority of Americans oppose the idea that we help the Chinese Nationalists to attack the Chinese Communists. The most common ground for this opposition is the fear that such action would involve us in war—either with Communist China or on a grander scale.

On the question of what the United States should do if Communist China is admitted to the United Nations, there is almost unanimous agreement (only five per cent dissenting) that we should stay in the United Nations rather than withdraw. Among the many reasons offered for this viewpoint, the advantage of our retaining a voice in the United Nations and support for the United Nations as an organization are prominent.

An attempt was made to assess the willingness of the public to follow possible Presidential initiatives aimed at improving relations with Communist China. A large majority say they would favor following a Presidential suggestion that there be visits between Americans and people from Communist China—such as newspapermen from each country visiting the other. A possible Presidential suggestion that we talk over Asian problems with Communist China and try to come to some agreements with it likewise draws a favorable reaction from a large majority of those interviewed. A third possible Presidential initiative, to which a majority react favorably, is the suggestion that we exchange ambassadors with Communist China.

However, a clear majority say they would oppose any Presidential suggestion that we let Communist China join the United Nations. A possible suggestion from the President that we sell things like wheat to Communist China draws a mixed reaction. A slight majority of those with opinions oppose this idea.

Willingness to follow Presidential proposals on some issues is shown by many who had previously expressed a general opposition to dealing with China. On the other hand, some of those who are generally willing to increase our dealings with China stop short of accepting several specific Presidential suggestions—such as admitting Communist China to the United Nations. Reaction to possible Presidential suggestions aimed at increasing contact with China is more favorable among younger people, is somewhat more favorable among those with better education, is somewhat less favorable in the South, and tends to be less favorable among Republicans.

As with knowledge of the government of China, about one-fourth of those interviewed say they have not heard anything about the fighting in Viet Nam. Those who say they have heard something about the fighting were asked their feelings about four possible actions that the United States might take. A large majority oppose complete U. S. withdrawal from Viet Nam and favor continued military aid to the South Viet Nam government. The suggestion that American forces be used in Viet Nam if the Communists are winning evokes an approximately equal split in opinion. However, the idea of making a compromise agreement with Communist China on this problem, such as making all Viet Nam neutral, draws a favorable response from a majority of those questioned. As with other opinions, views about policy in Viet Nam vary according to education, level of information, age, political party affiliation, and region. The use of American forces if necessary is most likely to be favored by those with more education, by those with more information about the Far East, and by younger people. The most highly educated, the better informed, and strong Republicans are more likely to oppose a compromise such as neutralization of Viet Nam—though this proposal draws a large measure of support from all portions of the population.

Both those who favor increased contact with Communist China and those who oppose such contact are equally opposed to U.S. withdrawal from Viet Nam. Similarly, regardless of their opinions about dealing with Communist China, most Americans are in favor of continued military aid to South Viet Nam.

However, people who favor increased contact with Communist China are generally more likely than others to oppose the use of American forces in Viet Nam. Also, those people who favor contact with Communist China are generally more likely than others to be willing to make some compromise agreement with China on the issue of Viet Nam. These data indicate that a general willingness to deal with Communist China is usually accompanied by a preference for a non-military solution in Viet Nam.

The general tendency of these attitudes to go together, however, is counter-balanced by the effect of education and age, both of which tend to produce a different pattern of attitudes. Better educated and younger people are somewhat more likely than others to favor increased contact with Communist China at the same time that they approve of a relatively militant policy in Viet Nam.

INTRODUCTION

At the time of this writing, in mid-1964, the American public has ample reason to be interested in Communist China and in our policy toward China. The United States effort to support South Viet Nam has brought us close to another direct confrontation with China in Southeast Asia. Moscow and Peking have publicly debated the merits of trying to "co-exist" with the United States; in this debate China has favored a "hard" policy. And the question of what the United States should do if Communist China is admitted to the United Nations has threatened to become a Presidential campaign issue. In the context of these events, what view does the American public take of Communist China, of our policy toward China, and of our policy in Viet Nam, where United States and Chinese interests clash? The annual Spring survey conducted by the Survey Research Center of The University of Michigan in May and June of 1964 provided an opportunity to obtain some information on this subject.

The survey sample consisted of 1,501 persons, almost all of whom are heads of households and wives of heads of households.[1] The specific persons to be interviewed were chosen by advanced methods of probability selection.[2] The sample of persons interviewed is generally representative of the adult American population.[3]

---

[1] The universe sampled was all families living in households in conterminous United States (exclusive of Alaska and Hawaii). Persons living on military reservations or in group quarters such as rooming houses or institutions were not included in the sample.

[2] Appendix A provides estimates of the probable margin of error in the percentages reported above as the result of sampling error.

[3] See Appendix C for a description of the sample.

AWARENESS OF A COMMUNIST GOVERNMENT IN CHINA

First we asked people if they knew what kind of government China now has. It turns out that a sizable proportion of Americans—28 per cent—is not aware that most of China is now ruled by a Communist government. The proportion of those who are aware of this fact rises, as we might expect, with educational level (see Table 1). Also, men are more likely to be informed about the existence of a Communist China than are women (Table 1). Age is not generally related to such knowledge except for a drop in knowledge among the oldest age group, 65 and over.

TABLE 1

"First, do you happen to know what kind of government most of China has right now—whether it's democratic, or Communist, or what? [If answer unclear]: Do you happen to know if there is any Communist government in China now?"

(Read rows across)

	Know Communist Government Controls Most of China	Do Not Know[a]	Total	Number of Persons
By Education				
Grade school	46%	54%	100%	(396)
Some high school	61	39	100	(242)
Completed high school	83	17	100	(497)
Some college	94	6	100	(179)
College degree	97	3	100	(167)
By Sex				
Men	81	19	100	(647)
Women	66	34	100	(854)
Total Sample[b]	72%	28%	100%	(1501)

[a] Includes for the total sample 24 per cent who said they did not know and 4 per cent whose answers indicated they did not know.
[b] Includes 11 persons whose education was not ascertained.

CONCERN ABOUT COMMUNIST CHINA

Of those Americans who are aware of Communist China's existence, an overwhelming majority (86 per cent) feel that the United States should be concerned about Communist China (see Table 2).

A large proportion of people mention aggressive intentions of China as a reason to be concerned (see Table 3). Only a few thought of possible attack on such neighbors of China as India and Viet Nam. A much larger number of Americans are afraid that China might want to attack the United States or to rule the whole world or picture Communist China as warlike in general terms without specifying whom she might attack. For example, a housewife in Chicago said: "I think they are one of our most potent enemies and even more dangerous than Russia. They seem bent on annihilating this country." A man in San Diego explained his concern by saying: "Communist China is out to run the whole world if it can."

Many Americans speak of the present or potential strength of China as reasons for concern. An Air Force man living in Alabama pointed to "their population and industrial resources" as reasons for concern. "They are becoming a nuclear power now," a truck driver in Los Angeles commented.

Other reasons for concern frequently given include the very fact that China is Communist, the fear that China may help spread communism to other (usually unspecified) countries, and negative or dangerous qualities of the Chinese such as unconcern for human life.

TABLE 2

"Do you think there is any reason for the United States to be concerned about Communist China, or that we should not be too concerned about Communist China?"

(Asked only of those who are aware of Communist government)

Should be concerned	86%
Should not be concerned	7
Don't know	6
Not ascertained	1
Total	100%
(Number of persons,	1088)

Among the small proportion of people who say we need not be concerned about Communist China, the most frequently given reason is that China is too weak now to harm us. Other reasons given by this small group of people include the idea that we should pay more attention to the United States than to foreign countries and that China's troubles with Russia will keep her too occupied to become a problem for us.

TABLE 3

Reasons Given Why the United States Should be Concerned about Communist China[a]

Aggressive intentions of China suspected:		
Toward the United States or the whole world	21%	
Toward specific countries other than United States	3	40%
Target unspecified	16	
China's strength or bigness:		
Present strength	18	30
Potential strength	12	
Communism anywhere is bad; bad features of how China is governed		14
China may help spread communism to other countries		8
Negative or dangerous qualities or values of Chinese people or leaders (unconcern for human life, don't believe in God, etc.)		8
Have to keep informed about events in China as a part of the world		2
Other reasons		5
No reason given for concern		18
		—[b]
(Number of persons, 1088)		

[a] All persons who know about Communist China, regardless of whether they said we should be concerned about China or not, are included in this table. Some persons who said we should not be concerned nevertheless indicated some reasons for concern when questioned further.

[b] Total adds to more than 100 per cent because each respondent could give more than one answer.

PERCEPTION OF AMERICAN POLICY TOWARD COMMUNIST CHINA

Of those Americans who realize that China is ruled by a Communist government, a majority (60 per cent) are aware that the United States has been more willing to have dealings with Russia than with Communist China (see Table 4). Those who are aware of this difference mention such specifics as our having diplomatic relations with Russia but not with China; trade, such as selling wheat to Russia; talks with Russia; and the presence of Russia, but not China, in the United Nations.

A small proportion—less than 10 per cent—see the United States as treating both Russia and China pretty much the same. Of these people, the largest number give general, non-specific answers. Some say that we have tried to get along equally with both, and some say that we have kept aloof from or been firm with both.

TABLE 4

"Now Russia and China are both Communist countries. Do you happen to know whether the United States has been treating Russia and China the same up to now, or whether we've been treating them differently? In what ways would you say we've been treating them differently (the same)?"

(Asked only of those who know China is ruled by Communist government)

Treating Russia and China the same	9%
Closer or friendlier to Russia	60
Closer or friendlier to China	1
Treating them differently, nature of difference is unclear; or other difference; or not ascertained	5
Don't know	24
Not ascertained	1
Total	100%
	(Number of persons, 1088)

Almost one-fourth of those asked this question do not know whether we have treated Russia and China differently or the same.

Those who are aware that the United States has had more to do with Russia than with Communist China give a variety of explanations for U. S. policy toward China (see Table 5). The reasons most often given are that Communist China is aggressive, that we have preferred to support the Nationalists, and that it is China (rather than the United States) which has been unfriendly. No single reason is, however, given by as many as one-fifth of those asked this question. Almost one person in five says he does not know why the United States has treated China in the way we have.

TABLE 5

"What reasons do you think the United States has had for treating Communist China in the way we have?"

(For those who are aware that United States has been closer
to Russia than to Communist China)

China has made aggressive actions or plans	19%
U.S. support of Nationalists or non-legitimacy of Communist government in China	16
China has been unfriendly or uncooperative	16
Different or bad qualities of Chinese or Chinese government other than communism or aggression: race, religion, untrustworthy, etc.	12
China is Communist; Communist ideology or way of life	9
Fear of Chinese motives or expansion; wish to keep China from expanding	6
China is weaker; we're more afraid of Russia	6
U.S. unfriendliness, errors, or stupidity	2
Don't know	18
Other	5
No reason given	5
	—ᵃ

(Number of persons, 653)

ᵃ Total adds to more than 100 per cent because each respondent could give more than one answer.

AWARENESS OF THE NATIONALIST
GOVERNMENT

Those people who know that most of China is ruled by a Communist government were asked whether they have heard of another Chinese government besides the Communist one. Only 60 per cent were able to think of the name, or the leader, or the location of the "other Chinese" (Nationalist) government.

As with knowledge of the Communist government, there is no general relation between age and knowledge about the Nationalists; however, there is an indication that knowledge of the existence of the Nationalists is less widespread among the youngest age groups (18-24) than among other age groups. As with awareness of the Communist government, awareness of the Nationalists increases sharply with educational level, and men are better informed than are women (see Table 6).

If we assume that all of those who are not aware of the existence of the Communist government also do not know about the Nationalist government, then only 43 per cent of the total sample can be classified as knowing about the Nationalists. It may be that some of those who did not know "what kind of government most of China has now" would, nevertheless, have mentioned the Nationalist government if asked about the subject. It is likely, also, that some persons who could not think of the name, leader, or location of "another Chinese government" would have recognized names such as Chiang Kai-shek or Nationalists if they had been asked directly about them. However, these data do indicate that for only a relatively small portion of the American public—probably under 50 per cent—is the existence of the Nationalist government a salient reality.

TABLE 6

"Have you happened to hear anything about another Chinese government besides the Communist one? [If respondent has not mentioned one of the following—Nationalists, Republic of China, Chiang Kai-shek, Formosa, or Taiwan—go on]: *Do you happen to remember anything about this other Chinese government—like what it is called or who its leader is, or where it is located?"*

(Asked only of those who know that most of China is ruled by Communist government)
(Read rows across)

	Know about Nationalist Government	Don't Know about Nationalist Government[a]	Not Ascertained	Total	Number of Persons
By Education					
Grade school	49%	51%	0%	100%	(183)
Some high school	48	52	0	100	(148)
Completed high school	56	43	1	100	(415)
Some college	67	32	1	100	(169)
College degree	86	14	0	100	(162)
By Sex					
Men	71%	29%	0%	100%	(520)
Women	50	49	1	100	(567)
Total Sample[b]	60%	39%	1%	100%	(1088)

[a] Persons who had mentioned the Nationalists, or Chiang Kai-shek, or Formosa in a previous part of the interview were automatically credited with knowledge of the Nationalist government.

[b] Total includes several persons whose education was not ascertained.

ON DEALING WITH THE COMMUNIST
GOVERNMENT

Among those Americans who are aware of both Chinese governments, there is a considerable division of opinion about whether we should deal with the Nationalists as the government of all China or whether we should deal with the Communist government as well as with the Nationalists (see Table 7).

About one person in three advocates dealing with the Communist government as well as with the Nationalists. The most common reason given for this position (see Table 8) is that it fits the reality of the situation we face. For example, a retired Army officer in California commented: "None of these things will go away if we close our eyes. ... We have to deal with communism. It's there and will not vanish or go away." A supervisor in a manufacturing company in Missouri said: "We will have to deal with them both as separate governments. We can't ignore those people for they are there and will not stand still to be ignored." Other reasons mentioned for dealing with the Communist government include the importance of Communist China and the possibility that such dealings may lead to increased cooperation or an easing of tensions.

One person in four who is aware of both Chinese governments is against our having any dealings with the Communist government and in favor of dealing with the Nationalist government only. Some of those who take this position mention our commitment to the Nationalist government, virtues of the Nationalist government, or advantages of supporting the Nationalists. A ferryboat captain in California said: "We should deal with Chiang Kai-shek as the government of China. I think they are more for the free world than the Reds." A housewife in Chicago said: "I think we have more respect for the Nationalists and should just deal with them."

Some who oppose dealing with Communist China give as reasons their opposition to dealing with a Communist government. A distillery worker in Detroit said: "We're committed against communism in any form and I just can't see recognizing a nation we're committed against."

Other reasons given for not dealing with Communist China include perceived aggressive attitudes by Communist China and negative qualities of the Communist Chinese—such as lack of respect for religion and for human life.

Eight per cent of those who are aware of both Chinese governments emphasize their wish for United States support of the Nationalist government but do not directly indicate opposition to dealing with the Communist government. A small number of persons—2 per cent—express opposition to the Nationalists or to their leader Chiang Kai-shek but do not indicate directly that we should deal with the Communist government.

A large number of persons who are aware of both Chinese governments— more than one in five—say they have no opinion about whether we should deal with the Communist government.

Opinion about whether the United States should deal with the Chinese Communist government varies considerably among different segments of the American population—depending on education, age, sex, region, and political affiliation (see Table 7).

Willingness to deal with the Communists as the government of most of China increases sharply as education increases. Among those with a grade school education or with some high school, a clear majority of almost two to one (of those with opinions) is against dealing with Communist China. At the other end of the educational scale, there is a similar majority of about two to one in favor of dealing with the Communist government.

There is a progressive decline in willingness to deal with the Communist Chinese as the age of respondents increases. Among those groups aged 44 and under, a clear majority favors dealing with the Communists. Opinion becomes almost equally divided in the age group of 45-54. In the age groups of 55 and above, a majority is opposed to dealing with the Communists as the government of most of China.

About an equal proportion of men and women—one in three—favors dealing with the Communists, but a much smaller percentage of women than men—17 per cent compared to 31 per cent—directly opposes dealing with the Communists. Also, more women than men express no opinion on this question.

Regional differences are not large, but there is a tendency for the West to be the most favorable toward dealing with the Communist Chinese government and for the South to be the least.

When those with different political affiliations are compared, the Independents and those who are Democrats, but not strongly so, indicate the greatest support for dealing with Communist China. Those who express a strong tie to either major party, especially to the Democrats, are less likely to support dealings with the Communists. Those who are Republicans, but not strongly so, tend to resemble the strong Republican group in their opinions more than they resemble the Independents and less strong Democrats.

In general, then, dealing with the Communists as the government of most of China is more likely to be favored by those with high education, by younger people, by women, to a slight degree by those living in the West, and by those who are Independent or moderately Democratic in politics.

TABLE 7

"Some people say we should deal with Chiang Kai-shek's Nationalist government on Formosa as the government of all China, and have nothing to do with Communist China. Other people say we should support the Nationalists as the government of Formosa, but should deal with the Communists as the government of the rest of China. Do you have an opinion about this or not? [If yes]: *How do you feel about this?"*

(Asked only of persons who are aware of the existence of both Chinese governments)

	A. By Education					
	Grade School	Some High School	Completed High School	Some College	College Degree	Total Sample*
Against having anything to do with Communist China; in favor of dealing with Nationalists only	30%	40%	22%	21%	23%	25%
In favor of supporting the Nationalists; no direct statement on dealing with Communist China	8	6	9	6	6	8
In favor of dealing with Communist government as government of most of China	21	20	31	43	48	34
Against supporting Nationalists; no direct statement on dealing with Communist China	2	0	3	2	3	2
No opinion	30	27	25	19	11	22
Other; it depends	4	3	4	2	2	3
Not ascertained	5	4	6	7	7	6
Total	100%	100%	100%	100%	100%	100%
Number of persons	(90)	(70)	(235)	(114)	(140)	(656)

* Total sample includes persons whose education was not ascertained.

TABLE 7 (*Continued*)

	B. By Age					C. By Sex		
34 and under	*35-44*	*45-54*	*55-64*	*65 and over*	*Total Sample*[b]	*Men*	*Women*	*Total Sample*
21%	20%	24%	36%	34%	25%	31%	17%	25%
7	9	8	3	11	8	6	9	8
44	39	29	27	18	34	35	33	34
2	2	2	2	2	2	3	1	2
15	21	27	22	30	22	18	27	22
5	3	2	3	2	3	4	3	3
6	6	8	7	3	6	3	10	6
100% (185)	100% (163)	100% (126)	100% (98)	100% (83)	100% (656)	100% (370)	100% (286)	100% (656)

[b] Total sample includes persons whose age was not ascertained.

TABLE 7 (continued)

D. *By Region*°

	Northeast	North Central	South	West	Total Sample
Against having anything to do with Communist China; in favor of dealing with Nationalists only	26%	24%	29%	21%	25%
In favor of supporting the Nationalists; no direct statement on dealing with Communist China	7	8	9	5	8
In favor of dealing with Communist government as government of most of China	35	33	28	39	34
Against supporting Nationalists; no direct statement on dealing with Communist China	2	1	3	3	2
No opinion	22	22	10	26	22
Other; it depends	3	5	2	3	3
Not ascertained	5	7	10	3	6
Total	100%	100%	100%	100%	100%
Number of persons	(192)	(178)	(154)	(132)	(656)

° Northeast: Conn., Del., Maine, Mass., N.H., N.J., N.Y., Pa., R.I., Vt.
North Central: Ill., Ind., Iowa, Kansas, Mich., Minn., Mo., Neb., N. Dakota, Ohio, S. Dakota, Wis.
South: Ala., Ark., D.C., Fla., Ga., Ky., La., Maryland, Miss., N.C., Okla., S.C., Tenn., Va., W. Va.
West: Ariz., Calif., Col., Idaho, Mont., Nev., N. M., Oregon, Utah, Wash., Wyoming,

TABLE 7 (continued)

E. *By Political Affiliation*[a]

Demo- crat, Strong	*Demo- crat, Not Strong*	*Indepen- dent*[e]	*Repub- lican, Not Strong*	*Repub- lican, Strong*	*Total Sample*[f]
34%	19%	20%	28%	33%	25%
7	5	8	8	10	8
25	37	39	34	33	34
0	2	4	3	2	2
28	23	18	19	17	22
1	4	3	5	4	3
5	10	8	3	1	6
100%	100%	100%	100%	100%	100%
(134)	(135)	(169)	(116)	(88)	(656)

[a] The question was: "Generally speaking, do you usually think of yourself as a Republican, a Democrat, an Independent, or what? [If Republican or Democrat]: Would you call yourself a strong Republican (Democrat) or a not very strong Republican (Democrat)? [If Independent or other]: Do you think of yourself as closer to the Republican or Democratic Party?"

[e] Includes persons who said they are closer to one of the major parties as well as those who did not indicate any leaning.

[f] Total sample includes persons whose political affiliation was other or not ascertained.

TABLE 8

Reasons Given Why United States Should Deal With Communists as Government of Most of China

Facing reality; Communists are the real government of most of China; Nationalists don't represent Chinese people	67%
Importance of Communist China	15
May lead to cooperation with Communist China; may ease tensions	7
Permanence of Communist government; will control China for indefinite future; Nationalists can't regain control	5
To know what's going on in Communist China	4
China is Communist like Russia, and we deal with Russia	2
Other	5
No reason given	8
	—*
(Number of persons, 222)	

* Total adds to more than 100 per cent because each respondent could give more than one answer.

TABLE 9

Reasons Given Why United States Should Not Deal With Communist Government, But Only With Nationalists

Our commitment to Nationalists; virtues of Nationalists; advantages of supporting Nationalists	32%
We should oppose Communist governments	27
Present or future aggressive attitudes or intentions of Communist China	15
Negative or dangerous qualities or values of Chinese people or leaders	5
We wouldn't gain anything by dealing with Communist China	5
Dealing with Communist China means giving into them	4
Don't know	1
Other	8
No reason given	9
	—*
(Number of persons, 165)	

* Total adds to more than 100 per cent because each respondent could give more than one answer.

ON HELPING THE NATIONALISTS ATTACK COMMUNIST CHINA

Those people who are aware of the existence of both Chinese governments were also asked whether or not they think the United States should help the Chinese Nationalists to attack the Chinese Communists.

An overwhelming majority of those who expressed an opinion on this subject oppose our helping such an attack. Only one person in ten favors our aiding a Nationalist attack, while more than six times that proportion expresses opposition. Fifteen per cent questioned on the subject say they have no opinion (see Table 10).

The most frequently given reasons for opposing such an American action are that it would automatically involve us in war or lead us into war—either with China or with Russia as well as China. For example, an employee of an electronics firm in San Diego said: "I don't think we can help Nationalist China to attack Red China. It would lead to an all-out war. We should simply protect Nationalist China from Red China." A housewife in Chicago said "I think we should protect the Nationalists, but not start a war. We'd be starting a war if we did something like that—it would be another Korea, or lead to another world war."

TABLE 10

"Some people say we should give the Nationalists all the help they need to attack the Communists on the mainland of China. Other people say we should protect the Nationalists from a Communist attack, but should not help them to attack the Communists. Do you have an opinion about this or not? [If yes]: How do you feel about this?"

(Asked only of persons who know about both Chinese governments)

Against helping Nationalists to attack Communists	62%
In favor of helping Nationalists to attack Communists	10
In favor of protecting Nationalists; no indication whether we should help Nationalists to attack Communists	7
No opinion	15
Other; unclear	4
Not ascertained	2
Total	100%
	(Number of persons, 656)

Other reasons given in opposition to helping a Nationalist attack on the Communists include the beliefs that such an attack could not succeed and that it is wrong for the United States to be an aggressor (see Table 11).

The small minority of Americans who favor our helping a Nationalist attack give among their reasons the belief that the United States should help all those who are fighting communism and simply the aim of overthrowing the Communist government (see Table 12).

Whereas opinion on whether to deal with the Communists as the government of most of China varies greatly among different segments of the American population, overwhelming opposition to an attack on Communist China is fairly consistent throughout the population. There is a tendency for opposition to an attack to increase among the better educated, but the relation is not strong. Opposition is relatively constant among those with different political affiliations, among both men and women, across all regions of the country, and for all age groups.

TABLE 11

Reasons Given Why United States Should Not Help *Nationalists to Attack Communists*

Might involve us in a war:		
With Communist China	6%	
With Russia as well as China; world war	10	45%
General, nonspecific	29	
Attack by Nationalists couldn't succeed; Communist China is too strong	25	
Wrong for U. S. to be an aggressor	10	
Let the Nationalists fight their own battles	9	
We should protect Formosa and the Nationalists	7	
Not the right time for an attack now	2	
Other	9	
Don't know or no reason given	8	
	—ᵃ	
(Number of persons, 407)		

ᵃ Total adds to more than 100 per cent because each respondent could give more than one answer.

TABLE 12
Reasons Given Why United States Should Help Nationalists to Attack Communists

Should help those fighting communism	36%
In order to overthrow Communist government	12
To protect ourselves against Communist China	11
Moral superiority of Nationalists or Chiang Kai-shek	8
Bad qualities of Chinese Communists or communism in general	5
Other	15
Don't know or no reason given	17
	—*
(Number of persons, 66)	

* Total adds to more than 100 per cent because each respondent could give more than one answer.

ON U.S. WITHDRAWAL FROM UNITED NATIONS
IF COMMUNIST CHINA IS ADMITTED

We asked our sample of Americans whether, if Communist China gets into the United Nations, the United States should stay in or get out of the world organization. This question was asked of all persons who know that most of China is ruled by a Communist government.

Three out of every four persons say that the United States should remain in the United Nations, even if Communist China is admitted (see Table 13). Only one American in 20 favors our withdrawal from the United Nations in the event of China's admission. Fourteen per cent say they have no opinion on the matter.

Among the vast majority who favor our staying in the United Nations with Communist China, many persons give as a reason the idea that staying in would enable us to retain some influence on what goes on in the United Nations (see Table 14). The wife of a salesman in Ohio said: "I don't think we ought to get out because all the other countries would be in and we wouldn't be able to vote on anything." A man in South Carolina, an employee of an electric utility company, commented: "We've got to try to keep things going. China and Russia both, they'd like to rule the world and we sure don't want that."

Others who favor our staying in the United Nations give as reasons their support of the United Nations as an organization. A woman in New Jersey, the wife of the head of a small manufacturing company, explained her feeling that we should stay in the United Nations by commenting: "At the present time the United Nations is an organization which tries to deal effectively with world problems or coordinate things among the nations of the world." Others spoke of the United Nations as "mankind's best hope."

Some of the great majority who favor staying in the United Nations if Communist China is admitted say that we'd be worse off outside the United Nations than inside—e.g., that we'd be isolated or wouldn't know what's going on. Among other reasons given for staying in the United Nations are that it wouldn't accomplish anything to get out and that withdrawal would constitute an admission of defeat for the United States.

Among the small minority who favor United States withdrawal from the United Nations if Communist China is admitted, the most frequent explanation given is in terms of general hostility to the United Nations unrelated to

Communist China's admission (see Table 15). A Missouri man, who works as a supervisor in a manufacturing firm, commented: "That United Nations is not worth a thing to us. It's just a waste of time and manpower; it never has served its purpose." This view appears, however, to be that of a very small minority.

The overwhelming support for our remaining in the United Nations, regardless of whether Communist China also gains admittance, is generally constant among all segments of the American population. The margin of endorsement of our continuing membership is of about the same magnitude among persons of different educational levels, among men and women, across different regions of the country, for persons of different political affiliations, and for persons with different levels of information about China. When different age groups are compared, only the oldest group, those 65 or over, shows any marked deviation from other groups. Withdrawal from the United Nations is favored by 12 per cent of the oldest group as compared to a figure of about 4 per cent in all other groups. However, even in the oldest age group, more than five to one favor remaining in the United Nations if Communist China is admitted.

TABLE 13
"Some people say that if Communist China gets into the United Nations, we ought to get out of the United Nations. Other people say that if Communist China gets into the United Nations, we should stay in and make the best of it. Do you have an opinion about this or not? [If yes]: How do you feel about this?"
(Asked of persons who know that most of China is ruled by Communist government)

In favor of *staying in* United Nations if Communist China gets in	75%
In favor of *getting out* of United Nations if Communist China gets in	5
No opinion	14
Other; answer not clear	3
No reason given	3
Total	100%
	(Number of persons, 1088)

TABLE 14

Reasons Given Why United States Should Stay in United Nations If Communist China Is Admitted

To have a voice, influence in United Nations	37%
Support for United Nations as an organization	22
We'd be worse off outside the United Nations: would be isolated; wouldn't know what's going on; etc.	16
Wouldn't accomplish anything to get out	11
Getting out would be a defeat	10
No objection to Communist China being in United Nations; advantages of having Communist China in United Nations	9
Getting out would be letting allies, other countries down	4
Advantages of debate or negotiation by staying in United Nations	2
Other	2
Don't know or no reason given	6
	—ᵃ
	(Number of persons, 821)

ᵃ Total adds to more than 100 per cent because each respondent could give more than one answer.

TABLE 15

Reasons Given Why United States Should Get Out of United Nations If Communist China Is Admitted

General hostility toward United Nations, unrelated to Communist China's admission	41%
United States would be outvoted, lose our influence	21
United Nations couldn't accomplish anything if Communist China was in it	12
United States shouldn't have anything to do with Communist China	9
Financial problem for United States or United Nations connected with Communist China's admission	9
Other	9
Don't know or no reason given	9
	—ᵃ
	(Number of persons, 56)

ᵃ Total adds to more than 100 per cent because each respondent could give more than one answer.

WILLINGNESS TO FOLLOW POSSIBLE
PRESIDENTIAL INITIATIVES IN DEALING
WITH COMMUNIST CHINA

After respondents had a chance to express their own opinions concerning American policy toward Communist China, they were asked how they would feel if the President of the United States suggested several new actions with regard to Communist China. For each possible action mentioned, the person interviewed chose from a card that answer which best showed how he would feel if the President suggested that action. This series of questions was asked both of those who are aware that there are two Chinese governments and of those who are aware of the Communist government but not of the Nationalists. These two groups of whom the questions were asked together constitute 72 per cent of the total original sample.

A large majority of those questioned—73 per cent—favors following a Presidential suggestion that there be visits between Americans and people from Communist China—such as newspapermen from each country visiting the other. Only 16 per cent oppose this idea (see Table 16).

Americans also appear overwhelmingly ready to endorse any Presidential proposal that we talk over Asian problems with Communist China and try to come to some agreements with her. Seventy-one per cent favor following this suggestion, while only 19 per cent indicate opposition.

A third possible Presidential proposal favorably received by a majority of persons is the suggestion that "we exchange ambassadors with Communist China the way we do with other countries." Fifty-one per cent indicate they would be willing to follow the President in such a move, while 34 per cent express opposition. However, the definiteness of opinion among those opposing an exchange of ambassadors appears to be generally greater than among the people who are willing to go along with this suggestion.

The idea of "selling things like wheat to Communist China" evokes an almost even split of opinion. Those opposing such a step are slightly in the majority. As with the proposal to exchange ambassadors, those opposing trade with Communist China generally appear to feel more definitely about this than do those who express a willingness to go along with such a move.

The one possible Presidential initiative which meets with opposition, and usually definite opposition, from a clear majority of Americans is any suggestion that "we let Communist China join the United Nátions." Fifty-three per cent oppose this idea, while 31 per cent say they would be willing to follow this suggestion if the President made it.

Reaction to possible proposals for dealing with Communist China is somewhat different among various segments of the American population.

In general, willingness to follow the Presidential initiatives described is greater among younger age groups than among older groups (see Table 17). The relatively greater resistance among older people is particularly noticeable on the subjects of exchanging ambassadors with Communist China and of talking over Asian problems with Communist China.

People of higher education are somewhat mor likely than those with less education to favor Presidential initiatives to im rove relations with Communist China. The more highly educated are especially likely to favor an exchange of visits—such as those of newspapermen—between Americans and Communist Chinese (see Table 18).

In addition to comparing persons of different education, it is also possible to compare people according to their knowledge about China. People were scored in this instance on the basis of (a) whether they were aware of the Nationalist government and (b) whether they were aware that the United States now has more dealings with Russia than with Communist China. While moves to improve relations with Communist China are somewhat more favored by the better educated, those with more information about China and our policy toward China do not consistently favor such initiatives. (see Table 19). The better informed are more likely to favor visits between the two countries. However, these better informed people are also somewhat more likely to oppose meetings with Communist China on Asian problems, to oppose an exchange of ambassadors with Communist China, and to oppose letting Communist China into the United Nations. The differing effects of education and of level of information suggest that the tendency of the better educated to follow Presidential initiatives is not primarily a result of their being better informed. Of course, the measure of information about China used is a very rough one. It is not possible from these data to tell whether, among those we classified as well-informed, further differences in information affect attitudes toward Presidential initiatives and, if so, in what direction this effect operates.

Differences according to geographical regions in willingness to follow Presidential initiatives are generally quite small (see Table 20). Southerners as a group show more opposition to several possible Presidential initiatives aimed at improving relations with Communist China. Most notably, they are less likely than those in other regions to go along with the ideas of exchanging ambassadors with Communist China and of selling her wheat.

Since any President is not only a national leader but a political party leader as well, it is especially relevant to see whether political affiliation is related to willingness to follow policy suggestions made by the President. (The President in office was Lyndon Johnson, a Democrat, although the questions referred only to "the President.") In general, differences between Republicans, Democrats, and Independents are small (see Table 21). Republicans tend to be less likely to follow the possible Presidential suggestions mentioned—but this attitude is consistent with their relatively low willingness to have dealings with Communist China as expressed in answer to a previous question. A somewhat less consistent picture is shown by strong Democrats. In expressing their own opinions in answer to a previous question, strong Democrats resemble strong Republicans in their degree of opposition to dealing with Communist China. However, strong Democrats generally express as much willingness to follow Presidential suggestions aimed at improving relations with Communist China as do other Democrats and Independents. This attitude may reflect the fact that strong Democrats react to the President, at least in part, as a party leader.

Finally, in comparing different segments of the population, we find no notable differences between men and women in their willingness to follow the Presidential initiatives described.

One additional comparison of interest concerns people who differ in their own general viewpoint about how to treat Communist China. In answer to a previous question, some persons expressed opposition to dealing with the Communists as the government of most of China, while others favored dealing with the Communist government as well as with the Nationalist government. It is revealing to examine the reactions of each of these groups to possible Presidential suggestions aimed at improving relations with Communist China (see Table 22).

Among those who had previously indicated opposition to dealing with Communist China, a clear majority is, nevertheless, willing to follow two Presidential suggestions—that visits between the two countries be arranged and that talks to discuss Asian problems be held. A large majority in this "no-dealings" group opposes the ideas of selling wheat to Communist China and of exchanging ambassadors with her—although almost 30 per cent of it is willing to follow each of these possible Presidential suggestions. The idea of admitting China to the United Nations evokes the clearest opposition in the "no-dealings" group. Only 10 per cent of it is willing to follow a Presidential suggestion of this kind.

Among those persons who had previously indicated approval of dealing with the Chinese Communist government, the overwhelming majority expresses willingness to follow Presidential suggestions that we exchange visits with the Chinese Communists and that we discuss Asian problems with them. A large majority of this "deal-with-Communist-China" group is also willing to follow suggestions that we exchange ambassadors with Communist China. On the two other possible steps mentioned—selling wheat and admitting Red China to the United Nations—a majority of the "deal-with-Red-China" group is willing to follow such Presidential suggestions, but a sizable minority is not ready to go that far in establishing relations with China.

In summary, willingness to follow Presidential suggestions aimed at improving relations with Communist China increases as one moves into younger age groups; increases somewhat as education improves; is inconsistent, but generally decreases, when persons have some information about China; decreases somewhat in the South; tends to decrease among Republicans; and is about the same regardless of sex. A majority of those who previously expressed opposition to dealing with the Chinese Communist government is, nevertheless, willing to go along with some specific Presidential suggestions, while a sizable minority of those generally in favor of dealing with the Communist government balks at following some specific Presidential suggestion.

TABLE 16

"Now the President of the United States might decide that it was in our best interests to take certain new actions with regard to Communist China. For each thing I mention, would you tell me how you would feel about it if the President suggested that action?"

(Asked only of persons who know that most of China is ruled by a Communist government)

"Suppose the President suggested visits between Americans and people from Communist China—like newspapermen from each country visiting the other?"

Definitely in favor	41%	} 73%
Probably in favor	32	
Probably against	6	} 16
Definitely against	10	
No opinion		10
Not ascertained		1
Total		100%

(Number of persons, 1088)

"Suppose the President suggested that we exchange ambassadors with Communist China the way we do with other countries?"

Definitely in favor	24%	} 51%
Probably in favor	27	
Probably against	11	} 34
Definitely against	23	
No opinion		14
Not ascertained		1
Total		100%

(Number of persons, 1088)

"Suppose the President suggested that we talk over problems of Asia with Communist China and try to come to some agreements with them?"

Definitely in favor	37%	} 71%
Probably in favor	34	
Probably against	7	} 19
Definitely against	12	
No opinion		9
Not ascertained		1
Total		100%

(Number of persons, 1088)

TABLE 16 (*Continued*)

"Suppose the President suggested selling things like wheat to Communist China?"

Definitely in favor	19%	} 43%
Probably in favor	24	
Probably against	14	} 47
Definitely against	33	
No opinion		9
Not ascertained		1
Total		100%

(Number of persons, 1088)

"Suppose the President suggested that we let Communist China join the United Nations?"

Definitely in favor	13%	} 31%
Probably in favor	18	
Probably against	13	} 53
Definitely against	40	
No opinion		15
Not ascertained		1
Total		100%

(Number of persons, 1088)

TABLE 17

Reactions to Possible Presidential Initiatives, for Persons of Different Ages

Possible Presidential Suggestions.	Age					
	18-24	25-34	35-44	45-54	55-64	65 and Over
Visits between Americans and Communist Chinese						
In favor	78%	78%	76%	71%	67%	61%
Against	15	13	15	16	19	23
No opinion	6	7	8	12	14	15
Not ascertained	1	2	1	1	0	1
Total	100%	100%	100%	100%	100%	100%

TABLE 17 (*Continued*)

Possible Presidential Suggestions	Age					
	18-24	*25-34*	*35-44*	*45-54*	*55-64*	*65 and Over*
Sale of Things Like Wheat to Communist China						
In favor	40%	45%	42%	46%	47%	34%
Against	51	45	46	45	45	54
No opinion	8	8	11	8	8	12
Not ascertained	1	2	1	1	0	0
Total	100%	100%	100%	100%	100%	100%
Discussion of Asian Problems with Communist China						
In favor	75%	72%	78%	69%	70%	58%
Against	12	17	16	20	21	27
No opinion	11	9	5	10	9	14
Not ascertained	2	2	1	1	0	1
Total	100%	100%	100%	100%	100%	100%
Exchange of ambassadors with Communist China						
In favor	61%	55%	55%	47%	50%	39%
Against	27	31	32	37	32	42
No opinion	11	13	12	15	18	18
Not ascertained	1	1	1	1	0	1
Total	100%	100%	100%	100%	100%	100%
Agreement to let Communist China into United Nations						
In favor	30%	34%	37%	30%	29%	18%
Against	51	47	47	59	57	66
No opinion	18	17	15	10	13	15
Not ascertained	1	2	1	1	1	1
Total	100%	100%	100%	100%	100%	100%
Number of persons	(89)	(243)	(258)	(201)	(155)	(140)

TABLE 18

*Reactions to Possible Presidential Initiatives, for Persons With Different
·Levels of Education*

Possible Presidential Suggestions	Education				
	Grade School	Some High School	Completed High School	Some College	College Degree
Visits between Americans and Communist Chinese					
In favor	59%	62%	79%	76%	82%
Against	24	19	12	17	14
No opinion	17	19	8	5	4
Not ascertained	0	0	1	2	0
Total	100%	100%	100%	100%	100%
Sale of things like wheat to Communist China					
In favor	41%	38%	41%	43%	54%
Against	50	49	46	48	43
No opinion	8	12	12	7	3
Not ascertained	1	1	1	2	0
Total	100%	100%	100%	100%	100%
Discussion of Asian Problems with Communist China					
In favor	59%	70%	75%	73%	72%
Against	25	18	15	19	22
No opinion	15	12	9	6	6
Not ascertained	1	0	1	2	0
Total	100%	100%	100%	100%	100%
Exchange of ambassadors with Communist China					
In favor	44%	46%	55%	50%	55%
Against	39	29	29	39	38 .
No opinion	16	25	15	10	7
Not ascertained	1	0	1	1.	0
Total	100%	100%	100%	100%	100%·

TABLE 18 (*Continued*)

Possible Presidential Suggestions	Education				
	Grade School	Some High School	Completed High School	Some College	College Degree
Agreement to let Communist China into United Nations					
In favor	25%	24%	32%	36%	38%
Against	58	54	51	53	53
No opinion	16	21	16	10	9
Not ascertained	1	1	1	1	0
Total	100%	100%	100%	100%	100%
Number of persons	(183)	(148)	(415)	(169)	(162)

TABLE 19

Reactions to Possible Presidential Initiatives, for Persons With Different Levels of Information About China

Possible Presidential Suggestions	Information Score[a]		
	(Low) 1	2	(High) 3
Visits between Americans and Communist Chinese			
In favor	64%	72%	78%
Against	17	16	16
No opinion	18	11	6
Not ascertained	1	1	0
Total	100%	100%	100%
Sale of things like wheat to Communist China			
In favor	41%	36%	48%
Against	44	52	47
No opinion	14	12	5
Not ascertained	1	0	0
Total	100%	100%	100%

TABLE 19 (*Continued*)

Possible Presidential Suggestions	Information Score[a]		
	(*Low*) 1	2	(*High*) 3
Discussion of Asian Problems with Communist China			
In favor	71%	72%	71%
Against	12	17	24
No opinion	16	10	5
Not ascertained	1	1	0
Total	100%	100%	100%
Exchange of ambassadors with Communist China			
In favor	49%	52%	51%
Against	24	32	40
No opinion	26	16	9
Not ascertained	1	0	0
Total	100%	100%	100%
Agreement to let Communist China into United Nations			
In favor	30%	26%	34%
Against	45	56	58
No opinion	24	18	8
Not ascertained	1	0	0
Total	100%	100%	100%
Number of persons	(264)	(279)	(505)

[a] The level of information score indicates how many of the following pieces of information the person knew: (1) most of China is ruled by a Communist government; (2) there is a Chinese government—identified by name of government, name of leader, or location—other than the Communist one; (3) the United States has had more dealings with Russia than with Communist China recently.

TABLE 20

Reactions to Possible Presidential Initiatives, for Persons in Different Regions of·the United States

Possible Presidential	Region*			
Suggestions	Northeast	North Central	South	West
Visits between Americans and Communist Chinese				
In favor	73%	77%	67%	72%
Against	15	13	21	17
No opinion	12	9	11	9
·Not ascertained	0	1	1	2
Total	100%	100%	100%	100%
Sale of things like wheat to Communist China				
In favor	48%	46%	34%	42%
Against	40	45	55	48
No opinion	12	8	9	8
Not ascertained	0	1	2	2
Total	100%	·100%	100%	100%
Discussion of Asian Problems with Communist China				
In favor	69%	75%	69%	69%
Against	21	15	19	23
No opinion	10	9	11	6
Not ascertained	0	1	1	2
Total	100%	100%	100%	100%
Exchange of ambassadors with Communist China				
In favor	51%	58%	40%	56%
Against	35	27	41	32
No opinion	14	15	18	·10
Not ascertained	0	0	1	2
Total	100%	100%	100%	100%

TABLE 20 (*Continued*)

Possible Presidential	Region[a]			
Suggestions	Northeast	North Central	South	West
Agreement to Let Communist China into United Nations				
In favor	32%	34%	26%	32%
Against	52	50	59	55
No opinion	16	16	·13	11
Not ascertained	0	0	2	2
Total	100%	100%	100%	100%
Number of persons	(292)	(317)	(272)	(207)

[a] For a listing of the states included in each region, see Table 7, note c.

TABLE 21

Reactions to Possible Presidential Initiatives, for Persons of Different Political Affiliation

	Political Affiliation[a]				
Possible Presidential Suggestions	Democrat, Strong	Democrat, Not Strong	Independent	Republican, Not Strong	Republican, Strong
Visits between Americans and Communist Chinese					
In favor	69%	74%	77%	75%	65%
Against	19	15	13	14	26
No opinion	12	11	9	11	9
Not ascertained	0	0	1	0	0
Total	100%	100%	100%	100%	100%

TABLE 21 (*Continued*)

Possible Presidential Suggestions	Demo-crat, Strong	Demo-crat, Not Strong	Indepen-dent	Repub-lican, Not Strong	Repub-lican, Strong
Political Affiliation[a]					
Sale of things like wheat to Communist China					
In favor	48%	42%	48%	34%	40%
Against	45	45	44	52	55
No opinion	6	13	7	14	4
Not ascertained	1	0	1	0	0
Total	100%	100%	100%	100%	100%
Discussion of Asian problems with Communist China					
In favor	73%	75%	71%	67%	67%
Against	18	14	18	22	26
No opinion	8	10	10	11	7
Not ascertained	1	1	1	0	0
Total	100%	100%	100%	100%	100%
Exchange of ambassadors with Communist China					
In favor	50%	55%	57%	47%	42%
Against	34	27	31	37	44
No opinion	15	17	11	16	14
Not ascertained	1	1	1	0	0
Total	·100%	100%	100%	100%	100%
Agreement to let Communist China into United Nations					
In favor	33%	28%	39%	24%	29%
Against	56	51	43	63	62
No opinion	10	21	17	13	9
Not ascertained	1	0	1	0	0
Total	100%	100%	100%	100%	100%
Number of persons	(244)	(240)	(255)	(187)	(133)

[a] For the questions used to assess political affiliation, see Table 7, note d.

TABLE 22
Reactions to Possible Presidential Initiatives, for Persons With Different Previously Expressed Opinions on Whether United States Should Deal with Communist China

Possible Presidential Suggestions	Previously Expressed Viewpoint*		
	Should Deal Only with Nationalists, Not with Communists	Should Deal with Both Communists and Nationalists	No Opinion
Visits between Americans and Communist Chinese			
In favor	63%	91%	86%
Against	30	6	14
No opinion	7	3	0
Not ascertained	0	0	0
Total	100%	100%	100%
Sale of things like wheat to Communist China			
In favor	29%	65%	36%
Against	67	30	48
No opinion	4	5	16
Not ascertained	0	0	0
Total	100%	100%	100%
Discussion of Asian problems with Communist China			
In favor	58%	87%	68%
Against	38	9	18
No opinion	4	4	14
Not ascertained	0	0	0
Total	100%	100%	100%
Exchange of ambassadors with Communist China			
In favor	28%	75%	41%
Against	65	19	37
No opinion	7	6	22
Not ascertained	0	0	0
Total	100%	100%	100%

TABLE 22 *(Continued)*

Possible Presidential Suggestions	Previously Expressed Viewpoint[a]		
	Should Deal Only with Nationalists Not with Communists	*Should Deal with Both Communists and Nationalists*	*No Opinion*
Agreement to let Communist China into United Nations			
In favor	10%	58%	24%
Against	87	34	54
No opinion	3	8	22
Not ascertained	0	0	0
Total	100%	100%	100%
Number of persons	(165)	(222)	(144)

[a] For the previous question, see Table 7.

INFORMATION AND OPINION ABOUT THE
FIGHTING IN VIET NAM

We asked everyone interviewed, regardless of whether he knew that China is ruled by a Communist government, whether he had heard anything about the fighting in Viet Nam. About three persons out of four say they have heard something about the fighting, but—despite the wide publicity given to the Viet Nam conflict over a long period of time—one American out of every four says that he has not heard anything about it.

As with information about China (discussed earlier), the presence of a minimal amount of information about fighting in Viet Nam increases sharply with educational level and is somewhat more widespread among men than among women (see Table 23).

Among those who have heard about the Viet Nam fighting, a majority expresses opposition, usually strong opposition, to the idea of "the U. S. getting out of the Viet Nam war completely," (see Table 24). However, about one person in four favors such withdrawal.

Among the proposals mentioned, strongest endorsement is given to "our continuing to give arms and training to the Viet Nam troops fighting the Communist rebels." Seventy-five per cent of those asked this question favor this policy—most of them strongly, while only 12 per cent expressed opposition.

The idea of "using American forces in Viet Nam if the Communist rebels are winning, even if this means our risking war with Communist China" evokes an approximately even split between those in favor and those opposed. The strength of feeling of those opposing use of American forces appears to be somewhat stronger than the strength of feeling of those favoring this idea.

The fourth possible action mentioned, "trying to make some compromise agreement with Communist China on this—like making all Viet Nam neutral," draws a favorable response from a majority of those with an opinion —usually strongly favorable. The sizable minority opposing this idea almost uniformly expresses strong opposition. Those expressing no opinion—a fair- , ly sizable group for all possible actions mentioned—number almost one person in four with respect to a possible compromise agreement with Communist China.

As with opinion concerning policy toward Communist China, opinion about U. S. policy in Viet Nam varies considerably among different segments of the American population.

As level of formal education increases, there is a sharp parallel increase in opposition to American withdrawal from Viet Nam (see Table 25). The better educated are more likely to favor our continuing to supply arms and training to South Viet Nam forces and are more likely to favor use of American forces if these are needed. While favoring these kinds of American involvement in Viet Nam, the best educated groups are more likely than others to oppose a settlement like neutralization.

While we did not assess the amount of information respondents had about the situation in Viet Nam, opinion among groups with differing amounts of information can be compared according to an indirect measure of information—that concerning China. With respect to opinions about Viet Nam policy, the effect of amount of information is parallel to the effect of education (see Table 26). The more information, the greater the opposition to withdrawal from Viet Nam; the greater the support for giving arms and training to the Vietnamese; the greater the willingness to use American forces if necessary; and the greater the opposition to a compromise agreement like neutralization of Viet Nam.

When the views of different age groups are compared, older people are seen to be less likely than younger people to oppose U. S. withdrawal from Viet Nam (see Table 27). Moreover, as age increases, there is somewhat less support, though still a clear favorable majority, for aiding the Vietnamese with arms and training. A striking reversal of opinion among age groups occurs on the idea of using American forces in Viet Nam if necessary. A clear majority of the youngest age group supports this suggestion, but as one moves successively to older age groups, the proportion favoring such a move steadily declines until for the oldest age group there is a heavy majority in opposition. With regard to the last suggestion of making Viet Nam neutral, the association of age and policy preference is not consistent.

With respect to political affiliation, those who identify themselves as strong Republicans are even more likely than others to oppose U. S. withdrawal from Viet Nam (see Table 28). Furthermore, whereas Democrats, Independents, and even less strong Republicans generally favor a compromise agreement like neutralization of Viet Nam, strong Republicans are likely to oppose the proposal for such a settlement. On another policy question concerning Viet Nam, strong Republicans are slightly more in favor of giving arms and training to the Vietnamese than other groups are.

In general, men are somewhat more militant than women in their commitent to the Viet Nam war—but the differences between sexes are modest. Men are more likely than women to oppose withdrawal from Viet Nam. Men are slightly more favorable to giving arms and training to the Vietnamese and somewhat more in favor of using American forces if necessary. Men are somewhat more likely to oppose a compromise agreement like neutralization, while a greater proportion of women than men express no opinion on this question.

Some differences in policy preferences also appear on the basis of geographical regions of the country (see Table 29). While a majority in all regions opposes withdrawal from Viet Nam, opposition to such a move is strongest in the West. And while there is little difference among regions on the question of providing arms and training to South Viet Nam, a majority of those living in the Northeast opposes using American forces, while a majority of those in the West favors such a move if necessary. Opinion on use of American forces is about evenly divided in the North Central and Southern states. With regard to the idea of a compromise agreement like neutralization, the South is about evenly split, while a majority in other regions favors such a settlement.

TABLE 23

"Have you happened to hear anything about the fighting in Viet Nam?"

(Read rows across)

	Yes	No	Not Ascertained	Total	Number of Persons
By Education					
Grade school	50%	49%	1%	100%	(396)
Some high school	64	36	0	100	(242)
Completed high school	85	14	1	100	(497)
Some college	94	5	1	100	(179)
College degree	96	4	0	100	(167)
By Sex					
Men	80	20	0	100	(645)
Women	70	29	1	100	(845)
Total Sample*	74%	25%	1%	100%	(1501)

* Total sample includes persons whose education or sex was not recorded.

TABLE 24

"Now as you may know, the United States has been helping the South Viet Nam government, while Communist China has been helping the Communist rebels in that country. I'm going to mention a number of things that the United States might do about the situation in Viet Nam. For each thing I mention, would you tell me how you feel about it? First, if you have no opinion, just tell me that. If you do have an opinion, choose one of the other answers on this card."

(Asked only of persons who have heard about the fighting in Viet Nam)

"How about the United States getting out of the Viet Nam war completely?"

Definitely in favor	18% }	28%
Probably in favor	10 }	
Probably against	16 }	53
Definitely against	37 }	
No opinion		18
Not ascertained		1
Total		100%

(Number of persons, 1127)

"How about our continuing to give arms and training to South Viet Nam troops fighting against the Communist rebels?"

Definitely in favor	51% }	75%
Probably in favor	24 }	
Probably against	5 }	12
Definitely against	7 }	
No opinion		11
Not ascertained		2
Total		100%

(Number of persons, 1127)

"How about using American forces in Viet Nam if the Communist rebels are winning, even if this means our risking war with Communist China?"

Definitely in favor	24% }	41%
Probably in favor	17 }	
Probably against	10 }	42
Definitely against	32 }	
No opinion		16
Not ascertained		1
Total		100%

(Number of persons, 1127)

TABLE 24 (*Continued*)

"*How about trying to make some compromise agreement with Communist China on this—like making all Viet Nam neutral?*"

Definitely in favor	28% ⎫	
Probably in favor	18 ⎬	46%
Probably against	6 ⎫	
Definitely against	23 ⎬	29
No opinion		23
Not ascertained		2
Total		100%
		(Number of persons, 1127)

TABLE 25

Reactions to Possible U. S. Actions in Viet Nam, for Persons with Different Levels of Education

	Education				
Possible Actions	Grade School	Some High School	Completed High School	Some College	College Degree
Complete withdrawal from Viet Nam war					
In favor	34%	31%	28%	24%	19%
Against	38	43	55	55	75
No opinion	24	25	16	19	5
Not ascertained	4	1	1	2	1
Total	100%	100%	100%	100%	100%

TABLE 25 *(Continued)*

Possible Actions	Education				
	Grade School	*Some High School*	*Completed High School*	*Some College*	*College Degree*
Continued military aid to South Viet Nam					
In favor	61%	71%	76%	82%	86%
Against	15	10	13	9	11
No opinion	21	17	10	8	2
Not ascertained	3	2	1	1	1
Total	100%	100%	100%	100%	100%
Use of American forces in Viet Nam if necessary					
In favor	33%	35%	41%	40%	53%
Against	41	44	42	43	37
No opinion	22	19	16	16	9
Not ascertained	4	2	1	1	1
Total	100%	100%	100%	100%	100%
Compromise agreement with Communist China— neutralization of Viet Nam					
In favor	44%	46%	51%	42%	39%
Against	20	24	25	38	47
No opinion	32	28	23	19	14
Not ascertained	4	2	1	1	0
Total	100%	100%	100%	100%	100%
Number of persons	(201)	(155)	(428)	(170)	(161)

TABLE 26
Reactions to Possible U. S. Actions in Viet Nam, for Persons with Different Levels of Information About China

	Level of Information Score[a]			
	(Low)			(High)
Possible Actions	0	1	2	3
Complete withdrawal from Viet Nam war				
In favor	32%	32%	28%	24%
Against	16	46	53	67
No opinion	45	22	18	8
Not ascertained	7	0	1	1
Total	100%	100%	100%	100%
Continued military aid to South Viet Nam				
In favor	45%	72%	75%	86%
Against	12	10	16	10
No opinion	35	17	9	4
Not ascertained	8	1	0	0
Total	100%	100%	100%	100%
Use of American Forces in Viet Nam if necessary				
In favor	22%	39%	38%	49%
Against	38	41	44	42
No opinion	32	19	18	9
Not ascertained	8	1	0	0
Total	100%	100%	100%	100%
Compromise agreement with Communist China—neutralization of Viet Nam				
In favor	35%	51%	53%	45%
Against	10	18	23	42
No opinion	46	31	23	13
Not ascertained	9	0	1	0
Total	100%	100%	100%	100%
Number of persons	(152)	(202)	(244)	(495)

[a] For an explanation of level of information scores, see Table 19.

TABLE 27

Reactions to Possible U. S. Actions in Viet Nam, for Persons of Different Ages

	Age					
Possible Actions	18-24	25-34	35-44	45-54	55-64	65 and over
Complete withdrawal from Viet Nam war						
In favor	25%	20%	25%	32%	38%	32%
Against	65	63	57	46	41	40
No opinion	10	16	15	21	19	26
Not ascertained	0	1	3	1	2	2
Total	100%	100%	100%	100%	100%	100%
Continued military aid to South Viet Nam						
In favor	84%	80%	78%	72%	67%	67%
Against	10	8	11	12	17	16
No opinion	6	10	8	16	15	14
Not ascertained	0	2	3	0	1	3
Total	100%	100%	100%	100%	100%	100%
Use of American Forces in Viet Nam if necessary						
In favor	55%	50%	43%	36%	29%	28%
Against	31	34	41	47	49	49
No opinion	14	15	14	16	21	20
Not ascertained	0	1	2	1	1	3
Total	100%	100%	100%	100%	100%	100%
Compromise agreement with Communist China— neutralization of Viet Nam						
In favor	49%	46%	44%	47%	57%	37%
Against	34	30	36	25	15	31
No opinion	17	23	17	27	27	29
Not ascertained	0	1	3	1	1	3
Total	100%	100%	100%	100%	100%	100%
Number of Persons	(92)	(260)	(256)	(225)	(150)	(142)

TABLE 28

Reactions to Possible U. S. Actions in Viet Nam, for Persons of Different Political Affiliations

	Political Affiliation[a]				
Possible Actions	Democrat, Strong	Democrat, Not Strong	Independent	Republican, Not Strong	Republican, Strong
Complete withdrawal from Viet Nam war					
In favor	28%	29%	28%	29%	22%
Against	47	53	56	51	62
No opinion	22	17	14	19	16
Not ascertained	3	1	2	1	0
Total	100%	100%	100%	100%	100%
Continued military aid to South Viet Nam					
In favor	71%	76%	78%	68%	84%
Against	13	11	11	16	8
No opinion	12	12	9	16	8
Not ascertained	4	1	2	0	0
Total	100%	100%	100%	100%	100%
Use of American forces if necessary					
In favor	37%	36%	46%	38%	45%
Against	45	44	37	41	45
No opinion	15	19	15	20	10
Not ascertained	3	1	2	1	0
Total	100%	100%	100%	100%	100%
Compromise agreement with Communist China— neutralization of Viet Nam					
In favor	47%	47%	45%	49%	39%
Against	24	27	31	29	41
No opinion	25	25	22	21	20
Not ascertained	4	1	2	1	0
Total	100%	100%	100%	100%	100%
Number of persons	(258)	(245)	(268)	(192)	(135)

[a] For question concerning political affiliation, see Table 7, note d.

TABLE 29

Reactions to Possible U. S. Actions in Viet Nam, for Persons in Different Regions of the United States

Possible Actions	Region[a]			
	Northeast	North Central	South	West
Complete withdrawal from Viet Nam war				
In favor	31%	30%	27%	20%
Against	54.	49	49	63
No opinion	14	20	20	16
Not ascertained	1	1	4	1
Total	100%	100%	100%	100%
Continued military aid to South Viet Nam				
In favor	77%	72%	73%	80%
Against	13	14	11	8
No opinion	9	14	12	11
Not ascertained	1	0	4	1
Total	100%	100%	100%	100%
Use of American forces in Viet Nam if necessary				
In favor	34%	42%	39%	48%
Against	50	41	36	39
No opinion	15	16	21	12
Not ascertained	1	1	4	1
Total	100%	100%	100%	100%
Compromise agreement with Communist China— neutralization of Viet Nam				
In favor	47%	51%	36%	50%
Against	25	25	34	34
No opinion	27	23	27	14
Not ascertained	1	1	3	2
Total	100%	100%	100%	100%
Number of persons	(295)	(336)	(286)	(210)

[a] For states included in each region, see Table 7, note c.

THE RELATIONSHIP OF OPINION ABOUT POLICY TOWARD CHINA TO OPINION ABOUT POLICY IN VIET NAM

Since actual American policy in Viet Nam is related to our policy toward Communist China, it is of interest to see what relation exists between public opinion on these two subjects.

It should be noted first that our questions about Viet Nam explicitly related the subject of Viet Nam to that of Communist China. For some people this connection is one that they would not readily have made themselves. We may therefore have encouraged people to answer questions about Viet Nam with somewhat more attention to Communist China than they would normally give.

The data show, first, that people who favor our dealing with Communist China are no more likely than others to want us to withdraw completely from Viet Nam. Those who favor various amicable contacts with Communist China are also just as likely as others to favor continued military aid to South Viet Nam. Willingness to deal with China is, then, no reflection of a desire to have the United States end its involvement in the Far East.

There are, however, general differences between those who favor contacts with Communist China and those who oppose such contacts. These differences concern two possible actions in Viet Nam: (a) "using American forces in Viet Nam if the Communist rebels are winning, even if this means risking war with Communist China" and (b) "trying to make some compromise agreement with Communist China on this—like making all Viet Nam neutral."

Those who favor contacts with Communist China are, in general, more likely than others to *oppose* using American forces in Viet Nam. They are more likely than others to *favor* a compromise agreement with China on Viet Nam (see Table 30).

This relationship is seen first by comparing the opinions about Viet Nam policy of people who favor dealing with the Communists as the government of most of China with the opinions about Viet Nam of those who feel we should deal only with the Nationalist government. Those who favor dealing with the Communist government, as well as with the Nationalists, are more likely to oppose using American forces in Viet Nam and also more likely to favor a compromise agreement. However, this relationship between opinion about dealing with the Communists as the government of China and opinion about Viet Nam policy is not a strong one.

A stronger association is found between opinions about Viet Nam policy and willingness to follow possible Presidential initiatives for closer contact with China. Those who say they would favor various Presidential suggestions of this type—such as selling wheat to Communist China and exchanging ambassadors with her—are more likely than others to oppose use of American forces in Viet Nam and to favor the alternative of a compromise agreement like neutralization. Conversely, those who said they would be against suggestions for greater contact with Communist China are more likely to favor the use of American forces and more likely to oppose a compromise settlement.

The relation between these two sets of opinions is shown most clearly when we give people an index score based on their reaction to all five possible Presidential suggestions for closer contact with China. Of those whose score shows the greatest willingness to follow such Presidential initiatives, only one out of three favors possible use of American forces in Viet Nam, while almost two out of three favor a compromise agreement in Viet Nam. At the other extreme, among those who are most opposed to Presidential initiatives for contact with China, the proportions favoring the two alternatives in Viet Nam are reversed. Almost two out of three favor the use of American forces if the war is being lost, while fewer than one in three favors a compromise like neutralization of Viet Nam. In general, then, willingness to have amicable contacts with Communist China and preference for a non-military solution in Viet Nam go together.

However, data presented earlier in the report indicate that a different. pattern of attitudes exists among certain segments of the population. Better educated people are likely to welcome contact with Communist China, but they are also likely to oppose a compromise like neutralization in Viet Nam. Younger persons are likely to favor contact with Communist China but tend to favor the use of American forces to prevent loss of the war in Viet Nam. In other words, more education and younger age tend to produce both willingness for contact with Communist China and preference for a relatively militant policy in Viet Nam. At first, these facts may seem to be inconsistent with the general tendency for willingness to accept contact with Communist China to accompany non-militant attitudes concerning Viet Nam. To clarify these results, it is useful to examine the pattern of attitudes within various educational and age groups.

As Figure 1 shows, those who favor following suggestions for increased contact with China are also more likely to favor a compromise settlement like neutralization in Viet Nam, regardless of their educational level. But Figure 1 also shows that the general level of support for such a compromise in Viet Nam is lower for those of better education. Among those with any given degree of willingness to have contact with Communist China, a smaller proportion of the well-educated than of others favor a compromise in Viet Nam. The result is that even though well educated persons are somewhat more likely than others to favor contact with Communist China, they are, as a group, more opposed than others to a compromise like neutralization in Viet Nam.

The pattern of attitudes for different age groups is similar. As Figure 2 shows, within any age group those who favor contact with Communist China are more likely than others to oppose the use of American forces in Viet Nam. But the total level of support for using American forces is higher among younger people than among older people. Among those with any given degree of willingness to have contact with Communist China, a greater proportion of younger people than of older people favor use of American troops in Viet Nam. The result is that while younger people as a group are more likely than others to favor contacts with Communist China, they are also more likely to favor the use of American forces to prevent loss of the Viet Nam war.

The general picture that emerges from the data is that there are different forces which tend to produce different patterns of attitudes concerning American policy in Asia. On the one hand, there are forces which produce both willingness for amicable contact with China and preference for a non-military solution in Viet Nam. This attitude pattern appears to reflect a general orientation of non-militancy as opposed to militancy in foreign policy. Several social characteristics discussed in previous sections, such as geographical location and political affiliation, sometimes appear to contribute to consistently militant or non-militant orientations. On the other hand, some social characteristics, principally education and age, appear to work toward producing a different pattern of attitudes—one in which approval of contact with China is accompanied by preference for a relatively militant policy in Viet Nam and vice versa. It is possible that this second pattern of opinions reflects another general policy orientation, perhaps the degree of willingness to see the United States actively involved in Far Eastern affairs. For the present, however, the reasons behind the opinion patterns found must remain largely a matter of speculation.

TABLE 30
Reactions to Two Possible U. S. Actions in Viet Nam, as Related to General Willingness to Deal with Communist China

(Read rows across)

	Reaction to Possible United States Actions in Viet Nam[a]									
	Use of American Forces if Necessary					Compromise Agreement with Communist China— Neutralization of Viet Nam				
	Favor	Against	No Opinion[b]	Total	N	Favor	Against	No Opinion[b]	Total	N
Willingness to deal with Communist government[c]										
Favor	42%	48%	10%	100%	(216)	54%	32%	14%	100%	(216)
Against	53	39	8	100	(159)	39	49	12	100	(159)
Reactions to possible suggestions by President[d]										
Index Score[e]										
Most favorable 5-7	33%	55%	12%	100%	(115)	64%	21%	15%	100%	(115)
8-10	44	44	12	100	(163)	58	26	16	100	(163)
11-13	55	36	9	100	(153)	45	43	12	100	(153)
14-16	50	44	6	100	(134)	43	48	9	100	(134)
Least favorable 17-20	62	26	12	100	(95)	31	60	9	100	(95)
Visits between Americans and Communist Chinese										
Definitely favor	42%	46%	12%	100%	(407)	54%	32%	14%	100%	(407)
Probably favor	44	42	14	100	(312)	47	30	23	100	(312)
Probably against	55	36	9	100	(64)	39	50	11	100	(64)
Definitely against	51	35	14	100	(97)	39	43	18	100	(97)
Sale of things like wheat to Communist China										
Definitely favor	33%	54%	13%	100%	(185)	55%	31%	14%	100%	(185)
Probably favor	42	44	14	100	(243)	55	26	19	100	(243)
Probably against	46	43	11	100	(139)	54	28	18	100	(139)
Definitely against	52	35	13	100	(319)	38	43	19	100	(319)

TABLE 30 (*Continued*)

	Use of American Forces if Necessary					Compromise Agreement with Communist China— Neutralization of Viet Nam				
	Favor	Against	No Opinion[b]	Total	N	Favor	Against	No Opinion[b]	Total	N
Discussion of Asian problems with Communist China										
Definitely favor	40%	47%	13%	100%	(366)	62%	24%	14%	100%	(366)
Probably favor	42	43	15	100	(339)	49	28	23	100	(339)
Probably against	49	47	4	100	(72)	39	44	17	100	(72)
Definitely against	57	30	13	100	(112)	23	68	9	100	(112)
Exchange of ambassadors with Communist China										
Definitely favor	36%	49%	15%	100%	(239)	59%	27%	14%	100%	(239)
Probably favor	45	44	11	100	(270)	56	24	20	100	(270)
Probably against	46	43	11	100	(102)	38	36	26	100	(102)
Definitely against	54	35	11	100	(231)	37	51	12	100	(231)
Agreement to Let Communist China into the United Nations										
Definitely favor	38%	54%	8%	100%	(132)	62%	28%	10%	100%	(132)
Probably favor	44	39	17	100	(174)	52	27	21	100	(174)
Probably against	47	43	10	100	(124)	51	33	16	100	(124)
Definitely against	48	38	14	100	(409)	42	40	18	100	(409)

[a] The wording of these questions is given in Table 24. They were asked of all those who said they had heard about the fighting in Viet Nam.

[b] Persons for whom a response was not ascertained are included in this category.

[c] The wording of this question is given in Table 7. It was asked only of those who were aware that there are two Chinese governments. Persons who did not indicate clear support for or opposition to dealing with the Chinese Communist Government are omitted from table.

[d] The wording of these questions is given in Table 16. They were asked of those who are aware that most of China has a Communist government. Persons not expressing an opinion on a question are omitted from the table.

[e] The index score was computed by assigning a score of 1 to the response "definitely favor," a score of 2 to "probably favor," a score of 3 to "probably be against," and a score of 4 to "definitely be against." An index score was computed for respondents who expressed an opinion on all five questions.

FIGURE 1

Reactions to the Idea of a Compromise Agreement in Viet Nam as Related to Willingness to Follow Presidential Suggestions for Contact with China, for Persons of Different Educational Levels[a]

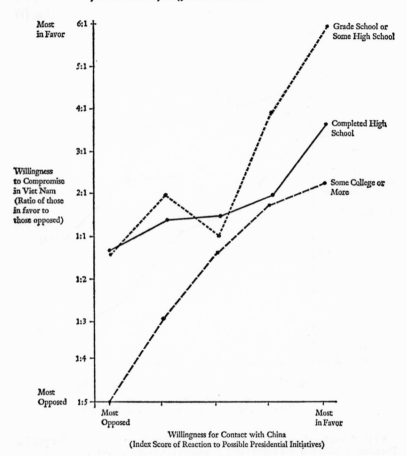

[a] This figure is based on an N of 590 persons who gave an opinion about five possible Presidential initiatives and about a compromise agreement in Viet Nam.

FIGURE 2

Reactions to the Idea of Using American Forces in Viet Nam, as Related to Willingness to Follow Presidential Suggestions for Contact with China, for Persons of Different Age Groups[a]

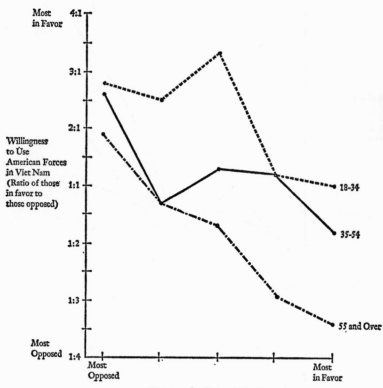

Willingness for Contact with China
(Index Score of Reaction to Possible Presidential Initiatives)

[a] This figure based on an N of 593 persons who gave an opinion about five possible Presidential initiatives and about using American forces in Viet Nam.

APPENDIX A

Approximate Sampling Errors of Percentages Reported

Since the percentages reported in the tables of this report are based on a sample of the American population, these percentages are subject to sampling variability—*i.e.*, the variations that might occur by chance because only a sample, rather than the whole population, is surveyed. The table below presents estimates of the amount of error which might be expected in the percentages reported. Consider, for example, the case where the number of interviews is 1,000 and the reported percentage is 50. The entry in the table for this case is 3.8. This figure indicates that the chances are 95 in 100 that the true percentage value figure in the population is within 3.8 per cent (plus or minus) of the sample percentage reported.

TABLE A
Approximate Sampling Errors of Percentages
(Expressed in Percentages)

Reported percentage	Number of Interviews							
	3,000	1,000	700	500	400	300	200	100
50	2.2	3.8	4.6	5.4	6.0	7.0	2.3	12.0
30 or 70	2.0	3.5	4.2	4.9	5.5	6.4	7.8	11.1
20 or 80	1.8	3.0	3.6	4.3	4.8	5.6	6.8	9.5
10 or 90	1.3	2.3	2.8	3.3	3.6	4.2	5.1	7.2
5 or 95	1.0	1.7	2.0	2.3	2.2	3.0	3.7	

APPENDIX B

Approximate Sampling Errors of Differences Between Subgroups

Some tables of this report compare subgroups of the entire sample—*e.g.*, groups with different levels of education—with respect to their responses to a question. Since differences between subgroups may be due simply to sampling error, we wish to estimate the probability that a difference as large as the one observed could occur by chance alone. To illustrate the use of this table, let us consider the case where the size of group A is 1,000, the size of group B is also 1,000, and the percentages for these groups are in the range of 35 to 65 per cent. The entry in the table for this case is 5.4. It indicates that a difference of 5.4 per cent or greater, in either direction, could occur by chance in less than 5 cases out of 100. That is, in this instance, a difference of 5.4 per cent or more between the subgroups would be considered as real and not the result of sampling error.

TABLE B
Sampling Errors of Differences
(Expressed as percentages)

Size of sample or group	Size of sample or group						
	1,000	700	500	400	300	200	100
For percentages from about 35 per cent to 65 per cent							
1,000	5.4	5.9	6.6	7.1	7.9	9.4	12.5
700		6.4	7.1	7.6	8.3	9.5	13.0
500			7.6	8.1	8.7	10.2	13.0
400				8.5	9.3	10.4	13.1
300					9.6	11.1	13.5
200						12.0	14.5
100							17.0
For percentages around 20 per cent and 80 per cent							
1,000	4.3	4.7	5.3	5.7	6.4	7.5	10.2
700		5.2	5.7	6.0	6.6	7.7	10.3
500			6.1	6.5	7.0	8.1	10.4
400				6.8	7.4	8.3	10.9
300					7.8	8.6	11.1
200						9.8	11.9
100							14.0

TABLE B (*Continued*)

Size of sample or group	Size of sample or group						
	1,000	700	500	400	300	200	100
	For percentages around 10 per cent and 90 per cent						
1,000	3.3	3.4	4.0	4.3	4.8	5.6	
700		3.9	4.2	4.6	5.0	5.8	
500			4.6	4.8	5.3	6.0	
400				5.1	5.6	6.3	
300					5.9	6.6	
200						7.1	
	For percentages around 5 per cent and 95 per cent						
1,000	2.3	2.6	2.9	3.3	3.5	4.0	
700		2.8	3.3	3.3	3.7	4.2	
500			3.4	3.5	3.9	4.4	
400				3.7	4.0	4.4	
300					4.3	4.8	

APPENDIX C

Description of Sample Used in Survey

TABLE C
Breakdown of Sample

Survey Research Center (SRC) Sample		U.S. Census Data	
REGION[a]			
1. Northeast	24.4%	1. Northeast	25.0%
2. North Central	28.0	2. North Central	28.9
3. South	30.9	3. South	30.8
4. West	16.7	4. West	15.2
AGE			
1. 18-24	7.7%	1. 20-24	9.7%
2. 25-34	20.7	2. 25-34	20.7
3. 35-44	22.5	3. 35-44	21.9
4. 45-54	19.3	4. 45-54	18.6
5. 55-64	13.7	5. 55-64	14.1
6. 65 and over	15.9	6. 65 and over	14.9
7. Not ascertained	0.2		
EDUCATION			
1. Grade school or less	26.4%	1. Grade school or less	32.4%
2. Some high school	13.1	2. Some high school	
3. Some high school plus		(1-3 years)	18.6
non-academic	3.0	3. High school (4 years)	30.4
4. Completed high school	20.7	4. Some college (1-3 years)	10.3
5. Complete high school plus		5. College (4 or more years)	8.3
non-academic	12.4		
6. Some college	11.9		
7. Has college degree	11.1		
8. Not ascertained	1.4		
SEX[b]			
1. Men	43.0%	1. Men	49.2%
2. Women	57.0	2. Women	50.8

[a] The region classifications in the SRC sample and the U.S. Census differ only in that the SRC sample includes Delaware with the Northeast and the Census includes it in the South.

[b] The smaller proportion of males in the SRC sample is probably due largely to the fact that the SRC sample is limited to adults in dwelling units and excludes persons in military reservations, large rooming houses, transient hotels, and similar places which have a higher proportion of males.

OCCUPATION OF HEAD OF HOUSEHOLD°

		SRC	U.S. Census
1.	Professional, technical, and kindred workers	14.7%	9.7%
2.	Non self-employed managers and officials	6.8	7.0
3.	Self-employed businessmen, artisans, craftsmen, works for corporation of which he is substantial owner	7.4	5.3
4.	Clerical, sales, and kindred workers	11.6	10.2
5.	Craftsmen, foremen, and kindred workers	15.1	15.3
6.	Operatives and kindred workers (factory, mill, mine workers, etc.)	16.0	15.2
7.	Laborers (unskilled and farm) and service workers (cooks, barbers, practical nurses, etc.)	12.0	11.6
8.	Farmers and farm managers	6.0	4.3
9.	Housewives (if female is head), retired, students, or military on-base	10.4	—
10.	Housewives (if female is head), retired, students, military on- and off-base, and unemployed	—	21.4

POLITICAL PARTY AFFILIATION

		Present SRC Sample	Fall 1962 SRC Sample
1.	Strong Democrat	23.9%	22.9%
2.	Not very strong Democrat	21.9	23.1
3.	Independent closer to Democrats	7.0	7.1
4.	Independent	9.9	7.7
5.	Independent closer to Republicans	4.7	6.1
6.	Not very strong Republican	17.0	16.1
7.	Strong Republican	10.7	12.2
8.	Other minor political party, apolitical, won't say	3.7	3.9
9.	Not ascertained	1.2	.9

° Unemployed persons were coded by SRC according to their usual occupation.

Sources:

Region: U.S. Bureau of Census, *Current Population Report,* February 7, 1963.

Age: U.S. Bureau of Census, *U.S. Census of Population: 1960, General Social and Economic Characteristics, U.S. Summary,* Final Report PC(1)-1C.

Education: U.S. Bureau of Census, *Current Population Report,* series P120, no. 121.

Sex: U.S. Bureau of Census, *Statistical Abstract of the United States, 1963* (84th edition).

Occupation of Head of Household: U.S. Bureau of Census, *Current Population Report,* series P60, no. 41.

Index

COUNCIL ON FOREIGN RELATIONS

PUBLICATIONS

FOREIGN AFFAIRS (quarterly), edited by Hamilton Fish Armstrong.
THE UNITED STATES IN WORLD AFFAIRS (annual). Volumes for 1931, 1932 and 1933, by Walter Lippmann and William O. Scroggs; for 1934–1935, 1936, 1937, 1938, 1939 and 1940, by Whitney H. Shepardson and William O. Scroggs; for 1945–1947, 1947–1948 and 1948–1949, by John C. Campbell; for 1949, 1950, 1951, 1952, 1953 and 1954, by Richard P. Stebbins; for 1955, by Hollis W. Barber; for 1956, 1957, 1958, 1959, 1960, 1961, 1962 and 1963, by Richard P. Stebbins, for 1964, by Jules Davids.

DOCUMENTS ON AMERICAN FOREIGN RELATIONS (annual). Volume for 1952 edited by Clarence W. Baier and Richard P. Stebbins; for 1953 and 1954, edited by Peter V. Curl; for 1955, 1956, 1957, 1958 and 1959, edited by Paul E. Zinner; for 1960, 1961, 1962 and 1963, edited by Richard P. Stebbins, for 1964, by Jules Davids.

POLITICAL HANDBOOK AND ATLAS OF THE WORLD (annual), edited by Walter H. Mallory.

INTERNATIONAL POLITICAL COMMUNICATION, by W. Phillips Davison (1965).

MONETARY REFORM FOR THE WORLD ECONOMY, by Robert V. Roosa (1965).

AFRICAN BATTLELINE: American Policy Choices in Southern Africa, by Waldemar A. Nielsen (1965).

NATO IN TRANSITION: The Future of the Atlantic Alliance, by Timothy W. Stanley (1965).

ALTERNATIVE TO PARTITION: For a Broader Conception of America's Role in Europe, by Zbigniew Brzezinski (1965).

THE TROUBLED PARTNERSHIP: A Re-Appraisal of the Atlantic Alliance, by Henry A. Kissinger (1965).

REMNANTS OF EMPIRE: The United Nations and the End of Colonialism, by David W. Wainhouse (1965).

THE EUROPEAN COMMUNITY AND AMERICAN TRADE: A Study in Atlantic Economics and Policy, by Randall Hinshaw (1964).

THE FOURTH DIMENSION OF FOREIGN POLICY: Educational and Cultural Affairs, by Philip H. Coombs (1964).

AMERICAN AGENCIES INTERESTED IN INTERNATIONAL AFFAIRS (Fifth Edition), compiled by Donald Wasson (1964).

JAPAN AND THE UNITED STATES IN WORLD TRADE, by Warren S. Hunsberger (1964).

FOREIGN AFFAIRS BIBLIOGRAPHY, 1952–1962, by Henry L. Roberts (1964.)

THE DOLLAR IN WORLD AFFAIRS: An Essay in International Financial Policy, by Henry G. Aubrey (1964).

ON DEALING WITH THE COMMUNIST WORLD, by George F. Kennan (1964).

FOREIGN AID AND FOREIGN POLICY, by Edward S. Mason (1964).

THE SCIENTIFIC REVOLUTION AND WORLD POLITICS, by Caryl P. Haskins (1964).

AFRICA: A Foreign Affairs Reader, edited by Philip W. Quigg (1964).

THE PHILIPPINES AND THE UNITED STATES: Problems of Partnership, by George E. Taylor (1964).

SOUTHEAST ASIA IN UNITED STATES POLICY, by Russell H. Fifield (1963).

UNESCO: ASSESSMENT AND PROMISE, by George N. Shuster (1963).

THE PEACEFUL ATOM IN FOREIGN POLICY, by Arnold Kramish (1963).

THE ARABS AND THE WORLD: Nasser's Arab Nationalist Policy, by Charles D. Cremeans (1963).

TOWARD AN ATLANTIC COMMUNITY, by Christian A. Herter (1963).

THE SOVIET UNION, 1922–1962: A Foreign Affairs Reader, edited by Philip E. Mosely (1963).

THE POLITICS OF FOREIGN AID: American Experience in Southeast Asia, by John D. Montgomery (1962).

SPEARHEADS OF DEMOCRACY: Labor in the Developing Countries, by George C. Lodge (1962).

LATIN AMERICA: Diplomacy and Reality, by Adolf A. Berle (1962).

THE ORGANIZATION OF AMERICAN STATES AND THE HEMISPHERE CRISIS, by John C. Dreier (1962).

THE UNITED NATIONS: Structure for Peace, by Ernest A. Gross (1962).

THE LONG POLAR WATCH: Canada and the Defense of North America, by Melvin Conant (1962).

ARMS AND POLITICS IN LATIN AMERICA (Revised Edition), by Edwin Lieuwen (1961).

THE FUTURE OF UNDERDEVELOPED COUNTRIES: Political Implications of Economic Development (Revised Edition), by Eugene Staley (1961).

SPAIN AND DEFENSE OF THE WEST: Ally and Liability, by Arthur P. Whitaker (1961).

SOCIAL CHANGE IN LATIN AMERICA TODAY: Its Implications for United States Policy, by Richard N. Adams, John P. Gillin, Allan R. Holmberg, Oscar Lewis, Richard W. Patch, and Charles W. Wagley (1961).

FOREIGN POLICY: THE NEXT PHASE: The 1960s (Revised Edition), by Thomas K. Finletter (1960).

DEFENSE OF THE MIDDLE EAST: Problems of American Policy (Revised Edition), by John C. Campbell (1960).

COMMUNIST CHINA AND ASIA: Challenge to American Policy, by A. Doak Barnett (1960).

FRANCE, TROUBLED ALLY: De Gaulle's Heritage and Prospects, by Edgar S. Furniss, Jr. (1960).

THE SCHUMAN PLAN: A Study in Economic Cooperation, 1950–1959, by William Diebold, Jr. (1959).

SOVIET ECONOMIC AID: The New Aid and Trade Policy in Underdeveloped Countries, by Joseph S. Berliner (1958).

RAW MATERIALS: A Study of American Policy, by Percy W. Bidwell (1958).

NATO AND THE FUTURE OF EUROPE, by Ben T. Moore (1958).

AFRICAN ECONOMIC DEVELOPMENT, by William Hance (1958).

INDIA AND AMERICA: A Study of Their Relations, by Phillips Talbot and S. L. Poplai (1958).

NUCLEAR WEAPONS AND FOREIGN POLICY, by Henry A. Kissinger (1957).

MOSCOW-PEKING AXIS: Strength and Strains, by Howard L. Boorman, Alexander Eckstein, Philip E. Mosely and Benjamin Schwartz (1957).

RUSSIA AND AMERICA: Dangers and Prospects, by Henry L. Roberts (1956).

ABOUT THE AUTHOR

A. T. Steele was for many years (1932–1950) a correspondent in China for leading American newspapers. He worked, alternately, for the Associated Press, *The New York Times*, the *Chicago Daily News* and the *New York Herald Tribune*. Leaving China shortly after the Communist occupation of Peking, which he witnessed, he spent nearly a decade roving the world, primarily Asia, for the *New York Herald Tribune*.

Mr. Steele was born in Toronto, Canada, but came to the United States as a youth. He attended high school in Salt Lake City, Utah, and later graduated from Stanford University with a B.A. in Economics-Journalism. Before going to China, he owned and edited community newspapers in California.